INSIGHTS ON INVESTIGATIVE JOURNALISM

Offering a critical overview of the state of contemporary investigative journalism, this book considers ways in which investigative journalism can bring about meaningful change and what conditions need to be in place for it to do so.

Combining theory and practice, each chapter introduces current issues and trends, including the impacts of Artificial Intelligence, evolving funding models, Freedom of Information, and SLAPPs. Applying these issues to some of the most pressing concerns of our time – misinformation, the climate crisis, inequality – this book demonstrates how journalists can draw on investigative skills to enact positive real-world change. Relevant chapters feature a practical guide to using the technique discussed and each is followed by a critical analysis of skills in practice, with case studies from around the world. All end with an exercise or discussion topic to help students make sense of what they've learned.

Shining new light on disruptions facing the industry, this book is recommended reading for anyone studying investigative journalism at an advanced level.

Neil Macfarlane is a senior lecturer in online journalism at The University of Sunderland, UK. He is a freelance investigative journalist and has written for titles including Private Eye, The Mirror, and HuffPost UK.

Barbara Longo-Flint is a PhD researcher at The University of Sunderland, UK. Previously, she worked as a journalist in Italy for 20 years.

John Price is a senior lecturer in journalism at The University of Sunderland, UK. He publishes research on topics including investigative journalism, sports, and discrimination and the media.

Journalism Insights

The Journalism Insights series provides edited collections of theoretically grounded case study analyses on an eclectic range of journalistic areas, from peace and conflict reporting to fashion and sports reporting.

The series has a bias towards the contemporary, but each volume includes an important historical, contextualising section. Volumes offer international coverage and focus on both mainstream and 'alternative' media, always considering the impact of social media in the various fields.

The volumes are aimed at both undergraduate and postgraduate students on journalism as well as media and communication programmes who will find the texts original, interesting and inspirational.

For information on submitting a proposal for the series, please contact the Series Editor Richard Lance Keeble, of the University of Lincoln and Liverpool Hope University, at RKeeble@lincoln.ac.uk

Insights on Literary Journalism
Edited by Kevin M. Lerner

Insights on Journalism and Human Rights
Edited by Sanem Şahin

Insights on Investigative Journalism
Edited by Neil Macfarlane, Barbara Longo-Flint, and John Price

For more information visit: https://www.routledge.com/Journalism-Insights/book-series/JI

INSIGHTS ON INVESTIGATIVE JOURNALISM

Edited by Neil Macfarlane, Barbara Longo-Flint, and John Price

Routledge
Taylor & Francis Group

LONDON AND NEW YORK

Designed cover image: Sean Gladwell/Getty

First published 2026
by Routledge
4 Park Square, Milton Park, Abingdon, Oxon OX14 4RN

and by Routledge
605 Third Avenue, New York, NY 10158

Routledge is an imprint of the Taylor & Francis Group, an informa business

British Library Cataloguing-in-Publication Data
A catalogue record for this book is available from the British Library

ISBN: 978-1-032-76346-0 (hbk)
ISBN: 978-1-032-76347-7 (pbk)
ISBN: 978-1-003-47815-7 (ebk)

DOI: 10.4324/9781003478157

Typeset in Galliard
by KnowledgeWorks Global Ltd.

For Zoe

CONTENTS

CONTRIBUTORS

Chris Arsenault is Assistant Professor and the Chair of the Master of Media in Journalism and Communication Program at Western University, Canada, and a former international correspondent with the Thomson Reuters Foundation and Al Jazeera. He has been based in Doha, Qatar, Rio de Janeiro, Brazil, and Rome, Italy and his reporting focuses on climate change, natural resources, and conflict. He has won the UN Correspondents' Prize, best national feature story from Canada's Radio Television Digital News Association, and the Kevin Tester Award for Marine Journalism for his investigations, and he is the author of *Blowback: A Canadian History of Agent Orange and the War at Home.*

Paul Bradshaw leads the MA in Data Journalism at Birmingham City University and works as a consulting data journalist with the BBC Shared Data Unit. He has written over 20 book chapters and research papers on online journalism, and authored a number of books in the field, including the Online Journalism Handbook, Mobile-First Journalism, Scraping for Journalists, Finding Stories in Spreadsheets, Snapchat for Journalists, and the Data Journalism Heist. He also publishes the Online Journalism Blog, which has been covering the field for two decades. The co-founder of the award-winning investigative journalism network HelpMeInvestigate.com, he has been listed on both Journalism.co.uk's list of leading innovators in media, and the US Poynter Institute's list of the 35 most influential people in social media, and has worked with news organisations including The Guardian, Der Tagesspiegel, Balkan Investigative Reporting Network and The Bureau of Investigative Journalism. His awards include the CNN MultiChoice Award for an investigation into people trafficking in football. Paul can be found on Twitter (@paulbradshaw).

Mathias-Felipe de-Lima-Santos, is a Lecturer at Macquarie University (Australia). He is also a Distinguished Researcher at the Pompeu Fabra University (Spain) and in the Digital Media and Society Observatory (DMSO) at the Federal University of São Paulo (Unifesp), Brazil. Previously, he was a Postdoctoral Researcher in the Human(e) AI and AI4Media projects at the University of Amsterdam, Netherlands and a researcher at the University of Navarra, Spain, under the JOLT project, a Marie Skłodowska-Curie European Training Network funded by the European Commission's Horizon 2020. He was also a Visiting Researcher at the Queensland University of Technology (QUT) in Brisbane, Australia. Mathias-Felipe is co-editor of the book "Journalism, Data and Technology in Latin America" and the upcoming two-volume book "Fact-Checking in the Global South" both by Palgrave Macmillan. Mathias-Felipe is currently part of the editorial board of Digital Journalism and Journalism Practice. His research interests include the changing nature of communications driven by technological innovations, particularly in journalism, media, and online social networks.

Philip Di Salvo is a Senior Researcher and Lecturer at the Institute for Media and Communications Management at the University of St. Gallen, Switzerland. His research interests include investigative journalism, digital surveillance, and the intersections between hacking, leaks, black box technologies, and information. He has previously held positions at the London School of Economics (LSE) and at Università della Svizzera italiana.

Neil Farrington is a Senior Lecturer in Sports Journalism, leading the delivery of the course across all undergraduate levels and also leading a module on MA Journalism/Journalism (Sports) at The University of Sunderland. He is the co-author of two books focusing on the socio-cultural landscape of the sports media, with particular reference to sports journalism's reporting of issues of race and religion, and sport-informed racism on social media.

Maria Konow-Lund is a Professor of Journalism at OsloMet University (Norway) and a Marie Curie Slodowska fellow at Cardiff University. Her recent research is featured in academic outlets such as Digital Journalism, Journalism Practice, Nordicom and Routledge Companion to Media and Humanitarian Action (2017). In addition to this, Maria has extensive experience as a journalist from broadcasting, both as a journalist and producer. She has won several awards for her journalism, as well as writing four books for children. At present, her research focus is on investigative journalism and changing technology, innovation and new funding models.

Barbara Longo-Flint is a researcher at the University of Sunderland. She worked as a journalist in Italy for 20 years, before moving to the UK and completing an MA in journalism from the University of Sunderland in 2021. Barbara is a chartered member of the Order of Journalists in Italy and has achieved the NCTJ Industry Gold Standard diploma in Journalism. Her research focuses on the impact of abuse and intimidation on investigative journalists and media freedom.

Carolyne Lunga is an Associate Professor of Journalism in the Department of Digital Communication and Media Production at the University of Doha for Science and Technology (UDST), Qatar. She is a visiting lecturer at City St Georges, University of London in the UK. Previously, she was a Senior Lecturer of Media Writing at the University of Portsmouth and a journalist. She is on the editorial board of Journalism Practice, where she is currently leading a Special Issue on Investigative Journalism in a Networked Age. She teaches digital journalism, data journalism, and media ethics. Her research interests include digital journalism, disinformation, artificial intelligence and journalism, investigative journalism and media ethics.

Neil Macfarlane is a Senior Lecturer in Online Journalism and leads the BA Journalism programme at the University of Sunderland. His specialisms include digital media, investigative journalism, and politics. He is a freelance investigative journalist and has written for the likes of Private Eye, The Mirror and Huff-Post UK. He previously worked as a staff reporter in newspapers in the UK and Taiwan. He has delivered training in investigative journalism for the likes of the BBC and has carried out research for the Google News Initiative.

Lucia Mesquita is a postdoctoral researcher at the FuJo Institute for Future Media and Journalism and a postdoctoral researcher at the Centre for Research in Applied Communication, Culture, and New Technologies at Lusofona University, Portugal. Lucia completed her PhD in DCU as a researcher on the JOLT Project, a Marie Skłodowska-Curie European Training Network funded by the European Commission's Horizon 2020. Before joining DCU, she was an MA student at the School of Social and Political Sciences (ISCSP), University of Lisbon. She was also a journalist, having graduated from Universidade Metodista de São Paulo (Brazil) in 2001. She is investigating the changing political economy of digital journalism and its impact on the plurality and the civic role of journalism.

Michelle Park is a teacher at the School of Journalism, Media and Culture at Cardiff University, UK, after the recent conferral of her PhD degree. Her PhD thesis was shortlisted for the 2023 Media, Communication and Cultural Studies Association (MeCCSA) Outstanding Achievement Award in the Doctoral Research of the Year category. Her research interests include nonprofit funding for news, investigative journalism, data and computational journalism and digital media.

John Price is Research Fellow and Senior Lecturer in Journalism at the University of Sunderland. He is co-founder of the Sport and Discrimination Network and organizes the annual International Sport and Discrimination Conference. He is Secretary of the Association for Journalism Education and on the Advisory Board of the International Sport and Society Research Network.

Tom Sanderson is the Deputy Director of the Centre for Investigative Journalism where he has overseen all aspects of the CIJ's training provision for more than a decade. He leads on the development of new curricula, funded projects and initiatives. His recent projects have focused on building capacity for in-depth climate investigations across the Global South and supporting new models of community and non-profit journalism with investigative training. He frequently works with national and international newsrooms and civil society organisations to deliver tailored investigative training for their research teams.

Bethany Usher is a journalist and author of Journalism and Celebrity (2020) and the forthcoming Journalism and Crime (2022), both published by Routledge's prestigious Media and Communications series. Before embarking on a career as a lecturer in journalism practice and studies, Bethany worked as a staff correspondent for national and regional newspapers. As an experienced leader in Learning and Teaching, Bethany is now an Associate Director of Education for the School of Arts and Culture. She has a proven track record in the development of pedagogy for journalism media and creative industries and was originally employed at Newcastle as Degree Programme Director for Media, Culture and Heritage's MA Media and Journalism and MA International Multimedia Journalism.

INTRODUCTION

Exploring Dark Corners That Some Wish to Keep in Shadow

Barbara Longo-Flint, Neil Macfarlane, and John Price

At the heart of investigative journalism lies the aim of revealing information that others would like to keep hidden. These 'others' are usually powerful or corrupt individuals or organisations. As such, the investigative journalist, more than any other type of journalist, embodies the watchdog role of journalism – the idea that journalism's fundamental mission is to hold power to account in the public interest, to expose wrongdoing and hypocrisy, and to shed light in the dark corners that some wish to keep in shadow.

Investigative journalism is widely recognised as a form of quality journalism that shares many subjects and methods with other forms of journalism but requires a more rigorous level of work and conceptualisation (Carson, 2019). McQuail (2013) considers investigative journalism the most active form of journalism, compared to the more passive role of transmission journalism, while Harcup (2021) argues that investigative journalism can often be seen as a battle between good and evil.

In the United Kingdom, investigative journalism's roots can be traced back to the 1880s, with W.T. Stead's undercover investigation of child prostitution serving as a landmark case. However, investigative journalism has never achieved the same institutional status in the UK as it has in the United States, where the Pulitzer Prizes have recognised it as a distinct category since 1953. The UK's first investigative journalism award was only established in 2005 (O'Neill, 2010).

Investigative journalism sits somewhere between myth and reality (Borins and Herst, 2020). In the United States, the Watergate scandal of the 1970s became a symbol of investigative journalism's power, although recent critiques have highlighted the mythologisation of this case. As Baker (2009) argues, the Watergate investigation was as much a product of elite rivalries as

DOI: 10.4324/9781003478157-1

of journalistic prowess, complicating the narrative of independent journalism acting solely in the public interest.

While some investigative journalists consider themselves as 'a breed apart' (Lanosga *et al*, 2017), for others, investigative journalism is just 'normal journalism' (Cancela, Gerber and Dubied, 2021). Hunter (2011) highlights the key differences between conventional and investigative journalism. In daily journalism, information is gathered and reported quickly, while investigative journalists cannot publish until the coherence and completeness of their findings are fully assured. Investigative journalists often work in relative secrecy, collecting information over long periods before publishing it. This work is typically original, systematic, and conducted in the public interest, often focusing on social justice and accountability. Investigations cover diverse topics, such as medical malpractice, education, and human rights. Investigative journalism usually starts with a hypothesis and involves analysing large datasets, both digital and on paper, and interviewing human sources. Should verification fail, the investigation must be abandoned. Errors expose reporters to sanctions that can destroy their credibility and that of the media outlet (Hunter, 2011).

Investigative journalism employs a distinctive set of tools and techniques that differentiate it from other forms of reporting. These methods are designed to uncover hidden information, verify facts, and construct comprehensive narratives that serve the public interest. As Hunter (2011) explains, investigative journalism is defined by its systematic and original approach, which often involves prolonged inquiry and innovative problem-solving.

One hallmark of investigative journalism is its reliance on data analysis. In recent years, the rise of data journalism has revolutionised investigative reporting, enabling journalists to handle vast quantities of information and uncover patterns that would otherwise remain hidden. By analysing datasets ranging from government records to corporate filings, journalists can identify irregularities and trace networks of influence (Carson and Farhall, 2018). For example, projects such as the Panama Papers investigation utilised advanced data analysis tools to expose global tax evasion networks involving politicians, celebrities, and corporations.

Open-Source Intelligence (OSINT) represents another transformative tool in modern investigative journalism. Derived from the intelligence community, OSINT involves gathering publicly accessible information through legal and ethical means. This can include mining social media platforms, analysing satellite imagery, and examining government databases. OSINT techniques have expanded investigative journalism's reach, allowing journalists to operate in digital environments where traditional methods may fall short. As Karan (2024) notes, the availability of open-source data has made it easier than ever to uncover evidence of corruption, human rights abuses, and other societal issues.

Traditional techniques, such as undercover reporting and whistleblower collaboration, remain critical components of investigative journalism. Undercover work – where journalists adopt false identities to gain access to restricted environments – has been used to expose unethical practices in industries ranging from healthcare to law enforcement. Whistleblowers, meanwhile, provide insider information that can be pivotal to uncovering hidden truths (Di Salvo, 2021). Platforms like WikiLeaks have further amplified the role of whistleblowers by offering secure channels for information sharing.

Freedom of Information (FOI) legislation is another indispensable tool to access publicly held data. However, navigating the bureaucratic hurdles and potential delays associated with FOI requests remains a significant challenge.

Ethically, investigative journalism often operates in a grey area, where methods such as hidden cameras, stings, and covert data collection may raise questions about privacy and consent. Journalists must weigh these concerns against the potential public benefits of their work. For example, investigative reporters have used hidden cameras to expose malpractice in care homes, revealing systemic failures that would otherwise remain concealed (Lashmar, 2013).

Immersive reporting is another method that sets investigative journalism apart from the others. By spending extended periods within specific communities, journalists can gain a deeper understanding of complex social issues. This technique has been particularly effective in exploring topics such as poverty, inequality, and environmental degradation.

Together, these tools and techniques illustrate the innovative and resourceful nature of investigative journalism. They enable journalists to uncover truths often obscured by powerful interests, making investigative reporting an essential component of democratic accountability. However, this pursuit of accountability does not come without significant risks.

Investigative journalism operates within a landscape fraught with economic, legal, and institutional constraints that pose significant challenges to its practice. These obstacles threaten the sustainability and efficacy of investigative reporting, yet journalists and organisations worldwide continue to innovate and adapt in response.

These challenges are compounded by the risks investigative journalists face in their work, such as threats to their safety and lives. The murder of Maltese journalist Daphne Caruana Galizia in 2017, targeted for exposing corruption, underscores the dangers inherent in holding powerful actors accountable. Similarly, Veronica Guerin, an Irish journalist killed in 1996, and Martin O'Hagan, assassinated in Northern Ireland in 2001, highlight how organised crime and political violence pose severe threats to journalists. According to the Committee to Protect Journalists (CPJ), journalists investigating sensitive issues such as corruption, organised crime, and human rights abuses are among the most frequently targeted worldwide.

At the same time, economic and structural changes in the media industry have significantly impacted investigative journalism. Newsroom cuts and the radical restructuring of news production have led to the disbanding of investigative teams across the globe, while many newsrooms have reduced or removed the role of investigative journalists from their newsrooms. In response, investigative journalists have sought new methods of organising, funding and doing investigative reporting (Carson and Farhall, 2018).

The rise of new media platforms and citizen journalism in recent years has brought both opportunities and challenges for investigative reporting. The democratisation of information has empowered citizen journalists and whistleblowers to reveal issues of public concern, but it has also contributed to the spread of misinformation and the erosion of traditional journalistic standards (Viner, 2016).

In terms of organisation, teamwork has been one of the most notable developments, shifting from investigations conducted by single newsrooms to large-scale international collaborations (Graves and Shabbir, 2019). The Panama Papers investigation serves as a prime example, where over 300 members of the International Consortium of Investigative Journalism (ICIJ) collaborated to expose a global tax evasion network, implicating politicians, celebrities, and financiers. Such collaborations have revolutionised investigative journalism, enabling the pooling of resources, data, and expertise from journalists worldwide. Large-scale investigations are now brought into being by partnerships of publications that may once have seen each other as hated rivals in a cutthroat market. Investigative reporters may now find themselves working more closely with journalists from different organisations – in different time zones – than they do with their own colleagues in the same newsroom. A shared desire to get the story out and to serve the global public interest trumps the territorial impulse to triumph over our rivals that led to the newspaper and network wars of the past.

The rise of collaborative models is not limited to international organisations like the ICIJ. Between 2010 and 2012, a record number of global investigative journalism start-ups emerged, including projects like The Bureau of Investigative Journalism, The Centre for Investigative Journalism, Open Democracy, and The Ferret Scotland (Price, 2017). These organisations sought to fill the gap left by mainstream media outlets and have contributed to a growing culture of independent, investigative reporting. However, these digital start-ups often face significant economic challenges. Many lack strong institutional backing and struggle to secure sufficient funding for essential services, such as legal defence. As libel lawsuits can easily lead to legal fees in the hundreds of thousands of pounds, small media organisations and freelance journalists are at risk of bankruptcy from a single lawsuit (Hanna, 2024).

The shift towards collaborative investigative journalism has not only changed the operational model of journalism but has also led to a rethinking of the roles and identities of investigative journalists themselves. As Cancela and Dubied (2022) point out, many journalists today must negotiate between their professional ideals and the realities of contemporary newsroom practices.

In an era of shrinking resources, journalists are increasingly adopting 'liquid' definitions of their roles, which allow for more pragmatic and flexible approaches to investigative work. Instead of rigidly adhering to traditional ideals, many journalists now juggle various roles and responsibilities, balancing investigative reporting with other journalistic tasks. Investigative journalists in staff jobs are less likely to work in silos, off diary, to flexible deadlines, and away from the routine demands placed on general reporters. This adaptability can foster creativity and innovation but also places additional demands on journalists to be versatile in a rapidly changing environment.

The collaborative nature of investigative journalism today, combined with the pragmatic negotiation of professional identities, represents the future of the field. As journalists continue to face economic, legal, and institutional challenges, the capacity to collaborate across borders and develop flexible strategies will be key to the sustainability of investigative reporting. Furthermore, the growing need for investigative journalism in addressing global issues such as climate change, corruption, and human rights violations highlights the essential role that collaborative efforts will continue to play in the evolving media landscape (Chacón and Saldaña, 2021).

This book aims to critically discuss the state and nature of investigative journalism today, with chapters containing new data and commentary about the challenges and opportunities outlined above. It includes case studies from across the globe covering recent developments in the field and addressing some of the most pressing issues of our time, including misinformation, the climate crisis, and inequality. In doing so, it asks readers to consider the ways in which investigative journalism can bring about meaningful change, and what conditions need to be in place for it to do so.

The book begins by exploring the historical and cultural roots of investigative journalism, tracing its evolution alongside the personas of those who practice it. **Bethany Usher's** chapter examines the origins of investigative crime journalism, from 19th century rogue and murder pamphlets to today's proliferation of true crime content. A former crime reporter herself, she argues that the development of investigative practices is closely tied to the public perception of crime journalists, offering insights into how these elements have shaped one another over time.

Following this historical grounding, the book turns to the Tools and Specific Techniques of Investigative Journalism.

Neil Macfarlane's chapter examines FOI as a vital tool in the armoury of any investigative journalist, one that is crucial in the media's role as watchdog for the public interest. The chapter provides an international, comparative analysis of FOI laws and assesses the achievements of FOI in increasing accountability, tackling corruption, and ensuring efficient governance. As an investigative journalist with decades of experience using FOI, the author provides guidance on using the legislation in a UK context by providing a recent case study, before evaluating quantitative data, including that obtained through new FOI requests, that indicates trends toward declining effectiveness.

Chris Arsenault offers practical strategies for investigating large-scale land and natural resource deals, drawing on testimonies from impacted communities and offering case-specific methodologies to navigate the challenges of this complex reporting area. The chapter examines strategies for investigative reporting on the land grabbing phenomenon, from the boardrooms of Toronto and Dubai to the parched farmland in Mali and expanding cattle farms in the Brazilian Amazon. The chapter offers a methodology for best practices in journalistic coverage of the deals, drawing on the author's own experience of leading investigations across the globe, and case-specific examinations of challenges, strategies, and opportunities for breaking original stories.

Covering and exposing the use of controversial digital technologies, algorithms and artificial intelligence (AI) applications has recently become a beat for journalists around the world. **Philip Di Salvo's** chapter sheds light on how these systems work. In a new form of investigative journalism, reporters use hacking and coding to open these 'black boxes' – exposing several cases of data injustice, discrimination, and abuses perpetuated through algorithmic decision-making, surveillance, or automation. The chapter will look at this phenomenon, discussing some international case studies and highlighting the implications for contemporary news-making.

The book then addresses Constraints on Investigative Journalism – and Ways to Challenge them.

Barbara Longo-Flint delves into the repercussions of legal intimidation on investigative journalists in Italy and the UK and explores strategies to bolster their resilience against such threats. It discusses how powerful entities increasingly use Strategic Lawsuits Against Public Participation (SLAPPs) to silence journalists through costly lawsuits. The chapter analyses the trauma triggered by these legal battles, assessing potential impacts on journalistic practice and self-censorship while offering a toolkit of advice for journalists, students, and educators.

Michelle Park contributes a comparative study of nonprofit newsrooms, focusing on the Korea Center for Investigative Journalism (KCIJ) in South Korea and The Bureau of Investigative Journalism (TBIJ) in the United Kingdom. Motivated by ProPublica's unwavering dedication to investigative journalism in the USA, these two nonprofit newsrooms have pioneered new approaches to financial sustainability. This has been made possible through nonprofit funding from the collective support of approximately 40,000 individuals (in the case of the KCIJ) and philanthropic benefactors (in the case of the TBIJ).

In conversation with journalists and academics, **Neil Farrington** and **John Price**, award-winning investigative journalist **David Conn** discusses how sports investigations are increasingly becoming big news stories and offers advice for young sports reporters looking to follow this path. From athletics to the Tour de France, some of the greatest athletes in history have been exposed as frauds by diligent sports reporters who ventured into the realm of investigative journalism. Sport has also become a geo-political plaything, with some of the world's most sacred institutions being used as sportswashing vehicles for authoritarian regimes and businesses with questionable ethical records. The chapter has a particular focus on the work of Conn and others in investigating the Hillsborough football stadium disaster.

The next section, The Impact of AI on Investigative Journalism, examines how AI has emerged as both a tool and a subject of investigation for journalists.

Investigative journalists have already used AI to hold power to account, while AI algorithms themselves have increasingly become a form of power that reporters seek to scrutinise. **Paul Bradshaw's** chapter examines the different branches of AI, how investigative journalists have used them, what recent developments mean for the future of the practice, and how both the industry and individual journalists are tackling the ethical challenges that new technologies present.

Mathias Felipe de Lima Santos takes a case-based approach to investigate how AI and data journalism are transforming environmental reporting in Latin America. The digital native media outlet InfoAmazonia (Brazil) and the legacy news organisation La Nación (Argentina) have launched initiatives dedicated to environmental data-driven storytelling. The chapter analyses how these two news outlets are using environmental data journalism and intelligent approaches to tackle the ongoing crisis of public trust, ultimately leading to the creation of award-winning investigative stories.

The final section of the book, Two Crucial Strands: Teaching and Collaborative Investigative Journalism, explores education and collaboration as critical pillars shaping the future of investigative journalism.

In recent years, cross-border investigative journalism has risen to global prominence, as evidenced by projects such as the Panama Papers. **Maria Konow-Lund, Lucia Mesquita, and Carolyne Lunga** analyse attempts to incorporate cross-border investigative projects into journalism education. This study examines the Erasmus+ project 'Cross-border Journalism Campus' (CJC), which unites institutions – Gothenburg University (Sweden), Universität Leipzig (Germany), and Centre de Formation des Journalistes (France) – with the guidance of seasoned investigative journalists who have been central to major global investigations. In doing so, the chapter assesses the potential of the CJC model as a blueprint for reshaping investigative journalism education.

The potential for collaborative investigative journalism (CIJ) to revitalise investigative reporting in the global south is explored in a further chapter by **Carolyne Lunga**. The chapter focuses on an award-winning CIJ project done in South Africa to understand the main actors, how they collaborated and the impact the collaboration had on traditional journalistic values and norms such as truth and transparency.

Finally, **Tom Sanderson**, Deputy Director of the Centre for Investigative Journalism, asks: How do we train students of investigative journalism to cope with the challenges of the next decade and beyond? His chapter interrogates a range of teaching techniques used by industry, academia and the wider education establishment and assesses whether they are fit for purpose. In doing so, the chapter provides an in-depth analysis of education's invaluable contributions to empowering journalists with the skills and knowledge necessary to uphold the principles of investigative journalism in the contemporary media landscape.

References

Baker, R. (2009) *Family of secrets*. New York: Bloomsbury Publishing. Available at: https://www.bloomsbury.com/uk/family-of-secrets-9781608191925/

Borins, S. and Herst, B. (2020) 'Beyond "Woodstein": Narratives of investigative journalism', *Journalism Practice*, 14(7), pp. 769–790. Available at: https://doi.org/10.1080/17512786.2019.1664927.

Cancela, P. and Dubied, A. (2022) 'Stay strong, get perspective, or give up: Role negotiation in small-scale investigative journalism', *Journalism Studies*, 23(9), pp. 1056–1076. Available at: https://doi.org/10.1080/1461670X.2022.2067585.

Cancela, P., Gerber, D. and Dubied, A. (2021) '"To me, It's normal journalism" professional perceptions of investigative journalism and evaluations of personal commitment', *Journalism Practice*, 15(6), pp. 878–893. Available at: https://doi.org/10.1080/17512786.2021.1876525.

Carson, A. (2019) 'What is investigative journalism', *Investigative Journalism, Democracy and the Digital Age*, pp. 53–82. Available at: https://doi.org/10.4324/9781315514291-3.

Carson, A. and Farhall, K. (2018) 'Understanding collaborative investigative journalism in a "Post-truth" age', *Journalism Studies*, 19(13), pp. 1899–1911. Available at: https://doi.org/10.1080/1461670x.2018.1494515.

Chacón, L.M.C. and Saldaña, M. (2021) 'Stronger and safer together: Motivations for and challenges of (trans)national collaboration in investigative reporting in Latin America', *Digital Journalism*, 9(2), pp. 196–214. Available at: https://doi.org/10.1080/21670811.2020.1775103.

Di Salvo, P. (2021) 'Securing whistleblowing in the digital age: SecureDrop and the changing journalistic practices for source protection', *Digital Journalism*, 9(4), pp. 443–460. Available at: https://doi.org/10.1080/21670811.2021.1889384.

Graves, L. and Shabbir, N. (2019) 'Gauging the global impacts of the "Panama papers" three years later', *Reuters Institute for the Study of Journalism*. Available at: https://doi.org/10.60625/RISJ-G00D-5906.

Hanna, M. (2024) 'SLAPPs: What are they? And how should defamation law be reformed to address them?', *Journal of Media Law*, 16(1), pp. 1–28. Available at: https://doi.org/10.1080/17577632.2024.2345982.

Harcup, T. (2021) *Journalism: Principles and practice*. 4th edn. Los Angeles: SAGE. Available at: https://uk.sagepub.com/en-gb/eur/journalism/book268232?_gl=1*1b7y9uj*_gcl_au*MzYzOTk4MjgxLjE3NDY2MTc0NDE.*_ga*MTY4NDkxODg5MC4xNzQ2NjE3NDM4*_ga_60R758KFDG*czE3NDczMDY5MDYkbzMkZzAkdDE3NDczMDY5MDYkajYwJGwwJGg1NTkwNDUwMDc.*_ga_B9E65QYXFE*czE3NDczMDY5MDYkbzEkZzAkdDE3NDczMDY5MDYkajYwJGwwJGgw

Hunter, M.L. (2011) *Story-based inquiry*. Unesco.

Karan, K. (2024) 'Open-source journalism: Innovations and ethical Challenges', in Dahiya, S. and Trehan, K. (eds.) *Handbook of digital journalism: Perspectives from South*

Asia. Singapore: Springer Nature, pp. 385–395. Available at: https://doi.org/ 10.1007/978-981-99-6675-2_33.

Lanosga, G. *et al.* (2017) 'A breed apart?', *Journalism Studies*, 18(3), pp. 265–287. Available at: https://doi.org/10.1080/1461670X.2015.1051570.

Lashmar, P. (2013) 'From the insight team to WikiLeaks: The continuing power of investigative journalism as a benchmark of quality news journalism', in Anderson, P., Ogola, G., and Williams, M. *(eds.) The future of quality news journalism*. Routledge.

McQuail, D. (2013) *Journalism and society*. London: Sage Publications.

O'Neill, E.P. (2010) *Investigative journalism after Watergate in the USA and UK : A comparative study in professional practice*.

Price, J. (2017) 'Can the ferret be a watchdog?', *Digital Journalism*, 5(10), pp. 1336–1350. Available at: https://doi.org/10.1080/21670811.2017.1288582.

Viner, K. (2016) 'How technology disrupted the truth', *The Guardian*. Available at: https://www.theguardian.com/media/2016/jul/12/how-technology-disrupted-the-truth.

PART I
Historical Background

1

WANDERING CRUSADERS

A Short History of the Investigative Crime Journalist

Bethany Usher

The investigative crime journalist is the oldest and arguably the most my-thologised professional persona of media industries (Usher, 2023). From its earliest origins in mid-16th century rogue pamphleteers and across vast socio-political, legal, cultural and technological change, this figure has endured and evolved, at times with evocative visual self-presentations. Professional persona construction allows for figures to represent ways to be and "organize themselves publicly as such" as both projection and performance (Marshall, Moore and Barbour, 2020, p. 3). The "crime journalist" is an intrinsic cultural figure of crime-as-genre – a male and often solitary investigator who wanders urban streets, appearing to seamlessly move between the criminal underworld, professional newsrooms and spaces of law, order and justice (Usher, 2023, pp. 148–150; 197–198). Across countless fictional and factual narratives, no other worker can be so visibly tracked through the history of popular media.

When journalism professionalised and modernised in the late 19th and early 20th centuries, the crime journalist became one of the most lauded figures of, and beyond, newsrooms (Root, 2018; Rowbotham, Stevenson and Pegg, 2013, pp. 153–158). But active mythologies drew on earlier popular cultures of crime, which were shaped by their historic place in legal and political systems. This established some of the contradictions of how sensationalised journalism and "true crime" can act in the public interest, but also how lines of meaningful investigation can become blurred with suspicion, rumour and conjecture. There is much to learn about the ethical parameters of contemporary crime investigation from picking through such complexities. This chapter explores three formative phases from the 16th to the 20th century that responded to shifts in media technology and shaped the symbolic, representative and professional aspects of investigative journalism, before considering

DOI: 10.4324/9781003478157-3

how such dimensions shape contemporary journalistic crime cultures and how we might rethink ethics-of-practice in response. Exploring the lineage of the crime journalist persona as both professional practice and self-performance and its unique place in the development of investigative journalism highlights the social significance and reasons for the enduring appeal of mediatised crime.

Newsgathering, Investigation and Early Crime Journalism (1550s–1750s)

Early modern societies were characterised by the first production and distribution systems for print. The seeds of crime news were sown here, in ballads and pamphlets first and then popular chapbooks and news books, and for some of the "new writers of this age" (Rich, 1593), it was soon their main area of work. They established "still active mythologies around class, gender, sexual immorality, outsiders and insiders and fears of what might lurk in our shadows" (Usher, 2023, p. 24). A genre of what were later named "rogue pamphlets" first evidenced the commercial benefits of speaking to audiences in "lively prose" and presented narrative accounts of newsgatherers as "wandering heroes" who exposed "criminal society" (Raymond, 2003, p. 18). Writers, some of whom were also magistrates, dressed as "common folk" to expose criminality in taverns and gambling houses, interview witnesses and sometimes criminals and began to report from court.

The first rogue pamphlet, *A Caveat or Warning for Common Cursitors* (1566 [1814 reprint], produced by magistrate Thomas Harman, described how he had "gathered and understood" his information, often from undercover work. He included transcripts of interviews with rogues and beggars – "men and women, boys and girls" – and named and shamed 215 "notorious" individuals, around 18 of whom were later verified from surviving assize court records (Aydelotte, 1913). It was hugely popular – reproduced in a variety of forms for at least the next 150 years – largely because of its tips to "gentle folk" to avoid falling foul of "wild rogues" including "beastly begotten" street children who "trade[d] up in treachery" (1566 [1814], p. 24) and influenced legislation around vagrancy and petty street crime. In *Pamphlets and Pamphleteering in Early Modern Britain*, Joad Raymond (2003, pp. 17–18) highlights *Caveat's* influence on the most prolific rogue pamphleteers of the 1590s and early 1600s, Robert Greene and Thomas Dekker, both of whom adopted its representational and linguistic techniques to "conny-catch" criminals across London. The term "conny" was Elizabethan slang for petty criminality, and Greene was responsible for a wave of ever more outlandish "catcher" pamphlets, adopting the image of a coney rabbit as his trademark or brand. He reprinted and inserted his own stories into *Caveat* under a new title, *The Groundworke of Conny-Catching* (1592), and urged authorities to act. Greene was criticised for his newsgathering techniques, including the use of subterfuge and his salacious and unsympathetic depictions of the poor, and was accused of producing "injurious pamphlets", which touched "small scrapes" but "let gross faults pass without reprehension" (A.I., 1592).

By the 1620s (and for the next 250 years or so) the production of crime pamphlets was centralised around London's Grub Street with the earliest surviving literary reference by the poet John Taylor (1630) already describing the "quintescence of Grub Street, well distild/Through Cripplegate in a contagious Map". Crime-in-print has an identifiable birthplace, and the "grubs" were a specific type of media worker who lived, worked and socialised, moving between nearby gaols and courts looking for stories and often interviewing criminals or producing biographies about them from hearsay. This made "grubstreet" the first popular news culture to be referenced in Samuel Johnson's *Dictionary of the English Language* (1755) as a commonly used adjective for popular low-cost print, something like "tabloid" today. Across generations, "grubs" produced crime content for countless pamphlets and newspapers and captured the eternal misery flowing from Newgate and the Old Bailey – inspiring generations of subsequent authors and journalists – and found means to turn such tools and techniques towards their own commercial and political ends. Crime news and biographies became "rooted in notions of a 'slippery slope'" from minor transgressions often driven by theft of property because of poverty or greed, "to steadily more serious crimes ending in rapes, robberies, murders and an ignominious end" (Ward, 2016, p. 18).

Grubstreet culture also established the city at night as the natural habitat of the investigative crime journalist. In *Nightwalking* (2015) Matthew Beaumont considers the "nocturnal picturesque" as a key part of early modern rogue pamphlets and how this influenced generations of writers and journalists. In 1696, moralist John Dunton published a short-lived but widely circulated journal entitled *The Night-Walker: Or, Evening Rambles in Search after Lewd Women* (1696) wherein he described how he meandered the streets of London, speaking to sex workers and their customers to provide a "moral map of the metropolitan night" (Beaumont, 2015, pp. 141–168). While he stopped publication within a year after accusations of titillating and corrupting material, it expanded links between cultural depictions of criminality, social commentary and discussions of law and order. From then, "walking the streets" became an "urban odyssey" in 18th century print, with narration often balancing sympathy for the poor with repulsion at their criminality (Corfield, 1990).

By the 1740s, investigations into crime linked to campaigns for improved systems of law and order were becoming more common and professionalised, with infamous magistrates Henry (1707–1754) and John Fielding (1721–1780) emerging as early pioneers. Across his pamphlets, newspapers and novels, Henry Fielding portrayed the criminal underworld in colourful detail and in *An Enquiry into the Recent Increases of Robbers* (1751) claimed that social freedoms for the poor had changed "manners, customs and habits" so that they demanded "luxury" and were "profligate", as part of moves towards "equality" with their superiors instead of "subjection" (p. xvii). He argued that the only way forward was to help them accept their rightful place through fairer systems of law and order. This also promoted the work of his Bow Street Runners (1749), London's first professional "thief-taking" force, which provided the model for the Metropolitan Police. Fielding engaged in proactive policing and investigative journalism, with the two practices indistinct from one another. He raided gaming houses, brothels and taverns as accounted in his short-lived newspaper *The Covent-Garden Journal* (1752), published from "His House in Bow Street" (4 April 1752). He looked to build support amongst the politically and socially influential and in adverts spoke directly "To the Public" and declared that "all persons who shall for the future suffer by Robberies, Burglaries" should send him "Description…to the Fact" so he could investigate. While it contained lots of crime news, its primary purpose was publicity, including for his novels and crime biographies that usefully also illustrated immoralities, causal factors and potential solutions. Although this led to accusations of "trading justice" for financial gain (Ward, 2016, p. 152), Fielding had established the close relationships between police and press that, for good and ill, have been part of investigative crime reporting ever since.

Investigation, the City at Night and the Professionalisation of Journalism

In the 19th century the crime journalist persona solidified with the modernisation of the press, but mythologised and indelible backdrops for both professional practice and cultural performance stayed largely the same. The authoritative journalistic investigator as narrator emerged as someone who wandered urban streets to expose causal factors, including social circumstances, injustices and corruptions.

Some American newspapers became explicit in their challenges to the social order, which they claimed were the principal reasons for criminality. For example, a column in the radical Philadelphia-based *Mechanics Free Press* (1828–1831), written anonymously by the "Night Hawk" revealed the "misdemeanours done under cover of the night" (12 January 1828) and the "pathetic lives of the poor and the depravity of the city's supposedly respectable people" (Osborn, 2017, p. 46). In Britain, Chartist[1] journalist and newspaper editor George W.M. Reynolds' fictional, but factually based, *The Mysteries of London* (1844–1845) and *The Mysteries of the Courts of London* (1848–1856) sold at least a million copies and focused on a central narrator, wandering the city and revealing scenes of desperate criminality. It was part of the hugely popular "city mysteries" genre across Europe and America where countless writers and investigators ventured into the darkest corners of the city to hold a mirror up to criminality and human suffering. Across his many publications, Reynolds' journalistic authoritative tone, even when penning fiction, both depicted the need for social change and directly argued for it. It is now considered the "tour de force" of an "editor, journalist, publisher and novelist" who seemed to "achieve an impossible synthesis: an unprecedented commercial success combined with an outspoken radical politics" (Haywood, 1998, p. 121).

The influence of Reynolds on pioneering investigative journalist Henry Mayhew (1812–1887) is clear, not least because Mayhew "waxed enthusiastically about Reynolds's appeal as a writer and activist" (Haywood, 1998, p. 121) in *London Labour and the London Poor* (1851–1861). Mayhew located his work around Haymarket and categorised different types of criminality, including the operating methods of thieves and sex workers. Countless histories of journalism highlight his more systematic newsgathering techniques, including the use of statistics from the authorities and first-person accounts gathered by interview as a shift towards press modernisation. There is less focus on how he was inspired by old Grub Street and spoke to news sellers and researched how crime biographies were produced (see Berridge, 1978, p. 252; Mountjoy, 1978, p. 267). The fourth and final volume of *London Labour and the London Poor* (1862) was produced with "several contributors", including penny dreadful writer and socialist Bracebridge Hemyng (1841–1901), who focused on the plight of sex workers. He included statistics on how many had committed suicide, were prosecuted for abortions or had asked for help from the "Midnight Meeting Movement" and were subsequently "restored to friends". As Hemyng night-walked, he considered the "intense horrors of Haymarket" and mused on differences between "lorettes of London, and the men by which they are kept", who worked from opulent night-houses, as compared to those who made their living "walking the Haymarket" and "promenade[d] the pavement… to pick up men" (volume 4, 1862 [1865 edn], pp. 210–262). Mayhew and his contributing team's investigative practices were better organised and more focused, which proved particularly influential for a new generation of journalists.

By the end of the 19th century, British and American newspaper editors were attuned to the commercial opportunities of populist news set against a backdrop of social upheaval, the city, industrial revolution, emigration and immigration, new senses of identity and ordinary people trying to make their way through it all (see Usher, 2023, pp. 155–169). "New" or "Yellow" journalism became the dominant form, and in the UK, prolific crime journalist, investigator and campaigner W.T. Stead was an early trailblazer. He first developed his investigative skills working for *The Northern Echo* (1870–present) in his native northeast England during the case of the "West Auckland Poisoner" and reports of Mary Ann Cotton's (1832–1873) arrest, the police investigation and her trial were widely syndicated by national and American newspapers. Stead linked banal details from the lives he observed while newsgathering to the sensational melodrama of the case. He trawled former addresses and spoke to those still living there, heard stories of other stepchildren and lodgers who had died in mysterious circumstances, with some later added to Cotton's charges. He convinced the authorities to exhume the bodies of two babies and spoke to the gravediggers as they did so. Other interviewees included the woman who adopted Cotton's gaol-born babe, chosen from applicants that "numbered nearer a hundred than fifty" (22 March 1873), shopkeepers who (perhaps) sold her poison on account (see Usher, 2023, pp. 155–169) and Cotton's stepfather shortly after a prison visit to her who suggested she might have also killed her mother (24 March 1873). Soon he was in competition with what *The Northern Echo* described a decade later as "pushing reporters", who also spoke to authorities or covered the trial for "a little fortune" (3 April 1882).

When Stead was headhunted by the London-based *The Pall Mall Gazette* he was repulsed by the widespread practice of rich and powerful men paying to rape the children of the poor and in response conducted his most famous investigation and campaign to tackle child sexual exploitation. *The Maiden Tribute of Modern Babylon*, first published in serial form in July 1885, was sensational in its demands for political and social change through the exposure of criminality. Published to coincide with parliamentary debates in relation to the age of individual consent (Herd, 1926), he appealed directly to politicians that they must read it but warned "the squeamish" and those "who prefer to live in a fool's paradise" against it. Stead spent "terrible weeks" in "a strange, inverted world…of the streets and the brothel" and began his work with a familiar description of nocturnal walks through the "labyrinth" of London, where "beneath the gas glare of its innumerable lamps" he witnessed "all the vices of Gomorrah" (6 July). *Maiden Tribute* owes much to Mayhew and Hemyng's accounts of sexual exploitation, George W.M. Reynolds' *Mysteries* and the traditions of criminal biographies (Usher, 2023, pp. 159–160). But this work was positioned at the crossroads of older traditions and a modern vision for "governance through journalism", and he was determined to force change. In an astonishing twist on older narratives, Stead described how he purchased the virginity of a 13-year-old child (later named as Eliza Armstrong), before taking readers on a degrading and humiliating journey for both the child and himself. He did not rape Eliza but left the reader under no illusions that he could have done so, and he was later imprisoned for the crime of not having her father's permission to purchase her virginity, which he used to further publicise his campaign. This provided him with further evidence of the need for an age of individualised consent, and he was exact as to what should be done. *Maiden Tribute* as a piece of campaigning investigative journalism was singular, achievable and timely, which forced the government to act.

Both these formative experiences proved fruitful during Stead's second big "serial murder" story – the Whitechapel Murders or "Jack the Ripper" case. This quickly became the first live news phenomenon where many journalists, including Stead and journalistic and political ally T.P. O'Connor, editor of

The Star (1888–1924), reimagined older mythologies and cultures to create a terrifying new archetype of a dangerous stranger lurking in the city's "dark shadows". The proximity of Whitechapel to booming Fleet Street at the peak of New Journalism's innovations made this the perfect case for ever more competitive on-scene "pack" reporting, which would come to characterise tabloid crime news as both an investigative practice and as a *visible extension* of criminal events, with the crime journalist as a central figure in the narrative. Those who consider how the Ripper case influenced American crime reporting often highlight how journalists investigating the "body in the river" in 1898 drew directly from the linguistic and newsgathering practices developed during the Whitechapel Murders. This case, which "scandalised a city and sparked the tabloid wars" (Collins, 2011), saw open competitive and at times even combative pack reporting between William Randolph Hearst's *New York Evening Journal* and Joseph Pulitzer's *New York World*. Hearst nicknamed his reporters the "Murder Squad" and invited readers to join in the investigation by sending "any information" that might identify the victim and his killer for large financial rewards, and Pulitzer soon followed suit. Such practices were primed for new media technologies and the rapid social and economic shifts of the early 20th century.

Golden Age: Investigation and the Tabloid Crime Reporter (1910–1980)

In the 20th century, the crime journalist persona morphed into the trilby and trench coat adorned crime hacks of mid-century Chicago, New York and London's Fleet Street. This iconographic visual form was characteristic of an age where systems and cultures of fame developed ever more complex and multifaceted spectacles of visibility. This was active imagery, as captured in American film and multiple print publications and was also the dress of the police detective and the mobster. Like in the early modern period when rogue pamphleteers and magistrates adopted the attire of common criminals to blend in, the criminal, the hack and the law might be indistinguishable, at least at first glance.

Crime reporters, now titled and by-lined as such, emerged as leading figures in the professionalisation of journalism, helped to establish unions and codes of practice and through personal contacts and "crime reporter associations" brokered ever closer relationships with police (Campbell, 2015; Root, 2018; Rowbotham, Stevenson and Pegg, 2013; Usher, 2023). Many were driven by a near cultish belief that exposing criminality was central to the public interest role in the press, and for some, that meant that anyone involved – victim, criminal or passing witness – was fair game. This developed gradually "across scores of spectacular exclusives, incredible investigations, significant campaigns, dubious dealings and ethically bankrupt doldrums of practice" (Usher, 2023, p. 175) and was one reason why the term tabloidisation came to "connote decay, a lowering of journalism standards that ultimately undermines the ideal functions of mass media in liberal democracies" (Gripsrud, 2008, p. 34). The techniques founded here degenerated ever further into forms associated with criminal tabloid practices as evidenced during Operation Elveden and Weeting in the early 2000s, which investigated payments by journalists to police and allegations of phone-hacking.

Crime journalism was a founding genre of tabloidism, broadly defined here as a "sensational, professionalised, transatlantic and multi-platform news media culture" (Usher, 2023, p. 175). As crime journalism became mass multimediated across print, radio, cinema and then television, tabloid hacks were at the forefront of modernisations that brought together crime as an ongoing news event, exclusive investigation and longer-form interviews, with the principal aim of staying ahead of competitors. This played a key, but often overlooked, part in the emergence of what is now known as "true crime" (Usher, 2023, pp. 190–195). While most studies focus on the influence of fictional American true crime detective magazines (Murley, 2008; Punnett, 2018), these shared a common lineage with crime news from the city mystery genre, detective pamphlets of the 19th century and older crime biographies. True crime might be better understood as an adjunct of the tabloid news cultures, with additional influences of fictionalisation, particularly in relation to how it portrays murder. Both newspapers and true crime magazines in the mid-20th century focused on the corrupting force of the city with its illegal entertainments of gambling, booze and vice. Evolutions of language, investigation and mythologies responded particularly to shifts in organised criminality, which, like journalistic investigation and production, was facilitated by modern technologies, transport and migration between Europe and America (Bell, 1960, pp. 139–150; Usher, 2023, pp. 190–195).

The founder of *Confidential* magazine (1952–1978), Robert Harrison (1904–1978), for example, trained as a crime reporter at the *New York Graphic* and turned his efforts towards an exposé of Hollywood stars and mafia criminals. True crime magazine *Chicago Confidential* (1952–present) had a "peep-hole writing team" (Bell, 1960, p. 139) led by former long-term *New York Daily Mirror* editor Jack Lait (1883–1954) and Lee Mortimer (1904–1963), both of whom began as "leg-men" in Chicago, hanging around police stations to telephone the office when a story broke. Alongside a New York sister-publication, it offered "shocking accounts" of the "fast fabulous, fascinating city" (1952) and Lait and Mortimer were given writing credits for the Hollywood film *Chicago Confidential* (1957). Together they forged the iconography of notorious "mobsters" as part of the dynamics of the modern city. In the UK, tabloid newspapers took much from their imagery, self-representations and linguistic styles and brought it together with their own investigative techniques and practices. In *The Murder Gang: Fleet Street's Elite Group of Crime Reporters in the Golden Age of Tabloid Crime* (2018), Neil Root accounts for how many spectacular exclusives were the result of their "nefarious collusions" with police and criminals alike (p. 11). Between the 1930s and 1960s, what became known as a "golden age" of tabloid investigative reporting, these "Sultans of the Newsroom" (Campbell, 2015, p. 91) led much of the work hailed as gold standard, but many paid money to, and were on first-name terms with, killers, and their tools of investigation were certainly unethical and often illegal by today's standards. Most were also active members of the National Union of Journalists and used the code of practice's public interest defence for "exposing or detection of criminality" as a shield against criticism (see Usher, 2023, pp. 195–198). When some of the Murder Gang helped found the Crime Reporters Association in 1945, it had the "dual function of pressure group for better facilities for gathering information" and *legitimising* their work as in the public interest (Chibnall, 1977, p. 50).

Founding member of the "Murder Gang" (*Picture Post*, 17 May 1947), infamous *News of the World* reporter Norman "Jock" Rae, solved murders and extracted confessions from killers. With better technologies for recording and organising evidence than police, fewer issues around legal jurisdiction, and quick responses to information in rival newspapers, he and other reporters were often far ahead of detectives and would exchange information for other exclusive lines (Campbell, 2015; Root, 2018). In the 1940s at the *Sunday People* (1881–present), crime correspondent Duncan Webb "expressly set out to crusade against criminal and moral wrongdoing and revamped the idea of the individual exposé of (un)deserving individuals" (Rowbotham, Stevenson and Pegg, 2013, p. 155). His investigation of the Messina Brothers' sex trafficking and vice racket in Soho and its links to Scotland Yard began with a startling front page that demanded the "arrest [of] these four men" and pictured them (3 September 1950). As part of their analysis of tabloid news cultures, *Time* magazine considered whether he might be the "greatest crime reporter of our time" (10 January 1955), but his investigation owed much to the mafia reports popularised in American "Confidential" magazines now turned to expose London's "Vice Empire". What Webb mastered was bringing investigatory practices together with the voices of victims, criminals and police. In some ways, this had much in common with 19th century pamphlets and "confessions" of sex workers, now extended by visual dynamics of tabloidism and links with police. While the influence of the American hacks was clear, the earlier origins of British investigation remained a key influence.

As in America, the work of the most celebrated crime correspondents inspired early broadcast crime narratives, and some also penned true crime books. To compete with television news bulletins, newspapers needed to carve out exclusive lines, but broadcasters and publishers alike saw potential in telling old narratives in new forms. The *Daily Express'* chief crime reporter Percy Hoskins (1904–1989) had, in his own words, first worked as a crime "legman" but told the Medico-Legal Society in 1959 that the days of reporters hanging around police stations and the courts in the hopes of an exclusive story were over. Instead, crime "specialists" made the news through investigation and looked to other mediums to tell their stories in new ways. Hoskins was a Murder Gang legend, having extracted a confession of one killer, found the location of the body before police and published dozens of sensational crime exposés (Root, 2018, pp. 76–77; 110). His primary source was police officers, whom he often paid or exchanged information with, and his access to Scotland Yard was unrivalled. In 1951, he published an early true crime book, *No Hiding Place*, which told the "authentic story of Scotland Yard in action", with a particular focus on murder and free access to files. This work provided the raw data for *Whitehall 1212* (1951–1952), produced for NBC radio in America and named after the first telephone line number installed in the Yard in 1934. The crime reporter was expanding in reach and medium, but in doing so was confirming their unique place in the archival history, not just of investigative journalism, but law and order itself.

Such investigatory practices also influenced the broadsheet newspapers. Many insider and outsider accounts highlight a similar golden age at *The Sunday Times* (1821–present) between the 1960s and 1980s, and this took much from how tabloids tied public interest and human interest together in interviews, investigatory practices and social campaigns. Under the leadership of Harold Evans (1928–2020), there was a reset of ethics, style, presentation, investigation and campaigning at the Sunday edition, which in turn influenced the daily edition to shift in style. As editor (1964–1981), he was known for his "independent editorial spirit" (Curran and Seaton, 2018, p. 101) and like New Journalist W.T. Stead, almost a century before, first edited regional *The Northern Echo* between 1961 and 1966, where he reinvigorated its reputation for strong campaigns, quality human interest interviews and exclusive crime content. In 1965, the paper campaigned for the pardon of Timothy Evans, wrongly convicted and hanged for the murder of his wife Beryl and infant daughter Geraldine, since proven to be victims of serial killer John Christie, whom they had lived alongside at 10 Rillington Place. At *The Sunday Times*, Evans created the "Insight" team, which brought the investigation together with emotive interviews, including with victims of crime and legal injustice. The team, which included famous reporters Philip Knightley, Murray Sayle and Elaine Potter, won many legal battles against limits on investigation from out-of-date contempt laws and exposed the Thalidomide Scandal, Kim Philby as a Russian spy, and Israel's secret nuclear weapons programme. In turn, they influenced tabloid investigatory practices such as those of Paul Foot, who throughout the 1980s examined the case of "The Bridgewater Four", who had been convicted of murdering 14-year-old Carl Bridgewater, ultimately leading to their successful appeal in 1997.

However, shifts in tabloid culture, including increasing interest in celebrity culture, meant that the tools and techniques of the great crime hacks were turned to other people, and for some, anyone in the public eye was fair game, including victims of crime. This was evidenced by phone-hacking revelations and the Leveson Inquiry, which heard testimony from victims and their families. Graeme Turner (2014, p. 83), Natalie Fenton (2012, p. 4) and James Curran (in Curran and Seaton, 2018) all suggest that the targeting of victims of crime, celebrities and politicians responded primarily to increased market competition, but the traditional thrill of the chase of the tabloids was also a factor. The consequences of crime journalism were vast. A combination of the exposure of wrongdoing and shifts in social media and digital technology resulted in the severing of direct and personal ties between lower-level police officers and reporters and the growth of a new type of investigatory crime content producer.

Reborn or Lost Forever?: Persona and the Investigative Crime Journalist in the 21st Century

Rampant commercialisation over the past 50 years and the triumph of neoliberal models of tabloidism aided owners and conglomerates of news media who spread their tentacles towards increased social, political and economic control. They seized the best narratives of popular crime and turned them to commercial ends, and as audiences diversified, the time and resources afforded to the hacks of the so-called golden age became a thing of the past. Pressure for exclusive investigation (or seedy revelation) without adequate resources was flagged as a key reason for criminality by reporters who were prosecuted and/or gave evidence against colleagues at the 2011 Leveson Inquiry and phone-hacking trials. At the same time, the affordance of digital technology meant that crime journalism became *mass-produced* with networks of content stretching across forms and platforms. Audiences who engage most often with tabloidised true crime now *cultivate* their interest in ways that can make them active participants (Jewkes, 2015; Usher, 2023). These fundamental changes to newsgathering practices, production and platforms, mean that the investigative crime journalist as lone, often unethical, sometimes spectacular and much lauded crusader, may be gone forever.

As large pockets of mainstream news – including some publications once at the forefront of crime investigation – offer fewer expensive exclusive investigations and more cheaply produced clickbait (Tong, 2022, pp. 21–23; Usher, 2023, pp. 234–241), journalists count as just one amongst a growing array of authoritative voices in crime media spheres that include professional and civilian (true) crime influencers, current and retired police officers, judges and lawyers, documentary makers and podcasters. The professional practice of influencers, citizen investigators and journalists blur together, and some amass vast followings. They draw on some of the same tools as digital crime news reporters but wrap them in presentational first-person narratives with insertions of emotion, shock and horror. Visibility *builds* through constant negotiation of authority (as if a journalist) and authenticity (as a fan), using digital tools of production, conversation and a sense of immediacy. This often replaces objective "fact" with subjective "truth" and, as a result, false accusations across social media can have terrible impacts on innocent people (Usher, 2023, pp. 213–246).

While the investigative reporter using subterfuge and undercover methods still exists, the traditional persona of the investigative crime journalist is no longer the lone restless male crusader, wandering the darkest areas of the city. A new breed of crime influencers builds visibility using similar production tools, investigatory practices and self-display, but they are also fundamentally different. True crime scholar Kelli Boling (2019, 2022) highlights how producers and listeners of such podcasts are more likely to be women and how they have reshaped true crime towards campaigning and tackling injustices. The American Society of Professional Journalists commented on how the hosts of *My Favorite Murder* (2016–present), Karen Kilgariff and Georgia Hardstark, draw from journalistic traditions of investigation, but bring in elements of humour to make stories of murders "like bedtime tales" with "wisecracks and general banter" (4 May 2022). *My Favorite Murder* now boasts more than 35 million listens a year, and fans describe themselves as "murderinos", buy memberships, merchandise and attend sell-out speaking events and participate in investigations. Another popular podcast *Crime Junkie* (2017–present), presented by Ashley Flowers and Brit Prawat, has 1.1 million Instagram followers and on its "about us" section declares that since 2017 it has "remained top of the charts" with "over 500 million downloads, 630 stories and $643,000 donated to charity". Questions around ethical responsibilities, accusations that they plagiarise the work of journalists or that they are too involved with law enforcement, who give them "exclusive content" in exchange for a say in production, led these women to publicly declare that they are "not journalists". The question becomes, can this reimagining of professional practice, persona construction and self-presentation be steered towards better ethics than what has gone before? In *Journalism and Crime* (Usher, 2023, pp. 252–268), I argue that just as codes of practice and relationships with police were founded by the pioneers of tabloid investigation, we now need an ethical movement amongst the broader production pool of those who produce "journalistic crime content". The proposed 10-point code (see below classroom exercise) is informed by the past and present of investigatory crime journalism and looks to future ethics for the realities of networked practice in the digital world. In an age where expansive and seemingly never-ending amounts of crime content are far too often focused on clicks first and care for victims later, learning from the history of the crime journalist might help build in greater care and tackle the potential corruptions and social repercussions.

CLASSROOM EXERCISE

The conclusion to *Journalism and Crime* proposes the below 10-point code for those involved in producing "journalistic crime content". In a small group, find a true crime influencer, a podcaster and a crime journalist. Look at their content and discuss: 1) do they follow the below code; 2) what would be your recommendations to them in order to improve the ethics of their practice?

The exposure of criminality or evidence-based risks of crime is in the public interest. This includes how it is dealt with by criminal justice authorities and the courts including potential miscarriages of justice or impropriety of process. There is a public interest defence in exposing malpractice by media professionals during the reporting of crime. It is not in the public interest to report crime only for commercial gain, nor to produce material based on rumour, conjecture or falsehoods.

When reporting on current, recent or historic events, producers of journalistic crime content:

1 Must not produce content based on speculation, rumour, conjecture or falsehoods.
2 Must not engage in intimidation, harassment or persistent pursuit of victims or their families when newsgathering or in publication.
3 Must adhere to media law relating to the exposure or reporting of criminality, particularly in relation to court proceedings, contempt of court and potential risks to justice.
4 Must not include references to class, race, religion, sexuality, nationality or disability unless there is a direct link to the crime itself.
5 Must not suggest or apply languages of crime to individuals or social groups when there is no specific evidence of criminality, and should identify those individuals specifically involved wherever possible.
6 Must not pay officials of criminal justice or those accused or convicted of criminality. Payment for the time of victims or to former officials of criminal justice may be permitted if the piece is of discernible public interest or to support actions that raise awareness on issues of public safety.
7 Must prioritise the rights of victims and/or their loved ones to privacy or to be heard as they choose. There must be discernible public interest to revisit a historic case where victims are living, and consent of victims and their next of kin must be sought wherever possible.
8 Must not identify the relatives or family members of accused or convicted criminals unless there is a public interest defence in the interests of open justice or clear relevance to the crime itself.

9 Should emphasise social, economic and political reasons for criminality, particularly survival, and give equal resources to the reporting or exposure of crimes of corruption.

10 Must protect the interests of children, either when victims or when involved in criminality, and recognise their inability to consent to interview until over the age of 18. This should not restrict the reporting of legal proceedings.

Note

1 Chartism was a working-class political movement of the 1830s–1850s, named for "The People's Charter (1838) which called for six reforms to make the political system more democratic and inclusive.

References

Aydelotte, F. (1913) *Elizabethan Rogues and Vagabonds.* Oxford: The Clarendon Press.

Beaumont, M. (2015) *Nightwalking: A nocturnal history of London.* London: Verso Books.

Bell, D. (1960) *The end of ideology.* 2000 edn. Boston, MA: Harvard University Press.

Berridge, V. (1978) 'Popular Sunday papers and mid-Victorian society', in Boyce, G., Curran, J. and Wingate, P. (eds.) *Newspaper history from the 17th century to the present day.* London: Sage, pp. 247–264.

Boling, K.S. (2019) 'True crime podcasting: Journalism, justice or entertainment?', *Radio Journal: International Studies in Broadcast & Audio Media,* 17(2), pp. 161–178.

Boling, K.S. (2022) 'it's that 'There but for the grace of god go I' piece of it: Domestic violence survivors in true crime podcast audiences', *Mass Communication and Society,* pp. 1–23.

Campbell, D. (2015) *We'll all be murdered in our beds: The shocking true history of crime reporting in Britain.* London: Elliott and Thompson Ltd.

Chibnall, S. (1977) *Law and order news.* London: Tavistock.

Collins, P. (2011) *Murder of the century: The gilded age crime that scandalized a city and sparked the tabloid wars.* New York: Crown.

Corfield, P. (1990) 'Walking the City streets: The urban odyssey in eighteenth-century England', *Journal of Urban History,* 16, pp. 132–137.

Curran, J. and Seaton, J. (2018) *Power without responsibility.* 8th edn. London: Routledge.

Fenton, N. (2012) 'Telling lies: Press, politics, power and the public interest', *Television and New Media,* 13(1), pp. 3–6.

Gripsrud, J. (2008) 'Tabloidization, popular journalism, and democracy', in Biressi, A. and Nunn, H. (eds.) *The tabloid culture reader.* New York: Open University Press, pp. 23–44.

Haywood, I. (1998) 'George W.M. Reynolds and the radicalization of Victorian serial fiction', *Media History,* 4(2), pp. 121–139.

Herd, H. (1926) *The making of modern journalism.* London: George Allen & Unwin Ltd.

Jewkes, Y. (2015) *Media and crime.* 3rd edn. London: Sage.

Marshall, P.D., Moore, C. and Barbour, C. (2020) *Persona studies: An introduction.* Hoboken, New Jersey: John Wiley & Sons Inc.

Mountjoy, P.R. (1978) 'The working-class press and working-class conservatism', in Boyce, G., Curran, J. and Wingate, P. (eds.) *Newspaper history from the 17th century to the present day.* London: Sage, pp. 265–280.

Murley, J. (2008) *The rise of true crime: Twentieth century murder and American popular culture.* Westport, CT: Praeger.

Osborn, M.W. (2017) "Crime journalism and the urban gothic novel". In *A history of American crime fiction.* C. Raczkowski (ed). Cambridge and New York: Cambridge University Press.

Punnett, I.C. (2018) *Toward a theory of true crime narratives: A textual analysis.* New York and Abingdon: Routledge.

Raymond, J. (2003) *Pamphlets and pamphleteering in early modern Britain.* Cambridge: Cambridge University Press.

Rich, B. (1593) *Greenes news from both heaven and hell.* [1911 reprint]. London: Sidgwick and Jackson.

Root, N. (2018) *The murder gang: Fleet Street's elite group of crime reporters in the golden age of tabloid crime.* Stroud: The History Press.

Rowbotham, J., Stevenson, K. and Pegg, S. (2013) *Crime news in modern Britain: Press reporting and responsibility 1820–2010.* London: Palgrave Macmillan.

Salkow, S. (1957) *Chicago Confidential.* [Film] Peerless Productions, United Artists.

Tong, J. (2022) *Journalism, economic uncertainty and political irregularity in the digital and data era.* Bigley: Emerald Publishing.

Turner, G. (2014) *Understanding celebrity.* 2nd edn. London: Sage.

Usher, B. (2023) *Journalism and crime.* London: Routledge.

Ward, R. (2016) *Print culture, crime and justice in 18th century London.* London: Bloomsbury.

Cited crime journalism and news publications (1550–2020)

A.I (1592) *Defence of cony-catching or the confutation of those two injurious pamphlets published by r.G. Against the practitioners of many nimble-witted and mystical sciences.* By cuthbert cony-catcher. London: T. Gubbins for J. Busby.

Chicago Confidential (1952–1978)

Chicago Confidential (1957) Sidney Salkew, Peerless Productions, United Artists.

Crime Junkie (2017-present)

Daily Express (1900–present)

Dunton, J. (1696) *The night-walker: Or, evening rambles in search after lewd women.* London: J. Orme.

Fielding, H. (1751) *An enquiry into the recent increases of robbers.* London: A Miller.

Greene, R. (1592) *The groundworke of conny-catching.* London: J. Wolfe for T. Nelson.

Harman, T. (1566) *A caveat or warning for common cursitors.* 1814 reprint. Fleet Street, London: T. Bensley.

Hoskins, P. (1951) *No hiding place.* Daily Express Publication.

Mayhew, H. (1861–1862) *London Labour and the London poor,* 4 vols. London: Frank Cass and Co. (1967 edn).

Mechanics Free Press (1828–1831)

My Favourite Murder (2016–present)

News of the World (1843–2011)

Stead, W.T. (1885) "The Maiden Tribute of Modern Babylon". *The Pall Mall Gazette.* 7–11 July.

Sunday People (also The People, 1881–present)

Telecrime (BBC, 1938–1939; 1946)

Time (1923–present)
The Covent-Garden Journal (1752)
The Northern Echo (1870–present)
The Mysteries of London (1844–1845)
The Mysteries of the Courts of London (1848–1856)
The Pall Mall Gazette (1883–1921)
The Star (1888–1924)
Whitehall 1212 (1951–1952)

PART II

Tools and Specific Techniques of Investigative Journalism

2
FREEDOM OF INFORMATION

Neil Macfarlane

Introduction

Freedom of Information (FOI) is your right to know, enshrined in law. More than 100 countries (Transparency International, n.d.) across the globe have introduced legislation that guarantees citizens access to information about the ways in which their governments are run. This can allow proper scrutiny of the performance of public services by tracking everything from the economy, health outcomes, education, and crime rates. It can help establish if the taxpayer is getting value for money, if elected officials are fulfilling their promises, and if those in power are staying honest. When used by investigative journalists, it has led to the imprisonment of criminals, the demise of corrupt politicians, and changes to public policy that have saved lives.

Sometimes known as sunshine laws (Reporters Committee for Freedom of the Press, n.d.), for their ability to cast light in areas that would otherwise be kept hidden in the dark, they have not always been popular with those who are subject to the resultant scrutiny. Former Prime Minister Tony Blair introduced FOI to the UK, but later wrote of his regret in his autobiography, chastising himself as a "naive, foolish, irresponsible nincompoop" (Campaign for Freedom of Information, 2010) for doing so. One of his successors, David Cameron, proclaimed "transparency, sunlight, fresh air, is the best disinfectant" (Knight, 2009) before later launching a failed attempt to curtail its reach.

The world's first FOI act came into being in Sweden in 1766 (Encyclopaedia Britannica, n.d.). The legislation has proliferated in recent years and has been established as a human right by the United Nations (United Nations, n.d.). Countries that champion transparency and freedom of the press typically

DOI: 10.4324/9781003478157-5

become more prosperous (World Economic Forum, 2018). As investigative journalist Heather Brooke, who played a key role in using FOI to expose political corruption during the MP's expenses scandal of the 2000s in the UK, writes:

> The public's right to know is not just a noble ideal for an enlightened society; it is thoroughly practical.
>
> Freedom of information is the most effective and inexpensive way to stop corruption and waste, and enhance efficiency and good governance.
>
> *(Brooke, 2007, p. 203)*

This chapter will offer a practical guide on how investigative journalists can use FOI, will compare the legislation in place in various countries across the globe, with a specific analysis of its operation in the United Kingdom. It will also offer a case study, outlining a firsthand account of the formation of a recent investigation completed using FOI.

How Does It Work?

Submitting an FOI request does not, or at least should not, amount to a complex challenge that can only be done after years of legal training and experience with the court system. It can be as simple as sending an email. It is usually free to do and open to any citizen of that country, not just journalists. Typically, legislation features the following key elements.

- Requests can be made to public authorities rather than private organisations.
- They should be made in writing.
- Information must be released within a specified time period.
- Some information is off limits. Exemptions can typically apply to some commercially sensitive data or information that could prejudice ongoing legal cases or put national security at risk. Cost limits are often in place to prevent the process from becoming too expensive for governments to abide by.
- A regulator is usually in place to ensure compliance and deal with appeals.

FOI across the World

Since its origins in Northern Europe hundreds of years ago, FOI legislation has proliferated across the globe. Investigative journalists have used it everywhere from North America to mainland Europe and continental Africa, with some success. What follows is an overview of the acts in action across a range of countries from different regions of the globe, featuring a mix of established and emerging democracies picked for their diversity in terms of the length of time the legislation has been in force and the unique characteristics of each act.

USA

The United States has a well-established Freedom of Information Act that was first enacted by President Lyndon B. Johnson in 1966 (George Washington University, n.d.). Upon signing the act into law, President Johnson said: "This legislation springs from one of our most essential principles: A democracy works best when the people have all the information that the security of the Nation permits. No one should be able to pull curtains of secrecy around decisions which can be revealed without injury to the public interest" (George Washington University, n.d.).

Requests are made in writing, can sometimes incur fees – although those for the news media can be waived – and authorities have a 20-day time limit for responses (Reporters Committee for Freedom of the Press, 2014).

It has been described, with some hyperbole, as a "leading legal export of the United States to the rest of the world" (Youm and Mendel, 2018); however, it does have its admirers elsewhere in the world. At the inception of the United Kingdom's own Freedom of Information Act, the British-American investigative journalist Heather Brooke pointed out that the stateside version had far fewer exemptions for public authorities to hide behind (Brooke, 2007). She wrote: "Reporters and lobbyists in the UK often file FOI requests with US government to glean information about the UK. Even under the new UK freedom of information law, this practice will probably continue" (Brooke, 2007, p. 45).

Investigative journalists have used FOI throughout its half a century of existence, including recently in the work of 2022 Pulitzer Prize-winner Azmat Khan and colleagues from the New York Times, who put it to good use to access thousands of Defense Department records that revealed the scale of civilian deaths on US-led airstrikes in Afghanistan, Syria, and Iraq (Reporters Committee for Freedom of the Press, 2022).

The legislation even played a notable part in the 2016 Presidential campaign, when it emerged that Democrat candidate Hillary Clinton had been using personal emails in her role as Secretary of State, which many claimed was to circumvent FOI scrutiny of her official emails (Nieman Reports, 2024). When FBI Director Jim Comey announced an official investigation days before polls closed, many attributed Donald Trump's subsequent victory to the intervention (Nieman Reports, 2024).

However, there is some evidence that journalists in the US may be losing faith in FOI. In an extensive study to assess the FOIA's first 50 years, Derigan Silver analysed data which showed the proportion of requests from journalists is in long-term decline (Silver, 2016). He writes: "While FOIA is failing journalists for many reasons – most notably … the long delays and processing inefficiencies associated with access requests – a key reason the law is failing journalists is because journalists simply do not use it nearly as much as corporations and other non-media individuals and organizations, a fact that stands in stark contrast to the history and purpose of the law" (Silver, 2016, p. 495).

In the John Dyer article *50 Years of FOIA*, published by Nieman Reports, University of Arizona journalism professor David Cuillier said: "I often wonder if we are better off without a law at all … Public record statutes in a lot of ways give government officials the ability to legally delay releasing information, to deny information on often questionable reasoning. They will just pick an exemption—personnel, or it's under investigation, or prejudicial discussions. The law allows those pegs to hang those denials on" (Nieman Reports, 2024).

Nigeria

Nigeria is one of the more recent countries to enact the law in 2011. Africa's largest country by population features a significant media market, with around 100 established national and local newspapers, plus more than 80 online startups (Reuters Institute for the Study of Journalism, 2024). In a study of its effectiveness for journalists in its first decade, Asogwa Fidelis Ndidiamaka, Ibe Nkechinyere Magdalene Awo and Orji-Egwu Agatha Bliageri question whether the act has met its initial promise, describing it as "a hope dashed" (Asogwa, Ibe and Orji-Egwu, 2021, p. 37). The act was 12 years in the making after it was initially proposed in 1999 (Asogwa, Ibe and Orji-Egwu, 2021, p. 37). There are limitations to its scope that can prove challenging for investigative journalists, such as a lengthy time limit for responses of 90 days (Asogwa, Ibe and Orji-Egwu, 2021, p. 45), a long list of exemptions – "there are more exemptions in the act than access and this has frustrated journalists, NGOs and individuals from accessing information held by the government and its agencies" (Asogwa, Ibe and Orji-Egwu, 2021, p. 44) – and scattered implementation across the states (Asogwa, Ibe and Orji-Egwu, 2021).

One of the biggest challenges in Nigeria appears to be a lack of awareness of its potential among the community of investigative journalists. One study found that only 22.3% of journalists have ever submitted an FOI request. Nnadi and Obot (2014) quoted in Asogwa, Ibe and Orji-Egwu, 2021, conclude: "The long awaited law is going through a trial by those who were supposed to be the major beneficiaries. Journalists are either unaware of the provisions of the law or have not utilised or tested the specific provisions of the law in their news gathering/information sourcing" (Asogwa, Ibe and Orji-Egwu, 2021, p. 43). Asogwa et al add: "Journalists and their media organisations have not shown enough interest, and commitment, to make FOI more effective as a legal instrument for journalism practice in Nigeria" (Asogwa, Ibe and Orji-Egwu, 2021, p. 46).

Kosovo

Another recent addition to the list of FOI countries is Kosovo, which formally declared independence from Serbia in 2008 and immediately vowed to establish fundamental principles outlined in the Ahtisaari Plan, set by UN Special Envoy Martti Ahtisaari (U.S. Department of State, 2008). These included a pledge "to embrace multi-ethnicity as a fundamental principle of good governance, and to welcome a period of international supervision" (U.S. Department of State, n.d.). Its own FOI law was formally adopted soon after in 2010 (Ebibi, 2022). In a study of its first decade of operation from 2010–2020, Dashnim Ebibi outlines provisions in the act that put it ahead of the legislation in many other countries. All routine requests by journalists are considered under the act, whether or not the legislation is mentioned or official request forms are filled in, and the time limit for responses is seven days (Ebibi, 2022). In contrast to Nigeria, FOI seemed to quickly become an established practice for journalists, with 73% of all requests coming from journalists in 2011, although this had dropped to 33% by 2016 (Ebibi, 2022). The study outlines that although there is a government body in charge of enforcing compliance with requests, its ineffectiveness may have led to a loss of faith in FOI's power among journalists, as disputes were delayed after being referred to an overstretched judicial system. "The continuous situation of overburdened courts has caused distrust of journalists to address indictments to public institutions who were denying the right of access to public documents" (Ebibi, 2022, p. 86). The inevitable lengthy delay might lead to journalists to be put off pursuing requests if the information is needed to meet the tight deadlines demanded by the daily news cycle (Ebibi, 2022, p. 86).

International Freedom of Information Index

In a 2009 study, republished in 2017, Johan Lidberg assesses a sample of five FOI acts across the world to gauge which most effectively fulfils the promise that "extensive independent access to government-held information will lead to increased transparency, prevention of corruption and maladministration and greater public participation in the political process" (Lidberg, 2009, p. 167.).

The study assesses the scope of the acts in the United States, Sweden, Australia, South Africa, and Thailand, and requests were submitted to authorities in each jurisdiction to test compliance. The resultant study ranks Sweden, the world's first FOI country, in first place. The author found that the country has a "very high FOI knowledge level among public servants" (Lidberg, 2009, p. 177) and supplied quick responses to requests at no cost. The United States, South Africa, and Australia were singled out for particular criticism, after all requests hit lengthy delays of more than nine months in some cases (Lidberg, 2009). Lidberg concludes: "FOI appears to be used by some nations as a way to convey an image of transparency and openness in governance that simply is not carried through in practice. In the present study, FOI as democratic 'window dressing' clearly applies to the US, Australia and South Africa" (Lidberg, 2009, p. 181).

Freedom of Information in the United Kingdom

With its entrenched class system, the United Kingdom is noted as having a history of secrecy in which only the select few were given privileged access to information (Žuffová, 2023 and Brooke, 2007). While the introduction of the Freedom of Information Act 2000 (which didn't come into force until 2005) went some way to correcting this, the country's own head of state remains almost entirely exempt. The Royal Family's official website states: "The Royal Household is not a public authority within the meaning of the FOI Acts, and is therefore exempt from their provisions" (The Royal Household, n.d.). The secret services also enjoy near-blanket immunity to their reach, and there have been high-profile legal hearings, such as the Hutton Inquiry into the death of government scientist David Kelly at the height of the Iraq War in 2003, that have been afforded similar long-term secrecy (The Scotsman, 2010).

The New Labour government led by Prime Minister Tony Blair wasted little time in bringing forward plans for FOI by publishing a White Paper in December 1997 (UK Government, 2018), only months after their historic landslide election win. The foreword, written by Mr Blair himself, promised: "The traditional culture of secrecy will only be broken down by giving people in the United Kingdom the legal right to know" (UK Government, 2018, p. 6).

David Clark, the Chancellor of the Duchy of Lancaster, who drafted the government's proposals, added: "Openness is fundamental to the political health of a modern state. This White Paper marks a watershed in the relationship between the government and people of the United Kingdom. At last there is a government ready to trust the people with a legal right to information. This right is central to a mature democracy" (UK Government, 2018, p. 7).

It wasn't until 2005 that the Act finally came into force and investigative journalists began to submit requests in earnest. Headlines soon appeared revealing embarrassing details about the previous Conservative government's Black Wednesday, the disastrous moment when the UK was forced to withdraw from the European Exchange Rate Mechanism in 1992, at a cost to the economy of £3.3bn (Summers, 2005). Also in those first few months of 2005 were revelations in the Daily Telegraph that back in 1956, the UK had asked the United States for two million tonnes of food supplies to protect itself in the event of a nuclear attack (FENTON, 2005) and a Sunday Times investigation that revealed thousands of overseas students had arrived in the country but never taken up their places at university (Waite and Chittenden, 2005).

Investigative journalism's real breakthrough achievement of the FOI era didn't come until 2009, when the Daily Telegraph exposed the parliamentary expenses scandal – a long-running probe into supplementary payments given to the 646 Members of Parliament, including the Prime Minister and cabinet. While it was public knowledge that the parliamentarians were paid £64,776 (LSE Government, 2012) a year in salary, there was an additional, opaque, expenses system, whereby legislators could – ostensibly – claim back payments to cover necessary costs, such as essential travel, subsistence or accommodation during official duties. However, it was long rumoured that some MPs may be using this system to top up their salaries. As The Telegraph's Robert Winnett and Gordon Rayner write in their account of the investigation, *No Expenses Spared*: "To a nation of cynics it seemed impossible that MPs, faced with such temptation, could have done anything other than misbehave" (Rayner and Winnett, 2009, p. 20).

Freelance journalist Heather Brooke, Jon Ungoed-Thomas of the Sunday Times, and Ben Leapman of London's Evening Standard didn't wait long to submit requests seeking full details of the claims (Rayner and Winnett, 2009). What followed was a four-year battle that involved the Information Commissioner and even Parliament's own attempts to keep the information hidden (Rayner and Winnett, 2009). Conservative MP David Maclean introduced a Private Members Bill – a mechanism by which the more junior backbench MPs can propose new legislation – seeking to retrospectively exempt MPs from the Act entirely. He ultimately failed, and the full database of claims was later leaked to the Daily Telegraph. Embarrassing revelations about Mr Maclean's own claims soon led to lurid headlines such as "One wife, two mistresses… and a quad bike on Commons expenses" (The Evening Standard, 2012). As The Telegraph published new revelations each day for several months, there were embarrassing headlines around claims for pornographic films, lavish home refurbishments, and expensive meals. One MP claimed £1,645 for a floating island home for the ducks in his garden pond (BBC News, 2020), while it was reported another was paid £2,200 to cover the cleaning of the moat around his vast country mansion (The Telegraph, 2009). Several MPs were later jailed for making fraudulent mortgage claims worth more than £30,000 (The Guardian, 2011).

The revelations led to public outcry and plummeting faith in politicians (The Guardian, 2009), but also to a new system, in which MPs' claims are now published online every three months by a new regulator, the Independent Parliamentary Standards Authority, which estimates that 99% of claims are now within the rules (Independent Parliamentary Standards Authority, n.d.).

Rather than celebrating the achievement of his own legislation in bringing about a cleaner, more efficient system of governance, Tony Blair later highlighted FOI as one of his biggest regrets. In his 2010 autobiography, he particularly resented the increased power it gave to investigative journalists.

"The truth is that the FOI Act isn't used, for the most part, by 'the people'. It's used by journalists. For political leaders, it's like saying to someone who is hitting you over the head with a stick, 'Hey, try this instead', and handing them a mallet. The information is neither sought because the journalist is curious to know, nor given to bestow knowledge on 'the people'. It's used as a weapon" (Campaign for Freedom of Information, 2010). This lack of understanding or appreciation for journalism's role in holding government to account to ensure a properly functioning democracy was apparently shared by the later Conservative government led by David Cameron. In 2015, Cameron's Leader of the Commons, MP Chris Grayling, announced a review of FOI's reach, saying it was too often being used as "a research tool to generate stories for the media, and that is not acceptable" (The Guardian, 2015a). The plans were later abandoned following a predictable media backlash (The Guardian, 2015b).

The UK Freedom of Information Act's Effectiveness in Its First Two Decades

The cooling of various governments' enthusiasm for the Freedom of Information Act may have played a part in a declining effectiveness of the legislation in the UK, or even a more obstructive attitude towards requests by the authorities. The Cabinet Office publishes data on requests and how they are dealt with each year. The statistics cover all requests processed by 22 government bodies, including key departments of state such as the Home Office, the Treasury, and the Department of Health and Social Care. They also include an analysis of 17 "other monitored bodies" such as HM Revenue and Customs, the National Archives, and the Crown Prosecution Service. The data goes back as far as 2005 and shows that in the first year of the Act, 66% of all resolvable requests were granted in full – the highest proportion of fully released requests over the period. By 2023, this fell to only 34% – nearly half of the figure 18 years previously, and the lowest on record (see figure 2.1). In 2023, there were 46,769 resolvable requests and 15,717 of those were fully withheld, with some being partially released (UK Government, 2023).

As compliance with FOI has reduced, so too has trust in government. The polling company Ipsos Mori carries out an annual survey in which members of the public are asked if they trust government ministers – and politicians, in general – to tell the truth. Their latest report shows trust has fallen to the lowest point in 40 years (see figure 2.2), with only 9% of respondents saying they trust politicians and only 10% saying they trust government ministers (Ipsos, 2023).

By 2024, Transparency International reported that the UK had fallen to an all-time low in its Global Corruption Perceptions Index – a metric used to assess which countries are least at risk of corruption. Tables show the UK falling

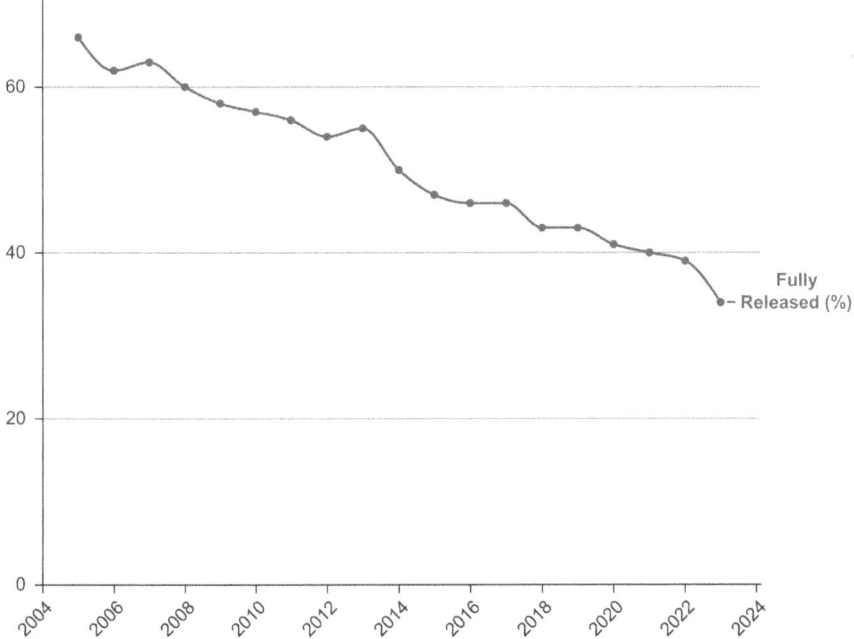

FIGURE 2.1   The proportion of fully released requests by UK authorities

from 8th in the world in 2012 to 20th in 2024 (Transparency International UK, 2023).

In a survey of 164 journalists in the UK, Mária Žuffová found that 84% of respondents classed FOI as "instrumental" to their work (Žuffová, 2023). In surveys and interviews, she found that 86% of journalists said they had been

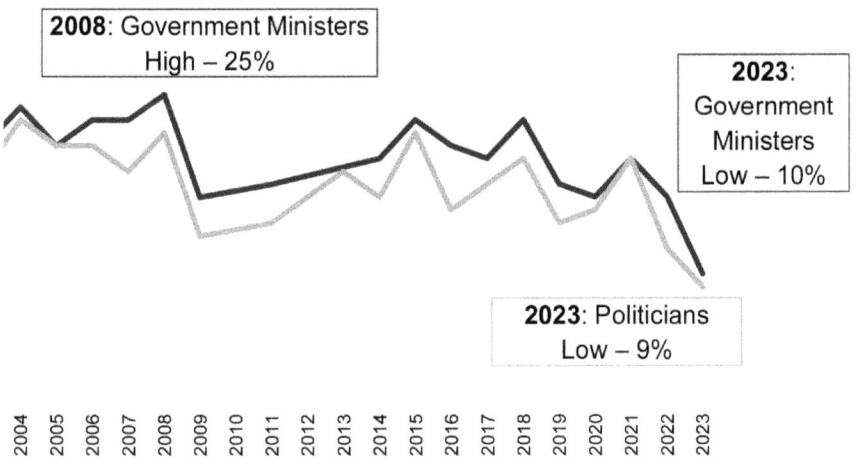

FIGURE 2.2   Trust in politicians: Highs and lows

refused an FOI request (Žuffová, 2023). The most common reason for refusal cited by authorities was cost grounds – 71% of respondents said they had met this refusal (Žuffová, 2023).

Authorities can legitimately refuse requests if it will cost more than £600 to comply (central government) or £450 to comply (local authorities). The cost limit was added to the Act in 2004 (perhaps a signal of the incumbent Blair government's waning enthusiasm for it). However, the figure has never been adjusted over a period of record inflation for the country. According to Bank of England estimates, £600 in 2004 would be worth £1052.48 by August 2024 (Bank of England, n.d.) By logical extension, this reduction of the real-world value of £600 would lead to a comparative increase in the number of times the opt-out could be used. The failure to set the limit as adjustable for inflation effectively added pre-planned secrecy by stealth, whether intentional or not. For every percentage point increase in inflation, more requests can inevitably be refused.

The enforcement body for the Freedom of Information Act is the Information Commissioner's Office (ICO). Anyone who believes their request has been inappropriately refused can appeal to the ICO, which has a sliding scale of powers, ranging from the ability to issue authorities with largely advisory Information Notices and Practice Recommendations, to the most stringent form of action – Enforcement Notices. Enforcement Notices are issued when an authority is a repeat offender or there are "significant or systemic issues in compliance" (Information Commissioner's Office, n.d.).

However, an FOI request submitted for this chapter asked how often Enforcement Notices were used to bring failing public authorities into line. The FOI sought the following information –

1 Which five authorities have received the most Enforcement Notices from the ICO since the Act became operational?
2 For each authority, how many Enforcement Notices have they received, when was each enforcement notice issued, and provide a brief summary of the reason for the notice?
3 How many times has the ICO commenced court proceedings under section 54 of the Act, which may be dealt with as contempt of court? Which authorities were subject to the proceedings in each case? What was the outcome of the proceedings in each case?

The response revealed that Enforcement Notices are rarely used. In the first two decades of operation, only 21 had ever been issued (correct up to October 2024) – a startlingly low number considering the body receives as many as 8,000 complaints a year (Information Commissioner's Office, 2024). Furthermore, no single authority has been served more than once. Most strikingly, the ICO's powers to take authorities to court have never been used at all.

In a blog post in April 2024, Warren Seddon, the ICO's Director of Freedom of Information and Transparency, wrote that recent years have seen an increase in Enforcement Notices, with a record eight being issued over a 12-month period. He also revealed that plans are in place to make better use of the option of court action. "We have also been working with our legal colleagues to develop a process for using our powers to refer a public authority for contempt of court if they fail to comply with a statutory decision or notice. This power has never been used in practice and compliance is usually very good – with bodies responding quickly when we chase them on the rare occasions a deadline is missed. But we are now in a much better position to go down this route if it's necessary at any point in the future" (Information Commissioner's Office, 2024).

It seems clear that work is needed to arrest the decline of FOI's reach in the UK, which could even help rebuild trust in public authorities. The act itself is in need of renewal, with an obvious starting point being the need to review the cost limits set in place decades before record inflation took place. The ICO's promises for stricter future enforcement action are to be welcomed, but there needs to be scrutiny from journalists over the coming years to see if this has taken place. The excellent Campaign for Freedom of Information outlines a list of further recommendations, which includes extending FOI to cover public sector contractors, tighter time limits for responses, and a strengthened ICO (Campaign for Freedom of Information, n.d.). Even David Clark, the original author of the act, has called for a revamp. In a recent interview with The Guardian, he said: "I think there really does need to be a serious re-examination of the situation … I would set up a parliamentary committee with a general view of examining FoI over the past 25 years, [and] the balance between confidentiality and openness" (The Guardian, 2023).

Freedom of Information: A Case Study

What follows is a case study outlining the process behind a recent investigation for The Mirror, the UK newspaper behind many of the Partygate investigations that led to the downfall of former Prime Minister Boris Johnson. This FOI investigation and subsequent data analysis were led by the author of this chapter, Neil Macfarlane, and written up for publication, with interviews, by Mirror reporter Katie Weston.

Most FOI requests, and indeed most investigations, start with a hunch. A journalist will have the kernel of an idea based on a gut feeling about something that *might* be happening in the world. In Story-Based Inquiry, the handbook for investigative journalism published as a free, open-resource by United Nations Educational, Scientific and Cultural Organization (UNESCO), the author Mark Lee Hunter defines this as the *hypothesis*: "You create a statement of what you think reality may be, based on the best information in your possession, and then you seek further information that can prove or disprove your statement" (Hunter, 2009, p. 20).

Awareness of the issues that dominate the news cycle is crucial for any journalist, and inspiration for story ideas will often flow from that. Three topics dominated UK headlines when the plan for this story began to take shape at the end of 2022: the cost of living crisis, the energy crisis, and the freezing winter temperatures. Inflation was reaching record highs of nearly 11% (Office for National Statistics, 2022), and bills for gas and electricity supplies to homes were increasing sharply following Russia's invasion of Ukraine in February 2022. Household gas and electricity bills increased by 74% (UK Government, 2022) in 2022 compared to 2021. The first two weeks of December were the coldest on record since 2010 (Met Office, 2022). This led to the hypothesis that many people could fall seriously ill because they were unwilling or unable to pay to heat their homes.

A quick search revealed that The Herald newspaper in Glasgow had a story in January 2023 which gave an early indication that this could be the case, in Scotland at least. Reporter Caroline Wilson obtained data from the Scottish Ambulance Service to show that 800 people were treated for hypothermia between December 1 and 18 in 2022 alone (Herald Scotland, 2023). It seemed logical to build on this by obtaining data for England and Wales, the core patch for the largest edition of The Mirror, and across a longer period of time to get fuller context. A single month of data would make it difficult to discern if this was a particularly high number due to the low temperatures and rising costs, or if it was fairly standard for that time of year.

The next step in the process was verification. While there are useful open-source resources that publish data on health outcomes in England, such as the Office for National Statistics and "NOMIS", there is usually a time lag of several months before publication, if that specific data is collated at all. There were a number of ways in which this story could be approached. It might have looked at deaths caused by hypothermia, although it can often be the case that lengthy inquests can take months or years to confirm the cause of death. It might have looked at the treatment of hypothermia cases at hospitals, although there are well over a hundred accident and emergency wards across the UK – possibly a task too vast for a single freelance journalist with limited time and resources to navigate. A more straightforward way to approach it would be to ask the first responders – the ten NHS ambulance trusts in England and Wales – for the data.

It is important to get complete data sets wherever possible, so FOIs were sent out in January 2023, so the response could include the full 12 months of the year.

The framing of the request was simple –

Please release the following information under the terms of the Freedom of Information Act –

How many patients were treated for hypothermia in each of the following months –

December 2022

November 2022

October 2022

etc.

All individual months from January 2020 to December 2022 were clearly listed, so that specific numbers for each month would be provided. Experience tells me that it is important to be literal with requests. A lack of clarity here might have led some authorities to reply with a single figure covering the entire period. This wouldn't allow for deeper interrogation to find specific spikes around certain dates.

This gave a three-year window, which would give a useful snapshot of data to see if there were any clear trends. Fewer than three years would have meant that any conclusions would be harder to reach, as there could be blips in the data. More than three years might have hit upon the cost limit for requests and been refused.

After drafting the request, I gathered the email addresses for the FOI contacts from each authority's website and pressed send. I made sure to save the addresses in my contact book so I could send ambulance trust requests more quickly in future.

Generic confirmation emails soon arrived from each authority to acknowledge that the request had been received and would be dealt with within 20 working days. As is common, some authorities got in touch to seek clarification on the request. It soon emerged that two of the authorities had trouble providing complete sets of data for the period requested, due to recent changes in the way their incident logs were recorded. At this point, there was a consideration of whether to abandon the story altogether or go ahead with responses from the remaining 80% of trusts. It is not unusual for there to be some missing data when making requests from multiple authorities. Some might take longer than others to respond. Northern Echo reporter Daniel Hordon (full disclosure: one of this author's own graduates) had to wait 819 days to get a response to a routine request sent to Greater Manchester Police (Hordon, 2024). George Greenwood of The Times waited 1,789 days for one response (Greenwood, 2023). Some authorities may have incomplete data; some may ignore the request altogether. It's a subjective call to decide at which point the investigation becomes unrepresentative. A survey of less than 50% is arguably not worth it, but eight out of ten seemed a reasonable sample to proceed with.

Once the responses were in, the data was logged in a Google Sheets spreadsheet (Excel is just as good), and some quick calculations were made to work out the totals for each month and the percentage increases across the period. It was quickly obvious that December 2022 did indeed feature the highest number of hypothermia cases, and this was in fact an 82% increase on the previous December.

It was nearly Spring by the time all the results could be properly analysed, and temperatures by that time had returned to normal, so there was a chance that the story might be less relevant to the news cycle by this point. However, inquests into the deaths of several victims soon began to report. In one case, the coroner ruled that 87-year-old Barbara Bolton had died after developing hypothermia in her home in Bury, Northern England, in December 2022. Hospital notes revealed the great-grandmother had not put her heating on because of "fear of high energy bills" (The Mirror, 2023a), and her son, Mark, said: "She was concerned about all her bills because she was a pensioner. She was careful, she was mindful of the prices and worried about them going up" (The Mirror, 2023a).

I then pitched the story to Mirror reporter Katie Weston and worked with her to flesh out the data findings, while she wrote it up for the final version. The findings were described as "heartbreaking" by the National Energy Action charity, and a spokesperson for the End Fuel Poverty Coalition said: "The energy bills crisis is now a public health crisis" (The Mirror, 2023b). Both organisations called for government intervention to reform the UK's energy sector.

Conclusion

This chapter has established that investigative journalists across the world have used FOI to expose ineffectiveness, incompetence or outright corruption among those in power. Without the diligent work of these journalists, many of the stories would have remained unknown to the wider public and allowed malfeasance to flourish.

While some FOI acts are decades, or even hundreds of years old, it is clear that there are signs of declining effectiveness in many countries, and there is evidence that this coincides with falling trust in the authorities and rising perceptions of corruption. Lawmakers in those countries cannot leave the legislation unaltered for several decades or more, if they are to avoid the accusation that FOI is merely a token gesture towards transparency. As Lidberg writes, if there is not a "genuine and continuous political will to make FOI work, you risk ending up with 'democratic window dressing'" (Lidberg, 2009, p. 181). It is important that the legislation is continuously reviewed, rigorously enforced, and that the journalism community – so crucial to its initial formation in many instances – is consulted.

However, we cannot leave reform to politicians, who often have a clear self-interest in keeping the status quo. Journalists must continue to use the legislation in their investigations, challenge any lapses in compliance, and make public their fight to do so.

CLASSROOM EXERCISE

- The website whatdotheyknow.com is a public database of FOI requests submitted to UK authorities, and their responses. Search the back catalogue by entering a keyword that relates to a subject that interests you, or the name of a particular organisation. Have a look through previous requests and responses to get a sense of how to frame a successful request.
- Have a look through today's newspapers online or in print. What are the biggest stories of the day? Can you think of an authority that would have involvement in the issues behind that story? Find an FOI email address for that authority and draft up a question in the email that seeks further information.
- Specify that this is a Freedom of Information request.
- Ask for data – stats and figures that will tell the story.
- Remember to get data for a number of years/months/days to spot trends. Be very, very specific – list the years you want data for (i.e., 2022, 2023, and 2024).
- Keep the request tightly focused to give you the best chance of success.
- Don't ask for a comment – that's what press offices are for after you have received and analysed your data to find a key angle.
- Hit send and review the response when it arrives (around 20 working days later) to see if you have the basis of a story.

References

Asogwa, F.N., Ibe, N.M.A. and Orji-Egwu, A.O. (2021) 'Freedom of information act and journalism in Nigeria 2011–2021: A review of a decade of utilisation and practice', *The Melting Pot*, 6, p. 34.

BBC News (2020) Sir Peter Viggers: 'Duck island' expenses claim MP dies aged 82. [online] Available at: https://www.bbc.co.uk/news/uk-england-hampshire-52219896 [Accessed 22 November 2024].

Brooke, H. (2007) *Your right to know*. London: Pluto Press.

Campaign for Freedom of Information (2010) *The Blair Memoirs and FOI*. [online] Available at: https://www.cfoi.org.uk/2010/10/the-blair-memoirs-and-foi-2/ [Accessed 20 Nov. 2024]

Campaign for Freedom of Information (2010) *The Blair memoirs and FOI*. [online] Available at: https://www.cfoi.org.uk/2010/10/the-blair-memoirs-and-foi-2/ [Accessed 22 November 2024].

Campaign for Freedom of Information, n.d. Improving FOI (2022). [online] Available at: https://www.cfoi.org.uk/campaigns/improving-foi/ [Accessed 22 November 2024].

DEBORAH SUMMERS UK, P.C (2005) Feb 10. Major's Black Wednesday defence Papers show Britain joined ERM based on 'wrong' forecast: [Final Edition]. *The Herald*, 6.

Ebibi, D. (2022) 'Freedom of information and journalism in Kosova 2010–2020', *SEEU Review*, 17(1), pp. 77–89.

Encyclopaedia Britannica (n.d.). *Freedom of the Press Act of 1766.* [online] Available at: https://www.britannica.com/topic/Freedom-of-the-Press-Act-of-1766 [Accessed 20 Nov. 2024].

FENTON, B. (2005) Mar 07. Britain begged America for food surplus to build nuclear war stockpile. *The Daily Telegraph*, 10. ISSN 03071235.)

George Washington University (n.d.) *LBJ and the Freedom of Information Act.* The National Security Archive. Available at: https://nsarchive2.gwu.edu/nsa/foia/lbj. html (Accessed: 21 November 2024).

Greenwood, G. (2023). *Tweet regarding response times to Freedom of Information requests.* [online] Twitter. Available at: https://twitter.com/GeorgeGreenwood/status/1703771394201272480/photo/1 [Accessed 22 November 2024].

Herald Scotland (2023) *Scots treated for hypothermia in hospital after cold snap.* [online] Available at: https://www.heraldscotland.com/news/homenews/23233387. scots-treated-hypothermia-hospital-cold-snap/ [Accessed 22 November 2024].

Hordon, D. (2024). *Direct message on Twitter regarding response times to Freedom of Information requests.* [Personal communication] 22 November 2024.

Hunter, M. (ed.) (2009) *Story-based inquiry: A manual for investigative journalists.* Paris: UNESCO. ISBN 978-9231041891.

Independent Parliamentary Standards Authority (IPSA) (n.d.) *How have things changed since IPSA's creation?* [online] Available at: https://www.theipsa.org.uk/news/how-have-things-changed-since-ipsas-creation [Accessed 22 November 2024].

Information Commissioner's Office (ICO) (n.d.) *FOI regulatory action.* [online] Available at: https://ico.org.uk/action-weve-taken/foi-regulatory-action/#:~: text=repeated%20and/or-,significant%20or%20systemic%20issues%20in%20 compliance,-with%20any%20of [Accessed 22 November 2024].

Information Commissioner's Office (ICO) (2024) *Director's update: The FOI year in review.* [online] Available at: https://ico.org.uk/about-the-ico/media-centre/news-and-blogs/2024/04/director-s-update-the-foi-year-in-review/#:~:text= It%27s%20fair%20to%20say%20that,six%20months%2C%20another%20record%20 high [Accessed 22 November 2024].

Ipsos (2023) *Trust in Professions: Veracity Index 2023.* [pdf] Available at: https:// www.ipsos.com/sites/default/files/ct/news/documents/2023-12/ipsos-trust-in-professions-veracity-index-2023-charts.pdf [Accessed 22 November 2024].

Knight, D. (2009) *NightJack, blogging and the police.* The Guardian, [online] 21 June. Available at: https://www.theguardian.com/commentisfree/2009/jun/21/nightjack-blog-blogging-police [Accessed 20 Nov. 2024]

Lidberg, J. (2009) 'The international freedom of information index', *Nordicom Review, Sciendo*, 30(1), pp. 167–182. https://doi.org/10.1515/nor-2017-0145

LSE Government (2012) *PSPE Working Paper 9/12: [Crime and Punishment the British Way: Accountability Channels Following the MPs' Expenses Scandal].* [pdf] Available at: https://www.lse.ac.uk/government/Assets/Documents/pdf/research-groups/pspe/working-papers/PSPE-WP9-12.pdf [Accessed 22 November 2024].

Met Office (2022) *Cold December concludes warmest year on record for UK.* [online] Available at: https://blog.metoffice.gov.uk/2022/12/30/cold-december-concludes-warmest-year-on-record-for-uk/ [Accessed 22 November 2024].

Nieman Reports, (2024) *Fifty years of FOIA.* [online] Available at: https://niemanreports.org/articles/fifty-years-of-foia/ [Accessed 22 November 2024].

Nnadi, E.C. and Obot, C. (2014) 'Akwa Ibom state journalists' reaction to the freedom of information act', *International Journal of Asian Social Science*, 4(4), p. 554.

Office for National Statistics (ONS) (2022) *Consumer price inflation, UK: December 2022.* [online] Available at: https://www.ons.gov.uk/economy/inflationand priceindices/bulletins/consumerpriceinflation/december2022#:~:text=The%20 Consumer%20Prices%20Index%20(CPI,of%200.5%25%20in%20December%20 2021 [Accessed 22 November 2024].

Rayner, G. and Winnett, R. (2009) *No expenses spared.* London: Bantam Press.

Reporters Committee for Freedom of the Press (n.d.). *Federal Open Government Guide.* [online] Available at: https://www.rcfp.org/foia/ [Accessed 20 Nov. 2024]

Reporters Committee for Freedom of the Press (2014) *Paying for public access.* Reporters Committee for Freedom of the Press. Available at: https://www.rcfp.org/ journals/news-media-and-law-spring-2014/paying-public-access/#:~:text=The%20 federal%20Freedom,pay%20full%20price (Accessed: 21 November 2024).

Reporters Committee for Freedom of the Press (2022) *RCFP FOIA litigation fuels Pulitzer Prize-winning NY Times investigation.* [online] Available at: https://www. rcfp.org/azmat-khan-civilian-casualties/ [Accessed 22 November 2024].

Reuters Institute for the Study of Journalism (2024) *Digital News Report 2024: Nigeria.* [online] Available at: https://reutersinstitute.politics.ox.ac.uk/digital-news-report/2024/nigeria [Accessed 22 November 2024].

Silver, D. (2016) 'The news media and the FOIA', *Communication Law and Policy*, 21(4), pp. 493–514. Available at: https://www.tandfonline.com/doi/abs/10.108 0/10811680.2016.1216686

The Evening Standard (2012) *One wife, two mistresses and a quad bike on Commons expenses.* [online] Available at: https://www.standard.co.uk/hp/front/one-wife-two-mistresses-and-a-quad-bike-on-commons-expenses-7290825.html [Accessed 22 November 2024].

The Guardian (2009) *Trust in politicians at all-time low.* [online] Available at: https:// www.theguardian.com/politics/2009/sep/27/trust-politicians-all-time-low [Accessed 22 November 2024].

The Guardian (2011) *MPs' expenses: Elliot Morley sentenced.* [online] Available at: https://www.theguardian.com/politics/2011/may/20/mps-expenses-elliot-morley-sentenced [Accessed 22 November 2024].

The Guardian (2015a) *Freedom of information: journalists warn Chris Grayling over FOI changes.* [online] Available at: https://www.theguardian.com/media/2015/ oct/29/freedom-of-information-journalists-chris-grayling-foi [Accessed 22 November 2024].

The Guardian (2015b) *Freedom of Information Act: Chris Grayling's claim of misuse 'misleading', say critics.* [online] Available at: https://www.theguardian.com/media/ 2015/oct/30/freedom-of-information-act-chris-grayling-misuse-foi [Accessed 22 November 2024].

The Guardian (2023) *Lord Clark calls for Freedom of Information review after data breaches.* [online] Available at: https://www.theguardian.com/politics/2023/ aug/18/lord-clark-calls-for-freedom-of-information-review-after-data-breaches [Accessed 22 November 2024].

The Mirror (2023a) *Great gran, 87, died of hypothermia after waiting hours for ambulance in freezing temperatures.* [online] Available at: https://www.mirror.co.uk/ news/uk-news/great-gran-87-died-hypothermia-29620736 [Accessed 22 November 2024].

The Mirror (2023b) *Hypothermia cases soar by 82% in UK as freezing temperatures persist.* [online] Available at: https://www.mirror.co.uk/news/uk-news/hypothermia-cases-soar-82-uk-29688206 [Accessed 22 November 2024].

The Royal Household (n.d.) *Freedom of Information.* [online] Available at: https:// www.royal.uk/freedom-information#:~:text=the%20Royal%20Household-, The%20Royal%20Household%20is%20not%20a%20public%20authority%20 within%20the%20meaning%20of%20the%20FOI%20Acts%2C%20and%20is%20 therefore%20exempt%20from%20their%20provisions.,-Despite%20its%20exemption [Accessed 22 November 2024].

The Scotsman (2010) *Classified documents released to support Dr David Kelly suicide verdict.* Available at: https://www.scotsman.com/news/classified-documents-released-to-support-dr-david-kelly-suicide-verdict-1699465 (Accessed: 3 December 2024).

The Telegraph (2009) *MPs' expenses: Clearing the moat at Douglas Hogg's manor.* [online] Available at: https://www.telegraph.co.uk/news/newstopics/mps-expenses/5310069/MPs-expenses-Clearing-the-moat-at-Douglas-Hoggs-manor.html [Accessed 22 November 2024].

Transparency International (n.d.). *Right to Information.* [online] Available at: https://www.transparency.org/en/our-priorities/right-to-information [Accessed 20 Nov. 2024]

Transparency International UK (2023) *Concerns over corruption at an all-time high as UK falls to its lowest-ever score in the Global Corruption Perceptions Index.* [online] Available at: https://www.transparency.org.uk/news/concerns-corruption-all-time-high-uk-falls-its-lowest-ever-score-global-corruption-perceptions [Accessed 22 November 2024].

U.S. Department of State (n.d.) *Kosovo.* [online] Available at: https://history.state.gov/countries/kosovo#:~:text=Kosovo%20declared%20its,of%20international%20supervision [Accessed 22 November 2024].

U.S. Department of State (2008) *Fact Sheet: U.S.-Russia Strategic Framework Declaration.* [online] Available at: https://2001-2009.state.gov/p/eur/rls/fs/101244.htm [Accessed 22 November 2024].

UK Government (2018) *Freedom of Information Act 2000: A Guide for Public Authorities.* [pdf] Available at: https://assets.publishing.service.gov.uk/media/5a7c5fcced915d6969f446d6/3818.pdf [Accessed 22 November 2024].

UK Government (2022) Quarterly Energy Prices – December 2022. [pdf] Available at: https://assets.publishing.service.gov.uk/media/63a2e8c78fa8f53911cfcd2c/quarterly-energy-prices-december-2022.pdf [Accessed 22 November 2024].

UK Government (2023) *Freedom of Information statistics annual 2023.* [online] Available at: https://www.gov.uk/government/statistics/freedom-of-information-statistics-annual-2023/freedom-of-information-statistics-annual-2023-bulletin#:~:text=Download%20data%20tables [Accessed 22 November 2024].

United Nations (n.d.). *Freedom of Information.* [online] Available at: https://www.un.org/ruleoflaw/thematic-areas/governance/freedom-of-information/ [Accessed 20 Nov. 2024].

Waite, R. and Chittenden, M. (2005) University scam lets in illegal migrants. *The Sunday Times,* 4 September. [online] Available at: https://www.thetimes.com/article/bd78a5c5-ea38-4ec8-9b04-3c7b665fd61b [Accessed 22 November 2024].

Winnett, R. & Rayner, G. (2009) *No expenses spared.* London: Transworld Publishers.

World Economic Forum. (2018). *How transparency can help grow the global economy.* [online] Available at: https://www.weforum.org/stories/2018/10/how-transparency-can-help-grow-the-global-economy/#:~:text=)%20Empirical%20evidence%20has%20shown%20that%20a%20lack%20of%20transparency%20and%20integrity%20can%20affect%20a%20country%E2%80%99s%20productivity%20and%20economic%20growth.%E2%80%9D [Accessed 20 Nov. 2024].

Youm, K. H. and Mendel, T. (2018) 'The global influence of the United States on freedom of Information', in Schudson, M. and Zelizer, B. (eds.) *Troubling transparency: The history and future of freedom of information.* New York: Columbia University Press, pp. 75–95.

Žuffová, M. (2023) 'Fit for purpose? Exploring the role of freedom of information laws and their application for watchdog journalism', *The International Journal of Press/Politics,* 28(1), pp. 300–322.

3

FRONTLINE STRATEGIES FOR LAND RIGHTS AND ENVIRONMENTAL JOURNALISM

Methodologies for Melding Ground Truth Interviews and Primary Records in Investigative Reporting

Chris Arsenault

Introduction

In providing counsel to his son, the television gangster Tony Soprano once advised, "Buy land, 'cause God ain't making anymore of it". While the fictional mob boss was hardly the first to make such a proclamation, the issue of large farmland acquisitions by wealthy investors, particularly in the Global South, has taken on new urgency since spikes in food and fuel prices in 2007 caused a rapid increase in the phenomenon known as land grabbing (Edelman, Oya and Borras, 2013; Hirsch, 2022; Von Braun and Meinzen-Dick, 2009). By 2024, the 21st century deals, covered an estimated 65 million hectares of land, an area twice the size of Germany (IPES-Food 2024). Millions of people and huge amounts of food, water, and capital are directly impacted by these deals (Liberti, 2013; Messerli *et al*, 2014; Oliveira, McKay and Liu, 2021).

In the western press, the term "land grab" gained popular media currency in the US in the late 1800s during the era of monopolies and pushes by white settlers to take control over Indigenous territories (Zoomers, Gekker and Schäfer, 2016). The "great land robbery" was frequently how commentators described the expansion of American railroads and the concentration of capital among a small group of oligarchs (Zoomers, Gekker and Schäfer, 2016, p. 151). In 1883, for instance, the New York Times ran a story about the behaviour of Texas railroad concerns headlined: "A Great Land Grab" (New York Times, 1883). The term gained renewed attention in North America during the Great Depression and Dust Bowl era of the 1930s, as indebted farmers hit by drought were forced to move en masse, as popularized in John Steinbeck's *The Grapes of Wrath* (1939). In short, large land deals are not intrinsically new

DOI: 10.4324/9781003478157-6

and have been well covered in scholarship, the press, and the popular imagination for more than 150 years (Basu, 2007).

In the 21st century itineration, there is near universal agreement that today's great land rush kicked off with global spikes in food and commodity prices in 2007–2008 (Ross, 2014; Zoomers, Gekker and Schäfer, 2016). Since 2005, more than 17,000 articles have been published including the phrase "land grabs," according to a review on Google Scholar (Google Scholar Search, 2025. In addition to "large-scale land deals," the terms "land deal" or the more direct "land grab" will be used on occasion for ease of syntax without implying a different political or economic configuration of the concession in question. For the purposes of this chapter, the term "large-scale land deal" refers to concessions bigger than 200 hectares involving investors primarily concerned with returns on capital, rather than local employment, community food security in the growing region or other social goods (Messerli *et al*, 2014). These investors could be nationals of the country where the concession is located or based internationally, but their concessions represent a "disarticulation from their host society" (Henderson, 2021, p. 262). Large-scale land deals can also refer to a form of neo-mercantilism, popularized by financiers from the Gulf states and northeast Asia, involving the wholescale export of crops out of a concession area and into the investing nation to meet its food security needs (Henderson, 2021). Lands where residents lack formal tenure security, including territories occupied by traditional Indigenous communities, or so-called frontier areas where climate shifts and increased demand from population growth elsewhere have elicited new interest from investors, are often particularly at risk from these deals (Arsenault, 2024; Henderson, 2021).

As noted above, there is a large volume of literature on land grabs, including: many case-specific studies, probes into the role of large land deals (or the lack thereof) in poverty alleviation and food security, and analyses on how colonialism, global power imbalances, and capital accumulation shape the agreements (Mihalik, 2012; Oliveira, McKay and Liu, 2021; Ross, 2014). However, there is minimal scholarship on best practices for journalistic coverage of the great land rush. No published academic monographs are specifically devoted to the issue, and "large-scale land deals" or "land grabs" mostly receive only tangential mention within broader studies of investigative journalism, best practices for the inclusion of marginalized voices in reporting, and environmental or resource journalism (Burrett, 2021; Hines, 2019; Lester, 2017; Radebe and Chiumbu, 2022; Schwartzstein, 2020). How reporters effectively uncover, report on, contextualize, and follow up on these deals in the era of climate change is fundamental for audiences and affected communities (Hines, 2019; Liberti, 2013; Radebe and Chiumbu, 2022). This chapter will explain an original methodology for journalists covering large land deals and offer some critiques of how it can be practised in the field. Next, it will analyse the utility of specific reporting tactics for obtaining primary records, including satellite mapping, social media, land registry records, stock price movements, investor disclosures, and contracting documents to determine their utility in bringing new information to light on land grabs. It will also explore how reporters covering large land and resource deals have used these tactics to break new ground in a series of short case studies. It will then provide a conclusion on key takeaways for journalists and media scholars.

The Methodology: Melding Ground Truth and New Primary Records to Advance Transparency

As a strategy for reporters investigating these agreements, melding ground truth interviews and primary records to identify previously unknown information on the causes, drivers, and impacts of large-scale land deals is arguably the most effective coverage methodology. This conclusion is based on a decade of frontline reporting on the land rush, based on hundreds of interviews on five continents, with government officials, lawyers, corporate executives, activists, scientists, politicians, policy experts, and residents facing displacement and the production of dozens of stories on the deals. These interviews are part of a journalistic methodology known as "ground truth," defined as "literally witnessing events" or talking to sources with direct insights on the issue in question to report the facts (Rohde and Roy, 2016, p. 116). In this land rights reporting methodology, ground truth from the field, literally in this case, is backed by primary records such as contracting documents, court filings, government data, official correspondence released via access to information requests and corporate disclosures (Chavkin, 2021; Lozada, 2022; Zoomers, Gekker and Schäfer, 2016).

The synthesis of ground truth and previously unreported official records form the backbone of this coverage methodology. Figure 3.1 provides a visual representation of what this methodology looks like in practice, including how source materials denoted as either ground truth or primary records can be selected, reported, and melded together to form a cohesive piece of investigative reporting. This methodology is underpinned by a broader theory of investigative environmental journalism. The deeper rationale for melding ground truth interviews and original primary records is to redefine how journalists understand transparency. This theoretical approach posits transparency as more than an idea or good policy, but as something journalists covering large land deals must wring out of powerful institutions through an ongoing praxis of engaged research and reporting. In essence, transparency is the product of active engagement from journalists, a continual process akin to political struggle but without partisan frameworks or predetermined conclusions. Rather than the ends justifying the means, the means themselves and the process of investigation based on journalistic rigour constitute a reframing of the idea of transparency in investigative reporting and the praxis underpinning how journalists can

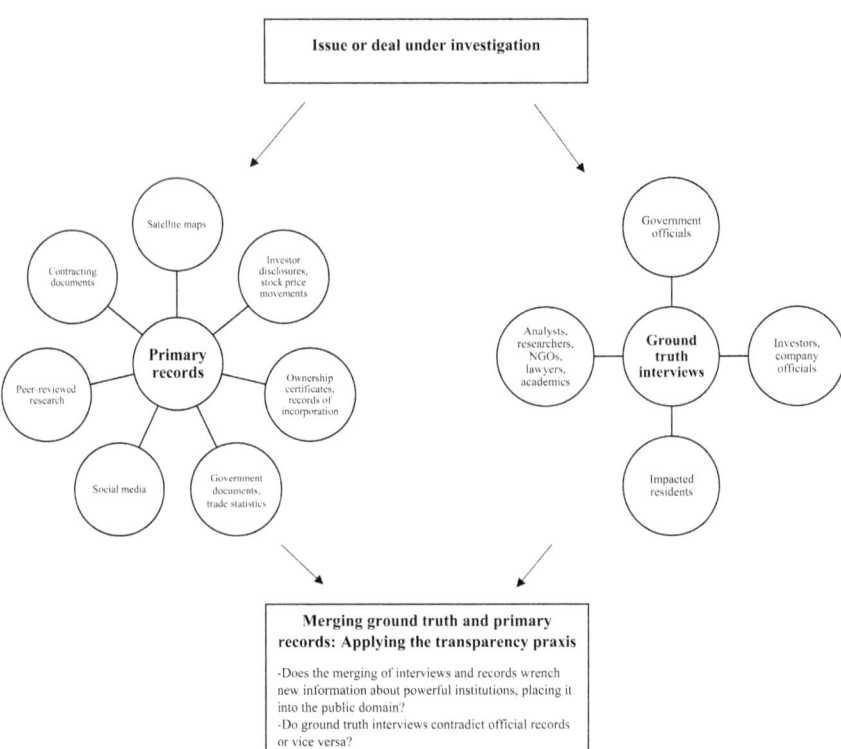

FIGURE 3.1 Visualizing the ground truth and primary records methodology

and should approach stories on land and natural resource deals. Full citations to journalistic work by the author exploring these themes through frontline coverage are available in the references section of the dissertation, *Covering the great land rush: The role of frontline journalism, and broader coverage strategies, for reporting on large land and natural resource deals in the 21st century;* most individual references to the author's past journalism have been removed from this chapter for clarity and cited directly to the dissertation (Arsenault, 2024).

Limits and Critiques of the Methodology

While the methodology of melding "ground truth" with primary records offers perhaps the most holistic approach to covering the great land rush, it still faces several theoretical, epistemological, and practical shortcomings. The first theoretical problem relates to the concept of ground truth itself. Insights from direct witnesses or participants in the same event are not universal. Two individuals can view the same proceedings and study the same primary records to draw radically different conclusions about key causes, historical drivers, and potential solutions. In environmental reporting, the writer William Cronon captured this dynamic in his essay *A Place for Stories: Nature, History and Narrative* (Cronon, 1992). Cronon analysed two competing works on the drought that struck much of the central United States in the 1930s. The authors, both respected scholars, had access to the same primary records on the Dust Bowl and agreed upon the basic facts around precipitation levels, migration, and food insecurity (Cronon, 1992). One argued the Dust Bowl was mainly a natural disaster due to a simple lack of rain, and it showcased the strength of American farmers who stayed on the land; their sacrifice during a period of drought improved the nation's food security in the long run (Bonnifield, 1978). The other called the period "one of the three worst ecological blunders in history" and said its toll showed the perils of industrial agriculture and the country's structural system of food production and class relations (Cronon, 1992; Worster, 2004, p. 4). The ground truth reporting methodology does not address competing interpretations of the same event, nor does it attempt to.

In addition to allowing for different framing, analysis, and conclusions from the synergy of ground truth through interviews and primary records, this methodology does not account for growing distrust among audiences of the accuracy and context of news reporting in much of the western world (Brenan, 2022; Strömbäck *et al*, 2020). In the US, for example, 38 per cent of respondents to a Gallup poll had no trust whatsoever in media reporting in 2022 (Brenan, 2022). The reasons for this drop in trust are hotly debated among journalists, scholars, and average citizens and addressing them is not the goal of this particular chapter (Farid, 2023; Markov & Markov, and Min, 2023). However, practised to near perfection, the reporting methodology outlined in this reporting methodology will not impact audiences who do not trust reporters in the first place.

Along with high-minded debates about interpretations for different events and rising distrust in the press, this methodology can be hampered by more practical problems. A lack of newsroom resources for international coverage and investigations makes ground truth nearly impossible for many working journalists to access given the costs of travelling to remote locations for interviews. The rise of video calling can, in some cases, help address this with secondary sources but obtaining ground truth voices from average farmers impacted by deals in rural areas in the Global South, isn't typically the kind of thing one can organize over Zoom due to poor internet connections and challenges in locating sources who are not affiliated with advocacy groups. Also, obtaining primary records such as corporate filings and contract documents can be expensive and logistically difficult or impossible in certain regions (Schwartzstein, 2020). In some authoritarian states which are also key backers of land investments, such as the UAE, China, Ethiopia, and Saudi

Arabia, employing this methodology to investigate land grabs often is not feasible due to visa prohibitions, a lack of public access to contracting records, and fears of potential sources of reprisals by state security (Bebawi and Bossio, 2014; Henderson, 2021; Schwartzstein, 2020). In Saudi Arabia, for example, on-the-record interviews with local tribesmen who will be displaced by NEOM, a proposed future city on the Red Sea spearheaded by Crown Prince Mohamed Bin Salman, cannot happen effectively (Hope and Scheck, 2020). Three residents who spoke out against the project were, for example, sentenced to death in October 2022; it's nearly impossible for foreign reporters to operate freely in the region to conduct on-the-record interviews with residents facing displacement or other government critics (Hope and Scheck, 2020; Rothwell, 2022).

In short, there are many regions where this methodology cannot be strategically employed due to safety, financial or logistical constraints. In these cases, other reporting strategies are more effective for garnering accurate information, such as interviews with diaspora communities who don't have "ground truth" perspectives and social media monitoring and verification (Bebawi and Bossio, 2014; Cooper and Owen, 2014). Those problems aside, in large swaths of the world, this journalistic methodology can provide the most transparent, fair, and complete picture of the impacts of the great land rush (Arsenault and Le Billon, 2022; Burgis, Clark and Peel, 2016; Lozada, 2022).

Best Practices for Sourcing in the Search for "Ground Truth"

So far, this chapter has introduced the basic idea of coverage of large land deals, offered a methodology for best practices when reporting on the deals, and outlined some theoretical and practical problems with employing this methodology. The next section offers some case studies of how this methodology was employed in different locations by journalists and then offers analysis on how various sourcing strategies were used to gain primary records. Before that, however, a bit of broader historical context is worth noting. Investigative environmental journalism, centred both on the lived experiences of sources on the frontlines of the land rush and empirical evidence from state or corporate-created primary sources such as contracting documents, is not new unto itself (Heidenblad, 2020). It's not a product of the most recent waves of economic globalization, the digitization of newsrooms or climate change pressure cooking inequalities and the scramble for resources (Friedman, 2004). It has, however, evolved due to these economic, environmental, and technological forces (Zoomers, Gekker and Schäfer, 2016). Technological shifts have made vast amounts of data easier for journalists to access. Corporate disclosures provided to financial regulators in London or New York, company press releases lauding the latest agreement, or satellite maps geolocating how land and water resource concessions overlap with local settlements are useful additions to a journalist's toolbox (Leigh, 2019; Lester, 2017; Lozada, 2022). But without context, confirmation, and insights sourced directly from people affected by the deals, they are not enough to produce accurate, engaging content for audiences. The next section will address cases where this methodology was utilized effectively in investigative reporting.

Mali: Following Up on Libya's Farmland Grab

The role of frontline journalism in creating broader understandings of the deals and their impacts was on display in a series of 2015 reports from Mali regarding a 100,000-hectare concession the late Libyan leader Muammar Gaddafi had signed in 2008 for some of the country's most fertile farmland (Arsenault, 2024). Prior to my arrival in the Segou region, no reporters had visited the site of the concession to follow up on what was happening there following Gaddafi's ouster from power in 2011, nor had the contract for the deal been previously made public. Based on interviews with local residents, government administrators, UN officials, and senior political advisers in the capital, Bamako, I was able to determine that much of the concession territory had been left fallow, despite Mali facing a hunger crisis (Arsenault, 2024; Bleck and Michelitch, 2015). Many local people living on and around the concession didn't know whether anyone from Libya would return to force them off the land, leaving them with particularly precarious tenure security.

I also obtained a copy of the original concession contract following extensive trust building with a law professor in the capital, under whom much of the country's political elite had studied. By melding ground truth and contracting documents to wrench transparency from powerful actors, the investigative reports from Mali brought original information into the public sphere. The New York Times also covered Gaddafi's Mali concession, interviewing local residents and economists in 2010, and using the transaction as part of a broader look at large land deals in Africa (MacFarquhar, 2010). But the report did not bring anything new into the public domain regarding the concession or land deals more broadly through contracts or other previously unreported primary source evidence (MacFarquhar, 2010).

Covering Brazil's High-Stakes Land Scams

With one of the world's largest agricultural industries, and powerful lobbies representing soy and cattle interests, Brazil consistently ranks among the world's most dangerous countries for land and environmental activists (Global Witness, 2022; Mollett 2021; Rodrigues, Campos and Santana, 2022). Its success as an exporter to global consumers, coupled with the importance of the Amazon as the world's largest rainforest, means stories about land rights struggles in South America's largest country can garner more audience interest compared to deals in smaller nations (Casado and Londoño, 2019; Fontes & Marques, 2023; Sampaio, 2022). Brazil's agricultural importance and the industry's ensuing political power are directly linked to violence against land rights activists (Global Witness, 2022; McCoy, 2022; Rodrigues, Campos and Santana, 2022). Between 2012 and 2021, 342 land and environmental campaigners were killed in Brazil, one of the highest rates on earth (Global Witness, 2022; Greenfield, 2022).

Through follow-up reporting, primary records, and interviews with residents directly impacted by these killings, my ground truth journalism was able to advance and deepen understandings of the country's land rights struggles. For example, by interviewing Elson Gomes a year after the killing of his friend, Indigenous land rights campaigner Clodiode Aquileu Rodrigues, I brought new information about the case to light, in the context of broader impunity for powerful agribusiness interests (Mollett, 2021). Prosecutors had originally arrested five men from an armed group of soy farmers in Mato Grosso do Sul, Brazil's farming heartland, following the murder. They were subsequently released, the reporting found, and no other arrests had been made for the murder. In an interview, the local prosecutor tasked with investigating the killing said "organized militias" of farmers had been attacking Indigenous rights campaigners in the area (Arsenault, 2024). "Land conflicts in Mato Grosso do Sul and the murder of Indigenous leaders are realities that go hand in hand," the prosecutor told me.

When it comes to coverage based on ground truth and primary records, court filings backed by original interviews can provide unique insights. One of the most common land grab tactics in Brazil, known locally as grilagem, involves investors illicitly registering state property or land used by small farmers as their own (Fearnside, 2008; Spadotto *et al*, 2021). The tactic can involve bureaucratic scams at local land registry offices, which are privately owned in Brazil and known as cartorios (Campbell, 2015; Fearnside, 2008). The problem is exacerbated by the lack of a central land registry demarcating ownership in any sort of systematic fashion and by the broader impunity which reigns in some rural areas (Mollett, 2021; Spadotto *et al*, 2021). Often, grilagem involves violence, as powerful local agribusiness interests, who are sometimes suppliers to larger international companies, forcibly evict or harass smaller farmers or Indigenous communities from land they seek to register as their own (Bledsoe, 2020; Fearnside, 2008; Mendonça and Pitta, 2022; Sampaio 2022).

The problem is well known in Brazil, but naming individuals or companies involved in criminality, tracing how specific pieces of land are usurped, and following the supply chains to determine how beef or minerals from territory taken through grilagem reaches global markets, is challenging (Campbell, 2015; Reydon *et al*, 2015; Spadotto *et al*, 2021). Primary interviews with members of impacted communities are important, but farmers who have been attacked or displaced typically have little insight into changes in ownership records for specific pieces of land and the legal tactics employed by agribusiness to take control over territory (Mollett, 2021; Reydon *et al*, 2015; Spadotto *et al*, 2021). In this regard, court documents, ownership certificates, and other primary records provide crucial primary evidence I have used to uncover the inner workings of land grab operations (Campbell, 2015; Spadotto *et al*, 2021).

In Piaui state, part of Brazil's MATOPIBA agricultural frontier, one key grilagem case I probed through court records involved a plan to usurp 124,000 hectares of farmland by registering property in the name of a dead man, among other illicit techniques. "The grilleros don't produce food," said the state prosecutor leading the investigation into the scam (Arsenault, 2024). "They're speculators ... the land is rich but the people face poverty," he told me, adding that the problem is getting worse. Bringing new insights about how these scams work on the ground, in the context of broader problems in Brazil's land governance regime, has value for audiences, along with regulators, reform campaigners, and government officials who are trying to combat the problem (Campbell, 2015; Fearnside, 2008; Mendonça and Pitta, 2022). The interplay between original ground truth interviews and primary records has also been used by other reporters breaking stories about land grabs and environmental crimes in Brazil, including the New York Times, The Washington Post, Mongabay, and The Intercept (Cowie, 2019; McCoy, 2022; Romero, 2015; Wenzel, 2023).

Cambodia: Ground Truth, Court Records, and Trade Data Interrogation

In Cambodia, a country hit hard by land grabs, bringing the voices of sources directly impacted by displacement to the fore is crucial for understanding how the land rush plays out on the ground (Baird, 2014). Melding official statements and contracting documents related to official compensation allotments following land deals with insights from residents who were forced out of their homes or farms, creates a more fulsome picture of what communities are being offered by government or corporate officials. Since 2000, more than 770,000 Cambodians have been forced from their land, according to a statement of claim filed by human rights lawyers against Cambodia's government at the International Criminal Court (Arsenault, 2024). In the capital, Phnom Penh, more than 10 per cent of the population was displaced between 1993 and 2013 to make way for new developments, including some 3,000 people forced out to make way for a luxury housing project at Boeung Kak Lake. Locating some of these displaced residents, now living in squatter camps outside the city or other makeshift accommodations, was not logistically easy, but crucial for investigative journalism. As part of the reporting, a leaked contract between the government and the Boeung Kak Lake developer for compensation was obtained via a whistleblower. It outlined three options for displaced residents: $800 in cash compensation, housing on the city outskirts, or upgrading existing homes near the site in central Phnom Penh. Displaced residents said they were never informed about the third option, and many wanted it. Once information about the third option became available due to the publication of the initial contract, residents and human rights groups organized protests demanding to stay in the city, prompting officials to offer higher compensation packages. In this regard, interviews with sources directly impacted by land grabbing and primary contracting documents produced unique insights for audiences and affected communities.

As these examples from Mali, Brazil, and Cambodia show, insights from residents impacted by large-scale land deals are crucial for accurately reporting basic facts about the agreements (Cancela, Gerber and Dubied, 2021; Rohde and Roy, 2016). One study of Chinese land deals in Africa, for instance, found that public announcements of large leases of African farmland totalled some 6 million hectares (Brautigam, 2015). After field visits to the sites in question and interviews with residents, Deborah Brautigam found that only 240,000 hectares had actually been transferred between 1987 and 2014 (Brautigam, 2015). After visiting the sites of 60 announced large-scale deals and conducting interviews, her study found that only 38 acquisitions led to some land being transferred. Ground truth through local verification and field interviews was crucial for establishing what was happening in the field around China's land deals in Africa (Brautigam, 2015). This section has outlined the importance of melding ground truth and primary records by way of specific coverage examples. The next section evaluates the utility of different sourcing options for obtaining primary records in the context of land rights journalism.

Methodologies for Social Media Inclusion: Marginal Potential for Land Coverage

Social media has been a sourcing bedrock for coverage of many 21st-century international news events, such as the Arab Spring or wars in Syria and Ukraine. For these sorts of stories, where social media is a dominant sourcing strategy for gathering ground truth information, the broader role of the foreign correspondent has shifted (Cooper and Owen, 2014). "Bearing witness" doesn't necessarily mean being on the ground; a plethora of YouTube videos, Facebook posts, and other social media content uploaded from protests in Egypt's Tahrir Square or Syrian rooftops as mortars hit neighbourhoods, offer primary source material for journalists in faraway newsrooms (Cooper and Owen, 2014). This citizen journalism, coupled with verification and contextualization, has offered new avenues, information streams, and source material for covering the world from the ground up, shifting the role of the foreign correspondent and re-centring digitally connected communities, advocacy groups, individuals, and citizen reporters, particularly in the Global South (Cooper and Owen, 2014; Hermida, 2012; Zayani, 2021).

However, covering what is often a slow burn of the great land rush typically requires a different, less digitally reliant journalism methodology compared to fast-moving stories such as the Arab Spring or Syria's civil war (Bebawi and Bossio, 2014). In rural areas where deals normally take place, internet connectivity is often poor. More importantly, key local sources, such as residents of Boco do Acre, Brazil, facing displacement from powerful local cattle interests, or plantation workers in the Democratic Republic of Congo (DRC) earning $1 per day, typically are not tweeting about their experiences on the frontlines of the global land rush, unlike Cairo's digitally savvy youth or Syrian aid workers ((Bebawi and Bossio, 2014). This connectivity divide between urban areas, where most news coverage is centred, and remote regions where most large land deals take place, coupled with the growing importance of data journalism on the issue, means the old-style role of the outsider foreign correspondent still has a place in covering large land deals. However, with current media technologies, the outsider correspondent needs more for sourcing than simply a recorder and a camera when trying to bring new information to light about the deals.

Methodologies for Leveraging "Big Data"

The growth of data journalism and easy-to-navigate mapping software has played an important role in land rights reporting as the rush for empirical evidence on global land grabs has coincided with broader cross-disciplinary discussions about "big data" (Graham and Shelton, 2013). A trending term in academia and journalism, "big data" suggests that the availability of datasets of increasing volume, velocity, and variety can help to better understand reality. (Zoomers, Gekker and Schäfer, 2016). Like social media, datasets alone are normally not enough unto themselves for creating a story. But they can play a role in helping reporters "find the needle in the haystack" for specific deals worth further investigation (Graham and Shelton, 2013). They can also help clarify connections between investors and different concessions while offering a broader, global look at the phenomenon. For instance, interactive maps curated by academic researchers at the project Land Matrix and informed by big data have been key tools for journalists around the world covering land deals (Graham and Shelton, 2013).

Raw data for land rights reporting has included comparisons of commodity import and export statistics from different jurisdictions, interactive timelines charting interlinked news developments in connected locations, and comparing land deal contract negotiation timelines with political trends. Stock price data for corporations involved in land deals compared with raw commodity prices, data on state subsidies and changing corporate ownership structures, and maps from different stakeholders and land registries showing competing information about concession ownership and custody chains have also been important inputs for investigative reporting.

When it comes to leveraging "big data" for land and natural resources reporting, official trade statistics cross-referenced with other sources can often show when authorities are hiding information. Government or corporate spokespeople can lie, obfuscate or simply refuse interviews; access to information requests from government agencies is often redacted (Hewitt, Larsen and Walby, 2012). But official trade data is normally untouched – government functionaries, even in undemocratic states, usually don't know what to censor, and basic statistical accuracy is key for functioning markets and official policy. By comparing big data sets, Reuters was able to show that some $15 billion worth of gold smuggled out of Africa ended up in the UAE (Lewis, McNeill and Shabalala, 2019). The reporters compared customs data on gold imports to the UAE with data from African gold exporters, indicating a massive discrepancy. The "UAE is cashing in on the unregulated environment in Africa," a senior African Union official responsible for mining industry oversight told Reuters, noting how the process is robbing some of the world's poorest nations of crucial tax revenue (Lewis, McNeill and Shabalala, 2019). Major legal gold mining companies operating on the continent told Reuters they do not send their ore to the UAE. Illegally mined gold is a prime cause of deforestation and contamination, as toxic mercury used to extract the ore is typically dumped into rivers in operations often controlled by criminal groups (Espin and Perz, 2021). While the reporting doesn't contain typical ground truth or interviews from illegal mining sites, it does an excellent job of merging big data and high-level sourcing from governments, mining companies, financial institutes, and transparency watchdogs to uncover unethical and environmentally destructive behaviour (Lewis, McNeill and Shabalala, 2019).

A similar strategy of comparing big data sets, coupled with ground truth established through field interviews, was leveraged in original reporting on illegal sand mining in rural Cambodia. Fishermen in Koh Sralau in the country's east had been complaining about industrial dredgers literally stealing the ground beneath their feet and the sand below their boats, decimating fish stocks and the broader environment. Until data journalism was employed, Cambodia's government had maintained that its sand dredging industry was small, showing less than 3 million tonnes of sand exports. Researchers compared this data with official import records contained in UN figures from neighbouring Singapore, which showed the wealthy entrepot imported 72 million tonnes of sand from Cambodia between 2007 and 2016. This data journalism, coupled with field interviews from coastal communities, and site visits showing dozens of large dredgers working openly in coastal estuaries, proved conclusively that the scale of the problem was huge and Cambodian officials were doing little about it, a lack of action local residents blamed on corruption. "Seven beaches have already disappeared because of the mining," said one local fisherman (Arsenault, 2024), "They're just gone and the people can't enjoy them anymore." After the data was published, Cambodian officials pledged to address the problem, underscoring the potential impact of merging ground truth and big data in land rights and environmental reporting.

The methodology of coupling big data with primary source interviews was employed during an original investigation into how a hedge fund based in the Cayman Islands acquired the largest palm oil plantation in the Democratic Republic of Congo (Arsenault, 2024). The story used stock price data and ownership records to track how this fund managed to lose money on the deal. Plantation owners were later bailed out by UK taxpayers via the Commonwealth Development Corporation, the private sector lending arm of Britain's international development department, since rebranded as British International Investment. Sources on the ground in the DRC explained that many workers were earning $1 per day, or less than the Congolese minimum wage, in a trend eventually confirmed by company officials. The investigation, leveraging ground truth and contracting records, broke open a previously unreported story and led to (unkept) promises by the company to improve housing for workers.

Satellite Mapping and Ground Truth Interviews: Emerging Coverage Approaches

For melding ground truth reporting with new data technologies including satellite mapping and artificial intelligence, the Global Investigative Journalism Network's collaboration with the Spanish newspaper El Pais and the Venezuela outlet Armando.info probing illegal mining activity in Venezuela's rainforest stands as an excellent example (Lozada, 2022; Ramirez, Poliszuk and Segovia, 2022). Accessing mining sites deep in the jungle controlled by drug traffickers and businessmen with connections to Venezuela's security services and Colombian rebel groups is exceptionally dangerous, even by the standards of rural land rights reporting. Moreover, even the most well-resourced news organizations couldn't send correspondents to the dozens of sites where deforestation and illegal mining were happening to paint a full picture of the scale of current environmental crimes. The project, observed one collaborator, "is a hybrid of data journalism" and "traditional, in-the-field reporting" (Lozada, 2022).

After using ground truth reporting to determine the locations of some illicit mines and to gain colour from the field, journalists partnered with artificial intelligence researchers at Stanford University and several non-profit journalism outfits (Lozada, 2022). Thanks to initial ground truth reporting, backed by interviews with experts, the team was able to build an algorithm programmed to recognize and associate images similar to aerial shots of open-pit mines and clandestine runways, in order to identify these patterns in the jungle. In an international investigative effort lasting nearly a year, the journalists identified over 3,000 mining locations; deforested areas equivalent to 40,000 soccer fields (Lozada, 2022). The problem of illegal mining fuelling deforestation and environmental contamination in the rainforest is nothing new. However, the scale of this project, according to one of the collaborators, allowed journalists "to show for the first time on a map the strategic points set up by the smuggling groups to take illicit cargo out of the country by air" (Lozada, 2022). The reporting was also able to name specific Venezuelan companies and individuals involved in deforestation and illegal gold trafficking through tracing contracts, field interviews, and other techniques (Ramirez, Poliszuk and Segovia, 2022). Overall, it's an excellent example of the journalistic methodology for international, collaborative natural resources reporting using big data, traditional reporting from the ground, and corporate records.

Conclusion

The idea of highlighting the importance of ground truth interviews for investigative journalism, unto itself, isn't novel (Friedman, 2004; Rohde and Roy, 2016). Striving to obtain primary records is also a well-documented tactic for investigative reporting (Hines, 2019). But merging these two approaches to create robust coverage in the context of large land deals is unique. With minimal existing journalism scholarship on best practices for this niche coverage area, this methodological contribution is part of expanding the research literature, primarily within journalism studies. The practical results of this approach, when practised in the field, uncovered new information about large land deals and their impacts.

While there have been new, significant land grabs globally following the COVID-19 pandemic, there has not been a spike in new land deals comparable to 2007–2008, despite the re-emergence of comparable economic trends such as rising food and fuel prices (German, 2022; Grain, 2023; Suwandi and Foster, 2022). Perhaps long-term problems emerging from the 21st century's first land grab wave – deals which don't lead to actual crop production, inexperience from some speculators in executing long-term agriculture projects, and increased journalistic scrutiny and community resistance, have spooked investors looking for market-beating returns or governments in politically unstable regions keen on boosting GDP (gross domestic product). Regardless of the trajectory of the great land rush, the original methodology for covering the agreements offers a practical, transferable guide and strategy for other journalists reporting on large land and resource deals. It also provides a framework on best practices and can serve as a rough guide for reporters and media scholars looking for different approaches to investigative journalism more broadly.

CLASSROOM EXERCISE

Create a pitch of about 300 words for a story in your coverage area, leveraging the methodology explained in this chapter. The pitch does not have to be related to large land deals or the environment: it can be about anything, including sports, business, politics, or social affairs. Make sure the pitch includes sourcing that leverages ground truth interviews and primary records when using the transparency praxis for investigative journalism.

Include the following in your written pitch:

- A working headline.
- Four to six sentences describing the basic story you plan to tell, with a nut graph explaining the core premise of your piece and why audiences will care.
- Include at least three named sources. For individual interview subjects, include a name and contact information.
- For primary records, explain what files you hope to leverage, how you will access them, and what you hope to obtain in terms of specific information for your story.

Be ready to make a short verbal presentation of your pitch to your class.

Bibliography

Arsenault, C. (2024) *Covering the great land rush: The role of frontline journalism, and broader coverage strategies, for reporting on large land and natural resource deals in the 21st century* (Doctoral dissertation, The University of Sunderland).

Arsenault, C. and Le Billon, P. (2022) 'Covering crude bargains: The impacts of investigative media reporting on oil deals', *The Extractive Industries and Society*, 12, p. 101144.

Baird, I.G. (2014) 'The global land grab meta-narrative, Asian money laundering and elite capture: Reconsidering the Cambodian context', *Geopolitics*, 19(2), pp. 431–453.

Basu, P.K. (2007) 'Political economy of land grab', *Economic and Political Weekly*, pp. 1281–1287.

Bebawi, S. and Bossio, D.(eds.) (2014) *Social media and the politics of reportage: The 'Arab Spring'*. Springer.

Bleck, J. and Michelitch, K. (2015) 'The 2012 crisis in Mali: Ongoing empirical state failure', *African Affairs*, 114(457), pp. 598–623.

Bledsoe, A. (2020) Afro-Brazilian resistance to extractivism in the Bay of Aratu. In McCarthy, J. (ed.) *Environmental governance in a Populist/Authoritarian era*. Routledge, pp. 192–201.

Bonnifield, M.P. (1978) The Dust Bowl: men, dirt, and depression [history, USA]. 1st.

Brautigam, D. (2015) *Will Africa feed China?* Oxford University Press.

Brenan, M. (2022) Americans' Trust In Media Remains Near Record Low. *Gallup*. Available at: https://news.gallup.com/poll/403166/americans-trust-media-remains-near-record-low.aspx (Accessed on November 9, 2022).

Burgis, T., Clark, P. and Peel, M. (2016) The great land rush. *The Financial Times.* Available at: https://ig.ft.com/sites/land-rush-investment/ethiopia/ https://pulitzercenter.org/projects/great-land-rush (Accessed June 28, 2022).

Campbell, J.M. (2015) *Conjuring property: Speculation and environmental futures in the Brazilian Amazon.* University of Washington Press.

Cancela, P., Gerber, D. and Dubied, A. (2021) "To me, It's normal journalism" professional perceptions of investigative journalism and evaluations of personal commitment', *Journalism Practice*, 15(6), pp. 878–893.

Casado, L. and Londoño, E. (2019) Under Brazil's far-right leader, Amazon protections slashed and forests fall. *The New York Times*, 28.

Chavkin, S. (2021) 'Exile, impunity, and covering Nicaragua's environmental crisis', *Columbia Journalism Review.* Available at: https://www.cjr.org/criticism/nicaragua-deforestation-ortega-press-freedom.php (Accessed June 19, 2022).

Cooper, A. and Owen, T. (2014) 'The new global journalism: Foreign correspondence in transition', *Columbia Journalism Review/Tow Center for Digital Journalism.* Available at: https://www.cjr.org/tow_center_reports/the_new_global_journalism.php (Accessed on June 4, 2022).

Cowie, S. (2019) Jair Bolsonaro praised the genocide of Indigenous people. Now he's emboldening attackers of Brazil's Amazonian communities. *The Intercept, 16.*

Cronon, W. (1992) 'A place for stories: Nature, history, and narrative', *Journal of American History*, 78(4), pp. 1347–1376.

Edelman, M., Oya, C. and Borras, S.M. Jr (2013) 'Global land grabs: Historical processes, theoretical and methodological implications and current trajectories', *Third World Quarterly*, 34(9), pp. 1517–1531.

Espin, J. and Perz, S. (2021) 'Environmental crimes in extractive activities: Explanations for low enforcement effectiveness in the case of illegal gold mining in madre de dios, Peru', *The Extractive Industries and Society*, 8(1), pp. 331–339.

Farid, A.S. (2023) 'Changing the paradigm of traditional journalism to digital journalism: Impact on professionalism and journalism credibility', *Journal International Dakwah and Communication*, 3(1), pp. 22–32.

Fearnside, P.M. (2008) 'The roles and movements of actors in the deforestation of Brazilian Amazonia', *Ecology and Society*, 13(1).

Feldstein, M. (2006) 'A muckraking model: Investigative reporting cycles in American history', *Harvard International Journal of Press/Politics*, 11(2), pp. 105–120.

Ferrante, L. and Fearnside, P.M. (2019) 'Brazil's new president and 'ruralists' threaten Amazonia's environment, traditional peoples and the global climate', *Environmental Conservation*, 46(4), pp. 261–263.

Friedman, S. (2004) And the beat goes on: The third decade of environmental journalism. *The environmental communication yearbook* (Vol. 1), pp. 175–187. Routledge.

Fontes, G. and Marques, F.P.J. (2023) 'Defending democracy or amplifying populism? Journalistic coverage, twitter, and users' engagement in Bolsonaro's Brazil', *Journalism*, 24(8), pp. 1634–1656.

German, L. (2022) *Power/knowledge/land: Contested ontologies of land and its governance in Africa.* University of Michigan Press.

Global Witness. (2022) Decade of defiance: Ten years of reporting land and environmental activism worldwide. Global Witness. Accessed Jan, 13, p. 2023.

Google Scholar Search. (2025 Available at: https://scholar.google.ca/scholar?q=%22Land+grabs%22&hl=en&as_sdt=0%2C5&as_ylo=2005&as_yhi=2025

Graham, M. and Shelton, T. (2013) 'Geography and the future of big data, big data and the future of geography', *Dialogues in Human Geography*, 3(3), pp. 255–261.

Grain. (2023) GRAIN's 2022 activity report. Available at: https://grain.org/en/article/6968-grain-s-2022-activity-report (Accessed on June 1, 2023).

Greenfield, P. (2022) More than 1,700 environmental activists murdered in the past decade'. *The Guardian. Available at:* https://www.theguardian.com/environment/2022/sep/29/global-witness-report-1700-activists-murdered-past-decade-aoe

Heidenblad, D.L. (2020) The emergence of environmental journalism in 1960s Sweden: Methodological reflections on working with digitalised newspapers. In Östling, J., Olsen, N., Larsson Heidenblad, D. (eds.) *Histories of knowledge in postwar Scandinavia.* Routledge, pp. 59–73.

Henderson, C. (2021) 'Land grabs reexamined: Gulf Arab agro-commodity chains and spaces of extraction', *Environment and Planning A: Economy and Space*, 53(2), pp. 261–279.

Hermida, A. (2012) 'Social journalism: Exploring how social media is shaping journalism', *The Handbook of Global Online Journalism*, 12, pp. 309–328.

Hewitt, S., Larsen, M. and Walby, K. (2012) He who controls the present, controls the past: The Canadian security state's imperfect censorship under the access to information act. *Brokering Access: Power, Politics and Freedom of Information Process in Canada*, pp. 194–208.

Hines, A. (2019) Global witness and investigative journalism. In Price, S. (ed.) *Journalism, power and investigation.* Routledge, pp. 137–159.

Hirsch, P. (2022) Land grabbing and exclusion. In Sims, K., Banks, N., Engel, S., Hodge, P., Makuwira, J., Nakamura, N., Rigg, J., Salamanca, A., Yeophantong, P. (eds.) *The Routledge handbook of global development.* Routledge, pp. 362–371.

Holleman, H. (2017) 'De-naturalizing ecological disaster: Colonialism, racism and the global dust bowl of the 1930s', *The Journal of Peasant Studies*, 44(1), pp. 234–260.

Hope, B. and Scheck, J. (2020) *Blood and oil: Mohammed bin Salman's ruthless quest for global power.* Hachette UK.

Hujanen, J. (2018) 'Renegotiating the journalism profession in the era of social media: Journalism students from the global north and south', *Journalism & Mass Communication Educator*, 73(3), pp. 282–292.

International Panel of Experts on Sustainable Food Systems. (2024). Land Squeeze. https://ipes-food.org/wp-content/uploads/2024/05/LandSqueeze.pdf

Leigh, D. (2019) *Investigative journalism: A survival guide* (Vol. 9). London: Palgrave Macmillan.

Lester, L. (2017) Rights activism, journalism and 'The new War'. *The Routledge companion to media and human rights, Routledge, London.*

Lewis, D., McNeill, R. and Shabalala, Z. (2019) Gold worth billions is smuggled out of Africa. *Reuters, April, 24.*

Liberti, S. (2013) *Land grabbing: Journeys in the new colonialism.* Verso Books.

Lozada, M. (2022) How They Did It: Uncovering a Vast Network of Illegal Mining in Venezuela. *Pulitzer Center on Crisis Reporting/Global Investigative Journalism Network.* Available at: https://pulitzercenter.org/stories/how-they-did-it-uncovering-vast-network-illegal-mining-venezuela (Accessed on June 25, 2022).

MacFarquhar, N. (2010) African farmers displaced as investors move in. *New York Times, 21.*

Markov, C. and Min, Y. (2023) 'Unpacking public animosity toward professional journalism: A qualitative analysis of the differences between media distrust and cynicism', *Journalism*, 24(10), pp. 2136–2154.

McCoy, T. (2022) The God of Sao Felix. *The Washington Post.* Available at: https://www.washingtonpost.com/world/interactive/2022/brazil-amazon-deforestation-politicians/ (Accessed on January 22, 2023).

Mendonça, M.L. and Pitta, F.T. (2022) 'Land speculation by international financial capital in Brazil', *Latin American Perspectives*, 49(5), pp. 146–160.

Messerli, P., Giger, M., Dwyer, M.B., Breu, T. and Eckert, S. (2014) 'The geography of large-scale land acquisitions: Analysing socio-ecological patterns of target contexts in the global South', *Applied Geography*, 53, pp. 449–459.

Michaelson, R. (2020) It's being built on our blood': the true cost of Saudi Arabia's $500 bn megacity. *The Guardian*, 4.

Mihalik, L.M. (2012) The Great African Land Rush: How foreign business is buying a continent.

Mollett, S. (2021) Resistance against the land grab: Defensoras and embodied precarity in Latin America. In Himley, M., Havice, E., Valdivia, G. (eds.) *The Routledge handbook of critical resource geography*. Routledge, pp. 92–102.

Oliveira, G., McKay, B.M. and Liu, J. (2021) Beyond land grabs: New insights on land struggles and global agrarian change. In de L. T Oliveira, G., Liu, J., McKay, B. M. (eds.) *Beyond the global land grab*. Routledge, pp. 1–18.

Poliszuk, J., Ramirez, M. and Segovia, M. (2022) The recruitment of Indigenous people in the Venezuelan Jungle. *El Pais*. Available at: https://elpais.com/internacional/2022-02-09/el-reclutamiento-de-indigenas-en-la-selva-venezolana.html (Accessed on June 22, 2022).

Radebe, M.J. and Chiumbu, S.H. (2022) 'Frames and marginalisation of counter-hegemonic voices: Media representation of the land debate in South Africa', *African Journalism Studies*, 43(1), pp. 89–106.

Ramirez, M., Poliszuk, J. and Segovia, M. (2022) The who's who of the criminal cartels south of the Orinoco. *Armando.info*. Available at: https://armando.info/el-quien-es-quien-de-los-carteles-criminales-al-sur-del-orinoco/ (Accessed on June 2, 2022).

Reydon, B.P., Fernandes, V.B., Bueno, A.P., Benatti, J., Simiqueli, R. and Treccanni, J. (2015) Land grab in Brazil caused by lack of land governance. In *Presentation at the 2015 World Bank conference on land and poverty*. The World Bank, Washington, DC, pp. 23–27.

Rodrigues, J.C., Campos, R.L. and Santana, J.R. (2022) 'Environmental defenders suffering death threats and "under protection" in the state of Pará, Eastern Amazonia, Brazil', *Journal of Political Ecology*, 29(1), pp. 430–454.

Rohde, D. and Roy, S. (2016) 'On the future of crisis reporting', *The Brown Journal of World Affairs*, 22(2), pp. 113–119.

Romero, S. (2015) TIAA-CREF, US investment giant, accused of land grabs in Brazil. *New York Times*, 17.

Ross, A.R. (2014) Editor's introduction: The global land grab. *Grabbing back. Essays against the global land grab*, AK Press. pp. 9–35.

Rothwell, J. (2022) Tribesmen face death sentence for resisting Saudi megacity. *The Telegraph*. Available at: https://www.pressreader.com/uk/the-daily-telegraph/20221010/281943136782604 (Accessed on November 12, 2022).

Sampaio, D.S. (2022) 'Brazil's return to the global environmental sphere and the hope for the dawn of a new day', *Biodiversity*, 23(3–4), pp. 152–155.

Schwartzstein, P. (2020) The Authoritarian War on Environmental Journalism.

Spadotto, B.R., Martenauer Saweljew, Y., Frederico, S. and Teixeira Pitta, F. (2021) 'Unpacking the finance-farmland nexus: Circles of cooperation and intermediaries in Brazil', *Globalizations*, 18(3), pp. 461–481.

Strömbäck, J., Tsfati, Y., Boomgaarden, H., Damstra, A., Lindgren, E., Vliegenthart, R. and Lindholm, T. (2020) 'News media trust and its impact on media use: Toward a framework for future research', *Annals of the International Communication Association*, 44(2), pp. 139–156.

Suwandi, I. and Foster, J.B. (2022) 'COVID-19 and imperial value: Commodity chains, global monopolies, and catastrophe capitalism', *International Critical Thought*, 12(3), pp. 426–447.

The New York Times. (1883) A Great Land Grab. Available at: https://timesmachine. nytimes.com/timesmachine/1883/02/20/102801389.html?pageNumber=4 (Accessed on July 6, 2022).

Von Braun, J., & Meinzen-Dick, R. S. (2009). Land grabbing" by foreign investors in developing countries: risks and opportunities: International Food Policy Research Institute Washington. *Policy Brief*, *13*, 1–9.

Wenzel, F. (2023) The $20m flip: The story of the largest land grab in the Brazilian Amazon. *Mongabay*. Available at: https://news.mongabay.com/2023/02/ the-20m-flip-the-story-of-the-largest-land-grab-in-the-brazilian-amazon/ (Accessed on February 21, 2023).

Worster, D. (2004) *Dust bowl: The Southern plains in The 1930s.* Oxford University Press.

Zayani, M. (2021) 'Digital journalism, social media platforms, and audience engagement: The case of AJ+', *Digital Journalism*, 9(1), pp. 24–41.

Zoomers, A., Gekker, A. and Schäfer, M.T. (2016) 'Between two hypes: Will "big data" help unravel blind spots in understanding the "global land rush?', *Geoforum*, 69, pp. 147–159.

4

INVESTIGATING BLACK BOX TECHNOLOGIES, DIGITAL POWER, AND ITS INVISIBILITIES

Philip Di Salvo

Introduction

Artificial intelligence (AI) and algorithms have now fully entered the field of journalism. On the one hand, these technologies are now part of the digital toolbox of journalists, and various AI-based applications are routinely used by journalists to perform different editorial tasks, including newsgathering, news production, and news distribution (Beckett and Jessen, 2023). Today, the debate around the use of AI in journalism is perhaps the most pressing in the industry, bringing together issues of automation, labor, journalistic ethics, disruption, and the balance of power between the media and the tech companies producing the tools (Simon, 2024). While much of the debate around AI in journalism studies is currently focused on assessing the impact of the technology *within* journalism itself, AI has also been a disruptive force *outside* of journalism, forcing journalism to respond to and report on new technology-enabled social and political issues. In particular, if we look at the evidence provided by the critical AI and data studies literature, which has extensively addressed the social issues arising from the widespread adoption of AI in society (Broussard, 2024; Crawford, 2021; Eubanks, 2019 – among others), discrimination, abuse of power, bias, and the other "errors" of AI and algorithmic systems (Barassi, 2024) now play a central role in the ongoing social negotiation around AI. As a result, this has also increasingly become a topic of journalistic reporting and investigation (Di Salvo, 2023). Research results show that the space that journalism devotes to covering the more critical aspects of AI is still a niche in the overall attention given to AI (Barassi et al., 2022), and that sensationalism still dominates the way journalists write about the technology, often contributing to fueling the hype around it (Nielsen, 2024).

DOI: 10.4324/9781003478157-7

Despite this scenario, some interesting approaches have emerged when it comes to investigative reporting. On the one hand, AI and machine learning tools have shown potential in assisting investigative reporters with various tasks related to sourcing and analyzing data and source material (Leiser, 2022; Stray, 2019). AI tools can be beneficial for investigations in various fields, from finance to climate, from conflict to politics. However, in recent years, AI and algorithmic tools have also become subjects of investigation themselves, particularly in relation to the direct study of the functioning and specifications of AI and algorithmic systems used in sensitive or even controversial areas of our society. From the investigation of predictive policing algorithms and their racial bias in the US,[1] to the scrutiny of the discriminatory outcomes of automated decision-making processes applied to welfare policies in Europe,[2] investigative reporters have begun to consider AI and algorithmic systems as *de facto* potential subjects of investigation and have done so also by adopting different computational strategies to effectively scrutinize and hold AI, algorithms, their producers, and users to account.

This trend is interesting for several reasons: firstly, it is a clear example of the evolving nature of investigative reporting and its ongoing innovation; secondly, it offers a glimpse into the nature of contemporary digital power and its dynamics; and thirdly, it can also be used as a lens to look at what resistance to algorithmic power can entail and how journalism also participates in it. The aim of this chapter is thus to provide an overview, through a case study discussion, of how the journalistic investigation of algorithms and AI systems is taking shape, and to discuss the broader implications of such a phenomenon for a datafied society increasingly built around AI. The chapter will also follow a twofold but interrelated line of inquiry: on the one hand, it will discuss changes and innovations within journalism; on the other hand, it will also connect these changes to broader reflections on digital power and its increasingly automated peculiarities. The chapter opens with a discussion of the concepts of "black box" and technological opacity, which is followed by an overview of the changes that occurred in investigative reporting in the wake of datafication and the progressive interest of journalists in investigating such technologies. After this, a series of prominent case studies are discussed, with the aim of offering insights about how investigative reporting has been digging into these technologies, while the discussion and conclusion sections will try to contextualize these investigations into broader notions of digital power and invisibility while simultaneously providing an overview of the major peculiarities of these projects.

Black Box Algorithms, AI Systems, and Obscurity

The metaphor of the "black box" is one of the most powerful in contemporary technology discourse. The origins of the "black box" concept can be found in science and philosophy, but when it comes to its application in the social sciences, Bruno Latour has provided the most functional use, defining a "black box" technology as one that reveals only its inputs and outputs, masking its "internal complexity" (Latour, 1999: 304). The metaphor is usually associated with technologies that, by design or obfuscation, hide some or all their properties, features or mechanisms, and do not allow external access, evaluation or transparency, and which therefore function and operate without the necessary accountability. Data-driven technologies, AI (Castelvecchi, 2016) and machine learning (Carabantes, 2020), among others, have been defined as "black boxes" due to their technical opacity, internal complexity and lack of transparency regarding their operational strategies and the communication tactics of technology companies, which aim to actively obfuscate the functioning of their products (Nguyen and Beijnon, 2023).

These "black box" traits are not only or necessarily connected to the technical sides but are also reflected in the way these systems function in reality and in society. The impact of black box technologies operating in society is political and social, and can lead to serious consequences for those affected, especially when AI and algorithmic systems are used to surveil, profile, judge, or automate decision-making about humans. It is therefore evident that the dangers of a "black box society" (Pasquale, 2015), where unaccountable AI and algorithms play a more and more central role, are of a clear newsworthy nature, especially when these machines provide controversial outcomes, commit errors or simply fail in their operations. Despite the techno-solutionist and sublime narratives that are used to describe AI systems and algorithms, these technologies are indeed prone to errors, not fairer than humans in their assessments and do often bring discriminatory outcomes (Gebru et al., 2021). According to Diakopoulos (2019: 208), and especially considering these almost mystical beliefs attributed to AI-driven technologies, it can be argued that these failures and mistakes make AI the most newsworthy. In this context, the act of "opening the black box" through journalistic investigation can also be framed in the broader concept of "witnessing", as proposed by Michael Richardson in his overview of artistic initiatives addressed against technological opacity and its ramifications (2024). Algorithmic accountability reporting can be considered as a strategy oriented towards "witnessing algorithms" or towards their explicability. The notion of "witnessing" is used here to describe strategies for exposing and revealing algorithms and their potential abuses by identifying the connections between the institutional, infrastructural, and techno-cultural contexts of technology and the production of race, gender, and class, which are inextricably linked (Richardson, 2024: 110–111). As it will be further discussed throughout the chapter, investigations into algorithms and AI are not conducted with the aim of explaining how the technology works, but rather with the goal of shedding light on the implications of their functioning within social reality.

Investigative Journalism from Datafication to AI

The advent of digitalization has had a profound impact on investigative reporting, giving rise to a plethora of new reporting and sourcing strategies, diverse styles and genres, and hybrid practices that combine computational elements with more traditionally journalistic ones (Carson, 2020: 171–193; Di Salvo and Porlezza, 2020). This has been particularly evident in the field of data journalism and the various computational elements involved in it, which has led to the emergence of a specific subgenre of reporting where data-driven approaches to muckraking are central. Furthermore, the integration of data journalism with computational strategies has led to the emergence of what Coddington (2015) defines as "computational journalism". This term encompasses a range of journalism practices that utilize computing and computational thinking to inform the processes of information gathering, sense-making, and information presentation (Coddington, 2015: 335). This computational approach to journalism is explicitly visible in the investigations of algorithms and AI systems. For instance, these investigations can entail the actual unveiling of the computer code of the applications they cover, or the explanation of their inner functioning. This can happen by practices such as reverse engineering, auditing, and code inspection, which are not journalistic in principle, but can become such when used to investigate computer systems (Diakopoulos, 2019: 216–222). These investigations are typically referred to as "algorithmic accountability reporting" (Diakopoulos, 2014), a definition that elucidates the rationale behind them: to provide accountability and/or transparency to computational and algorithmic systems that would otherwise be used without the necessary transparency or explainability.

"Algorithmic accountability reporting" (Diakopoulos, 2014) has become an identified genre, presenting a "reorientation of the traditional watchdog function of journalism toward the power wielded through algorithms" (Diakopoulos, 2019: 207). Whereas this is still a niche both for investigative reporting and technology journalism, a growing number of projects have been launched in the past few years, and the number of published stories of this kind has also grown. Dedicated newsrooms and projects now exist on both sides of the Atlantic, such as, among others, the US-based *The Markup*, which specializes in algorithmic accountability reporting or the AI + Automation Lab of German Public Broadcaster Bayerischer Rundfunk (BR), which routinely publishes investigations of this kind. At the same time, an identifiable group of journalists with background and experience in "opening" black boxes through computational practices is now also visible, as confirmed by the existence of various panels and sessions at international journalism conferences,[3] the launch of dedicated fellowships[4] and training[5] materials.[6]

Approach

This chapter is based on a series of case studies representing different kinds of algorithmic accountability reporting investigations. The case studies have been chosen for their ability to represent some of the most common traits of such projects. This is because they have been published by a different array of publications and in different countries, and because they rely on different sourcing and reporting strategies when it comes to their computational parts. The case studies presented here are intended to represent a diverse range of cases, selected to capture a broad spectrum of variations regarding algorithmic accountability reporting (Seawright and Gerring, 2008: 300). The selection process utilized purposeful sampling to identify case studies that are "information rich" (Emmel, 2014) and likely to provide significant insights for the analysis included in this chapter.[7] In particular, the case studies are informative of two different levels that are related to algorithmic accountability. On the one hand, they represent a wide array of reporting tactics journalists can employ when approaching algorithms and AI systems. These tactics vary from technical strategies derived from computer science to more classic journalistic approaches. On the other hand, they present a series of different reporting goals that algorithmic accountability reporting can achieve. These goals include disclosing the functioning of a specific algorithm, its training data, or the non-technical conditions influencing its problematic outputs or its own coding and programming.

The Case Studies

"Suspicion Machines" – Lighthouse Reports

"Suspicion Machines"[8] is a 2023 algorithmic accountability reporting series coordinated by the Amsterdam-based collaborative journalism newsroom Lighthouse Reports and published in partnership with technology magazine *WIRED*, the Dutch public broadcaster Vrijzinnig Protestantse Radio Omroep (VPRO) and the investigative journalism platform Follow The Money. The principal focus of the series has been on predictive algorithmic systems and their deployment in European public administrations. At the core of the project was an investigation into the fraud prediction system used by the city of Rotterdam, in the Netherlands, between 2017 and 2021. The algorithmic system had been used to rank every welfare benefit recipient in the city on a list according to their fraud risk, with the top decile referred for investigation. In terms of methodology, the Lighthouse Reports team also published an extensive background article outlining the methods employed by journalists to assess the algorithm (Lighthouse Reports, 2023b). Journalists obtained access to the machine learning model used to score recipients through public records requests and Freedom of Information Act (FOIA) access requests. Consequently, journalists were able to trace the data that was used to train the algorithm and how the machine was programmed to process it. Furthermore, journalists tested the algorithm with the profiles of personas created based on specific archetypes. As the investigation authors write, "it became clear that the system discriminates based on ethnicity, age, gender, and parenthood. It also revealed evidence of fundamental flaws that made the system both inaccurate and unfair" (Lighthouse Reports, 2023a)

"We Are All Raw Material for AI" – AI ± Automation Lab | Bayerischer Rundfunk

This 2023 investigation[9] was published by the AI + Automation Lab of German Public Broadcaster BR, focusing on training datasets used to build and train popular AI systems and on the information and images of individuals being involved in the training process. Journalists scrutinized the Large-Scale Artificial Intelligence Open Network (LAION-5B), the largest publicly accessible AI training dataset, which is involved in training popular AI applications such as Stable Diffusion. The dataset is based on over 5 billion links to images and their descriptions, all scraped from the Internet. As the investigation reports, images and text included in the dataset also feature sensitive and private data, such as "nude photos, bank data or precise information about where a particular photo was taken" through "exchangeable image file format" (EXIF) metadata. Furthermore, journalists discovered that the dataset includes problematic footage, such as pornography and explicit images and text pairs of rape, pornography, malign stereotypes, racist and ethnic slurs. The journalistic investigation was also centered around BR journalist Elisa Harlan requesting information about her portrait being included in the datasets through legal pathways, and particularly the EU's General Data Protection Regulation (GDPR) that allows citizens to request the deleting of images. The investigation revealed that OpenAI and Midjourney, whose applications rely on LAION datasets, did not respond to the journalist's requests despite being legally obliged to do so. OpenAI only replied following an official press inquiry. Overall, the journalist's image was deleted by only one LAION dataset out of the 50 that exist. Additionally, the removal will only be effective on new AI models being trained on the dataset, not on those already existing and in operation.

"Citizen Browser Series" – The Markup

This project encompasses a series of investigations conducted by the nonprofit US-based news outlet *The Markup*, a major player in algorithmic accountability reporting and one specializing in it. *The Markup* was founded by journalist Julia Angwin, who played a major role in establishing the algorithmic accountability reporting space with her pioneering work at ProPublica and the

"Machines Bias" investigation series (Cancela-Kieffer, 2021). With the "Citizen Browser" series[10] launched in 2020, *The Markup* aimed at measuring how disinformation travels across social media platforms over time and to do so by adopting a tailored technological solution to be used in cooperation with readers. As the initiative's webpage states:

> "At the center of The Citizen Browser Project is a custom web browser designed by The Markup to audit the algorithms that social media platforms use to determine what information they serve their users, what news and narratives are amplified or suppressed, and which online communities those users are encouraged to join. Initially, the browser will be implemented to glean data from Facebook and YouTube".
>
> *(The Markup, 2020)*

To conduct the investigation, *The Markup* established a statistically valid panel of 1200 US individuals. They were asked to surf the Internet using the browser extension, which was coded to gather data from YouTube and Facebook about how their algorithms operate when disseminating information online. Through the Citizen Browser, *The Markup* launched a crowdsourced experiment to gather data on different online experiences and to identify which content algorithms are amplifying and to whom. The insights gathered were subsequently analyzed by *The Markup* in collaboration with the *New York Times*. The project resulted in the publication of various articles and analyses. For instance, *The Markup* examined the dissemination of information about the January 6th assault on Capitol Hill in Washington, DC, comparing results from Trump and Biden voters on Facebook (Lecker and Keegan, 2021). The investigation and the data provided by the panelists through the Citizen Browser revealed that Biden voters were offered more news from nonpartisan outlets, such as the *Washington Post*, while Trump voters were more exposed to explicitly conservative news providers, such as *Breitbart*. In a joint investigation with the German daily newspaper *Süddeutsche Zeitung*, The Citizen Browser Project examined the visibility of German political parties on Facebook. The investigation revealed that the far-right party Alternative für Deutschland (AfD) has been the most visible party on the platform in the context of the 2021 German national elections (Waller and Lecher, 2021). The results of the investigation are particularly noteworthy given that most of the panelists involved in the analysis did not identify as AfD supporters.

"Online Gig Work Is Feeding Russia's Surveillance Machine"
(The Bureau of Investigative Journalism)

This is an algorithmic accountability reporting investigation led by the UK Bureau of Investigative Journalism, conducted in cooperation with *Le Monde*,

Follow The Money and Paper Trail Media.[11] The investigation dealt with the Russian surveillance apparatus and its use of AI-powered facial recognition technology to monitor dissent in the country and protests in the streets (McIntyre et al., 2024). The investigation, in particular, focused on how underpaid and extremely precarious gig workers in the Global South have been involved in improving the software when it comes to identifying individuals. According to the investigation:

> TBIJ reporting found workers in India, Turkey, Pakistan and Bangladesh had done tasks for the two companies, either providing photos to build their image libraries or labeling footage to improve automatic recognition of people and actions, since 2019.
>
> *(McIntyre et al., 2024)*

The investigation, which formed part of a broader research project into the implications of gig work and the human side of AI development, focused on a company that provides a platform for hiring gig workers to various clients, including some Russian EU-sanctioned suppliers of facial recognition systems to the Putin regime, which operate through a complex and obscure corporate scheme. The investigation also included the perspectives of the gig workers who were involved in the training of the facial recognition machine learning systems. These workers were largely unaware of the extent to which their work was being used in AI-powered surveillance operations in Russia. In a background story also published by the Bureau of Investigative Journalism, the journalists responsible for the investigation shared details about their methodology and approach (Jackson and McIntyre, 2024). The journalists conducted research on online forums where gig workers discussed their tasks on the gig work platform at the core of the investigation. They observed that some of the tasks included "drawing boxes around 'human bodies' in a security camera still of a girls' dance class" or "studying CCTV footage of people walking down the street to identify what they were doing" (Jackson and McIntyre, 2024). The journalists began their investigation by examining comments and questions posted by gig workers seeking support from their peers. This allowed them to identify which companies were requesting the seemingly innocuous tasks and to connect them to the companies supplying surveillance solutions to Russia.

Discussion

The case studies selected for this chapter illustrate some of the distinctive features of algorithmic accountability reporting and provide insights into how this field of investigative journalism is developing. While these case studies do not provide a complete picture of the field, they are illustrative of the range of reporting strategies involved in investigating AI and algorithmic technologies and the characteristics of such investigations. Considering the elements that emerge from the case studies, it is possible to analyze algorithmic accountability investigations in light of their subjects and the reporting strategies adopted. This analysis will focus on which "black box" elements of the algorithmic and AI systems being investigated are being looked at by journalists, how this is being done and what investigative tactics are being followed.

Opening the Black Box, One Layer at a Time

The case studies analyzed here allow an analysis of which aspects of black box technologies can be the subject of journalistic investigation. In particular, the case studies show that journalists can investigate opaque AI and algorithmic technologies when it comes to 1) the data used for their training and the related issues of "data justice" (Dencik, Hintz, Redden and Treré, 2022), as in the case of the "We Are All Raw Material for AI" investigation; 2) the functioning or rationale of algorithms with the aim of exposing their biases or discriminatory results, as in the "Suspicion Machines" investigation; 3) the effects of the behavior and operation of algorithms on citizens and their experiences, as in the case of the various "Suspicion Machines" investigations; 4) the impact of the behavior and operation of algorithms on citizens and their experiences, as for the various investigations in the Citizen Browser series; and 5) the political-economic dimensions of the training of AI and algorithms and the social justice issues involved in the development of technologies, as for the investigation "Online gig work is feeding Russia's surveillance machine". As Fuller and Weizman write (2021: 182), given the "multiple lines of conflict operating through computing in the present", it is inevitable that all these components can become "a space of investigation" (Fuller and Weizman, 2021: 182).

On the one hand, these areas of investigation pursued by journalists confirm the socio-technical relevance of black box technologies, especially when they're AI-driven or based on algorithmic, automated decision-making. On the other hand, they show that algorithmic accountability reporting can shed light on black box technologies not only in their technical aspects, but also in their offline and social justice implications. Overall, this overview of case studies shows that "black box" AI technologies can offer different possible journalistic approaches for reporters investigating their implications. While some coverage may be more technical and technology-oriented, focusing on exposing the material sides of the code or the coding issues involved in the malfunctioning of such machines, other coverage could be based on the implications of algorithmic invisibility outside of the technology itself. This comes as little surprise, as black box technologies are not only black boxes because of technical obfuscation strategies. In fact, black boxes are so because of what Frank Pasquale calls "legal secrecy" (2015: 8), put in place to prevent access to relevant information about the technology or the actors and companies producing it, which is common in the surveillance market (Rodrigues, 2019), as confirmed by the investigation into the role of gig workers in the coding of facial recognition software in Russia.

In summary, this overview of case studies shows that journalists, through algorithmic accountability reporting, are effectively trying to "open" black boxes by targeting different layers of their obfuscation, thus effectively contributing to the unmasking of AI systems and their "assemblage" nature made up of technical, material, economic and social components (Bennani-Taylor, 2024). In this light, AI reappears as a "mega-machine" or a "set of technological approaches that depend on industrial infrastructures, supply chains, and human labour that span the globe but are kept opaque" (Crawford, 2021: 48). Algorithmic accountability reporting also serves as a demystifying strategy, aimed at revealing what AI is, how it works, and what sublime and deterministic views about it hide.

The Different Technological Sophistication of Algorithmic Accountability Reporting

In the context of this book chapter, and following Anderson (2012)'s approach, the technological aspect of algorithmic accountability reporting has been intended as an embedded materiality intersecting with journalism at various levels. This is since a consistent part of these investigations is indeed technological in nature. Yet, the level of technological and computational sophistication involved in such investigative reporting varies. It is evident that certain strategies employed in the case studies analyzed here are more advanced in terms of computational complexity. This is exemplified by the "Citizen Browser" series, which has been developed using a browser extension specifically designed by *The Markup* technologists. The "Suspicion Machine" investigation employed a range of sophisticated statistical and data analysis techniques to assess the algorithmic system, including the machine learning model file, the pseudo-anonymized training dataset and the training data distributions (Lighthouse Reports, 2023b). Both these investigations, as well as the "We are all raw material for AI" project, are based on specific computational techniques that require dedicated expertise, knowledge, and training. However, algorithmic accountability reporting is not necessarily based only on such strategies.

The "Online gig work is feeding Russia's surveillance machine" investigation, for instance, has been conducted based on low-tech investigative approaches and by looking at online open sources, such as social media groups and discussion boards. While the digital component remains a significant aspect of the work, journalists did not apply statistical or computational techniques but rather employed more traditional methods of *muckraking*. Given the nature of the sources, which included social media postings and comments left by gig workers, journalists employed an open-source intelligence (OSINT) approach (Edwards, 2022; Reese and Chen, 2022), focusing on vetting and analyzing available source materials on the Internet.

The case studies demonstrate that the technical sophistication of algorithmic accountability investigations can encompass advanced computational practices and other, less technical approaches. This is not unexpected, given the nature of the issues involved in algorithmic injustice and invisibility, which are not solely of a technical nature. Rather, they are eminently political and increasingly connected with inequalities and pre-existing social issues originating and visible from outside of the digital realm. Algorithmic invisibility, in conjunction with the discriminatory and biased outcomes it can engender, is a phenomenon that transcends the scope of a mere technical glitch or coding error. It is a problem that requires a more comprehensive approach to address its underlying causes and effects (Broussard, 2024). Consequently, the various algorithmic accountability investigations are examining AI from disparate vantages and employing disparate methodologies, which are predominantly technical in nature. Collectively, they appear to investigate AI with the objective of elucidating its intrinsic dynamics and their intertwining with the "social, political, cultural, and economic worlds, shaped by humans, institutions, and imperatives that determine what they do and how they do it" (Crawford, 2021: 211). Some of these dynamics can be exposed by reverse engineering and software audits, while others may be identified by reading online comments and following the money through complex corporate conglomerates.

Conclusions

Over the past few years, algorithmic accountability reporting has established a presence in the journalistic field, becoming a recognizable area of investigative reporting. It has also evolved into a dedicated beat, constructed around "journalistic skills coming together with technical skills to provide the scrutiny that many algorithms warrant", as Diakopoulos notes (2019: 207). Algorithmic accountability reporting now occupies a position between technology journalism and other non-technological beats, contingent on the areas of application of the algorithms and AI systems that are the subject of scrutiny. In this sense, the reporting could take place in relation to social issues, economics and finance, law enforcement and even the military. Consequently, the application of this investigative approach to algorithmic and AI technologies is potentially extensive, given the wide range of uses of technology in society. While the presence of AI in society grows, together with its adoption in various areas, algorithmic accountability reporting investigations are becoming a crucial player for watchdog journalism, whose goal is to hold power to account, especially when power takes a digital shape. As McQuillan states, "AI is political because it acts in the world in ways that affect the distribution of power, and its political tendencies are revealed in the ways that it sets up boundaries and separations" (McQuillan, 2022: 2). As discussed by Verdegem (2022), AI is currently being produced at the center of various power dynamics, all of which come with accountability issues making the AI industry, which is dominated by Big Tech, particularly obscure. In light of this, investigating these black boxes fits entirely within the mandate of investigative reporting. Thus, the necessity of scrutinizing the changed distribution of power influenced by AI can be seen as one of the natural continuations of the mission of investigative reporting in the context of datafication. The case studies analyzed in this chapter do not, of course, show a complete picture of algorithmic accountability reporting, which is definitely more diverse and still in evolution (Diakopoulos, 2019: 204–239). Yet, it is certainly possible to isolate some insights from the case studies discussed here and try to conceptualize the field.

First, the technological component of these investigations is not a goal, but rather a tactic to expose more profound issues related to AI and algorithms. Second, that technological component of reporting can also be marginal when black boxing elements are embedded into algorithms and AI systems through non-technological means. This result is also in line with what has emerged from research conducted in other journalistic cultures and contexts, such as China (Ji, Kuai and Zamith, 2024), where these investigations are not necessarily conducted through advanced technical and computational practices. Even when conducted in more low-tech ways, these investigations always carry some interesting symbolic features in the context of datafication and its discontent. Especially when explicitly trying to look into black box technologies, they do represent a form of counteraction against digital power and its unaccountability. Analyzing algorithmic resistance in fields other than journalism, Tiziano Bonini and Emiliano Treré discuss a series of tactics that actors use to resist the power of algorithms and according to their framework that resistance can occur "to" algorithms or "through" algorithms (2024: 23–25), depending on how agency is negotiated or put into action vis-à-vis algorithms. This framework can also be applied to algorithmic accountability reporting and journalism at large, as they either resist the power of algorithms by shedding light on their operations or use computational strategies to do so. In both cases, what emerges is a quest for "tactical algorithmic agency" (Bonin and Treré, 2024: 43–47) that journalists gain in various ways while trying to disassemble, scrutinize and shed light on black box digital power.

CLASSROOM EXERCISE

- Think about the adoption of AI or automated systems used by public bodies or institutions: what potential abuses do you see?
- How would you set up an investigation into the problem? How would you approach access to data or code?
- Think about your local area: have instances of algorithmic abuses been investigated already?

Notes

1 See, for instance, the "Machine Bias" investigation by *ProPublica*: https://www.propublica.org/article/machine-bias-risk-assessments-in-criminal-sentencing
2 See, for instance, the "Suspicion Machines" series by Lighthouse Reports: https://www.lighthousereports.com/investigation/suspicion-machines/
3 See "Watchdogs of digital power" at Italy-based DIG Festival in 2023: https://dig-awards.org/en/event/watchdogs-of-digital-power-investigating-algorithms-artificial-intelligence/; "How to tame neural networks in AI models" at the International Journalism Festival in 2024: https://www.journalismfestival.com/programme/2024/here-be-neurons-how-to-tame-neural-networks-in-ai-models.
4 See the AlgorithmWatch's algorithmic accountability reporting fellowship: https://algorithmwatch.org/en/third-reporting-fellowship/.
5 See the 2023 "Tips for Investigating Algorithm Harm—and Avoiding AI Hype" by the Global Investigative Journalism Network: https://gijn.org/stories/tips-for-investigating-algorithm-harm-and-avoiding-ai-hype/.
6 See the 2019 "The Algorithms Beat: Angles and Methods for Investigation", published by datajournalism.com:https://datajournalism.com/read/handbook/two/investigating-data-platforms-and-algorithms/the-algorithms-beat-angles-and-methods-for-investigation.
7 This approach has already been followed by the author in another publication, dedicated to informational digital leaks and their different characteristics. See: Di Salvo (2024).
8 Available here: https://www.lighthousereports.com/investigation/suspicion-machines/.
9 Available here: https://interaktiv.br.de/ki-trainingsdaten/en/index.html.
10 Available here: https://themarkup.org/series/citizen-browser.
11 Available here: https://www.thebureauinvestigates.com/stories/2024-03-27/online-gig-work-is-feeding-russias-surveillance-machine/.

References

Anderson, C. (2012) 'Towards a sociology of computational and algorithmic journalism', *New Media & Society*, 15(7), pp. 1005–1021. https://doi.org/10.1177/1461444812465137.
Barassi, V. (2024) 'Towards a theory of AI errors: Making sense of hallucinations, catastrophic failures, and the fallacy of generative AI', *Harvard Data Science Review*. (Special issue 5). https://doi.org/10.1162/99608f92.ad8ebbd4.
Barassi, V., Scharenberg, A., Poux-Berthe, M., Patra, R. and Di Salvo, P. (2022) AI Errors and the Profiling of Humans: Mapping the Debate in European News Media, The Human Error Project: AI, Human Rights and the Conflict over Algorithmic Profiling, University of St. Gallen. https://thehumanerrorproject.ch/ai-errors-mapping-debate-european-media-report.
Beckett, C. and Jessen, M. (2023) 'Generating change a global survey of what news organizations are doing with artificial intelligence', *The London School of Economics and Political Science*. https://www.journalismai.info/research/2023-generating-change.
Bennani-Taylor, S. (2024) 'Infrastructuring AI: The stabilization of 'artificial intelligence' in and beyond national AI strategies', *First Monday*. https://doi.org/10.5210/fm.v29i2.13568.
Bonini, T. and Treré, E. (2024) *Algorithms of resistance*. MIT Press.
Broussard, M. (2024) *More than a glitch. Confronting race, gender, and ability bias in tech*. MIT Press.

Cancela-Kieffer, M. (2021) 'Journalism, algorithms, and the People's right to know', in Luengo, M. & Herrera-Damas, S. (eds.) *News media innovation reconsidered: Ethics and values in a creative reconstruction of journalism*. Wiley, pp. 155–173.

Carabantes, M. (2020) 'Black-box artificial intelligence: An epistemological and critical Analysis', *AI & SOCIETY*. https://doi.org/10.1007/s00146-019-00888-w.

Carson, A. (2020) *Investigative journalism, democracy and the digital age*. Routledge.

Castelvecchi, D. (2016) 'Can we open the black box of AI?', *Nature*, 538(7623), pp. 20–23.

Coddington, M. (2015) 'Clarifying journalism's quantitative turn', *Digital Journalism*, 3(3), pp. 331–348. https://doi.org/10.1080/21670811.2014.976400.

Crawford, K. (2021) *Atlas of AI. Power, politics, and the planetary costs of artificial intelligence*. Yale University Press.

Dencik, L., Hintz, A., Redden, J. and Treré, E. (2022) *Data justice*. SAGE.

Diakopoulos, N. (2014) 'Algorithmic accountability', *Digital Journalism*, 3(3), pp. 398–415. https://doi.org/10.1080/21670811.2014.976411.

Diakopoulos, N. (2019) *Automating the news. How algorithms are rewriting the media*. Harvard University Press.

Di Salvo, P. (2023) There's a Struggle over AI and Journalism Is at the Center. The Human Error Project. https://thehumanerrorproject.ch/journalism-ai-futures-narratives/.

Di Salvo, P. (2024) 'A typology of digital leaks as journalistic source materials', in Dunn, H., Ragnedda, M., Ruiu, M.L. and Robinson, L. (eds.) *The Palgrave handbook of everyday digital life*. Cham: Springer International Publishing, pp. 469–488.

Di Salvo, P. and Porlezza, C. (2020) 'Hybrid professionalism in journalism: Opportunities and risks of hacker sources', *Studies in Communication Sciences*, 20(2), pp. 243–254.

Edwards, M. (2022) Open-Source Journalism in a Wired World. *Nieman Reports*, December 7th. https://niemanreports.org/articles/open-source-journalism/.

Emmel, N. (2014) 'Purposeful sampling', in Emmel, N. (ed.) *Sampling and choosing cases in qualitative research: A realist approach*. SAGE, pp. 33–44.

Eubanks, V. (2019) *Automating inequality. How high-tech tools profile, police, and punish the poor*. Macmillan.

Fuller, M. and Weizman, E. (2021) *Investigative aesthetics. Conflicts and commons in the politics of truth*. Verso Books.

Gebru, T., Morgenstern, J., Vecchione, B., Vaughan, J. W., Wallach, H., Iii, H. D., & Crawford, K. (2021). Datasheets for datasets. *Communications of the ACM*, 64(12), 86–92.

Jackson, J. and McIntyre, N. (2024) 'How we found our gig work surveillance scoop', *The Bureau of Investigative Journalism*, March 28th. https://www.thebureauinvestigates.com/stories/2024-03-28/how-we-found-our-gig-work-surveillance-scoop/.

Ji, X., Kuai, J. and Zamith, R. (2024) 'Scrutinizing algorithms: Assessing journalistic role performance in Chinese news Media's coverage of artificial intelligence', *Journalism Practice*, pp. 1–18. https://doi.org/10.1080/17512786.2024.2336136.

Latour, B. (1999) *Pandora's hope. Essays on the reality of science studies*. Harvard University Press.

Lecker, C. and Keegan, J. (2021) Biden and Trump Voters Were Exposed to Radically Different Coverage of the Capitol Riot on Facebook. *The Markup*, January 14th. https://themarkup.org/citizen-browser/2021/01/14/biden-and-trump-voters-were-exposed-to-radically-different-coverage-of-the-capitol-riot-on-facebook.

Leiser, M.R. (2022) 'Bias, journalistic endeavors, and the risks of artificial intelligence', Pihlajarinne, T. and Alén-Savikko, A. (eds.) In *Artificial intelligence and the media*. Edward Elgar Publishing, pp. 8–32.

Lighthouse Reports. (2023a) Suspicion Machines. Lighthouse Reports. https://www.lighthousereports.com/investigation/suspicion-machines/.

Lighthouse Reports. (2023b) Suspicion Machine Methodology. Lighthouse Reports. https://www.lighthousereports.com/methodology/suspicion-machine/.

McIntyre, N., Kijewski, L., Munzinger, N., Huppertz, C. and Kotkamp, L. (2024) 'Online gig work is feeding Russia's surveillance machine', *The Bureau of Investigative Journalism*. March 27th. https://www.thebureauinvestigates.com/stories/2024-03-27/online-gig-work-is-feeding-russias-surveillance-machine/.

McQuillan, D. (2022) *Resisting AI. An anti-fascist approach to artificial intelligence.* Bristol University Press.

Nielsen, R.K. (2024) How news coverage, often uncritical, helps build up the AI hype. The Reuters Institute for the Study of Journalism. https://reutersinstitute.politics.ox.ac.uk/news/how-news-coverage-often-uncritical-helps-build-ai-hype.

Nguyen, D. and Beijnon, B. (2023) 'The data subject and the myth of the 'black box' data communication and critical data literacy as a resistant practice to platform exploitation', *Information, Communication & Society*, pp. 1–17. https://doi.org/10.1080/1369118x.2023.2205504.

Pasquale, F. (2015) *The black box society. The secret algorithms that control money and information.* Cambridge. Harvard University Press.

Reese, S.D. and Chen, B. (2022) 'Emerging hybrid networks of verification, accountability, and institutional resilience: The U.S. Capitol riot and the work of open-source investigation', *Journal of Communication*. https://doi.org/10.1093/joc/jqac030.

Richardson, M. (2024) *Nonhuman witnessing. War, data, and ecology after the end of the world.* Duke University Press.

Rodrigues, R. (2019) 'The surveillance industry in Europe', in Wright, D. and Kreissl, R. (eds.) *Surveillance in Europe*. Routledge, pp. 101–149.

Seawright, J. and Gerring, J. (2008) 'Case selection techniques in case study research: A menu of qualitative and quantitative', *Political Research Quarterly*, 61(294), pp. 294–308.

Simon, F. (2024) *Artificial intelligence in the news. How AI retools, rationalizes, and reshapes journalism and the public arena.* Tow Center for Digital Journalism, Columbia University. https://academiccommons.columbia.edu/doi/10.7916/ncm5-3v06

Stray, J. (2019) 'Making artificial intelligence work for investigative journalism', *Digital Journalism*. https://www.tandfonline.com/doi/full/10.1080/21670811.2019.1630289.

The Markup. (2020) The Citizen Browser Project—Auditing the Algorithms of Disinformation. *The Markup*. https://themarkup.org/citizen-browser.

Verdegem, P. (2022) 'Dismantling AI capitalism: The commons as an alternative to the power concentration of Big Tech', *AI & SOCIETY*. https://doi.org/10.1007/s00146-022-01437-8.

Waller, A. and Lecher, C. (2021) Germany's Far-Right Political Party, the AfD, Is Dominating Facebook This Election. *The Markup*, September 22th. https://themarkup.org/citizen-browser/2021/09/22/germanys-far-right-political-party-the-afd-is-dominating-facebook-this-election.

PART III

Constraints on Investigative Journalism

And Ways to Challenge Them

5

THE IMPACT OF LEGAL INTIMIDATION ON INVESTIGATIVE JOURNALISTS

Barbara Longo-Flint

Introduction

Investigative journalists play a vital role in functional democracies by holding power to account and unveiling what is kept secret. Nevertheless, powerful people and organisations prefer to keep their secrets hidden, sometimes weaponising the law to silence journalists. Strategic Lawsuits Against Public Participation (SLAPPs) are a form of legal intimidation aimed at silencing reporters by threatening them with expensive and baseless claims. These lawsuits can inflict substantial psychological, physical, and financial distress on journalists, potentially undermining journalistic practice and leading to self-censorship (Kerševan and Poler, 2023; Papadopoulou and Maniou, 2024).

This chapter delves into how powerful entities weaponise the law through SLAPPs, with a particular focus on Italy and the UK. It examines the chilling effect of these legal threats on journalistic practices, particularly how they compel journalists to redact or abandon public interest stories. By comparing the experiences of investigative journalists in these two countries, this chapter aims to uncover the varied social and emotional responses to abuse and intimidation within different legal frameworks.

The chapter also tracks implementation of legal protections in the UK and Italy and reviews international trends in Anti-SLAPP legislation, particularly in the United States, Canada, and Australia.

Empirically, this chapter is grounded in new comparative research, including an online anonymous survey of 52 investigative reporters in the UK and Italy and qualitative interviews with 16 practising investigative journalists from these countries. Integrating quantitative and qualitative methods enhances our understanding of the scope and depth of legal intimidation. The quantitative

DOI: 10.4324/9781003478157-9

survey establishes a statistical foundation, while the qualitative interviews provide nuanced personal narratives and detailed accounts of journalists' experiences with legal threats.

The chapter begins by providing an overview of legal intimidation before offering a global perspective on legislative efforts to counteract these threats. Drawing on empirical research conducted in the UK and Italy, the chapter examines the practical and emotional effects of SLAPPs on journalists' practice and mental health. To conclude, the chapter discusses strategies for building resilience and supporting journalists in the face of these ongoing challenges.

Background

When Maltese freelance journalist Daphne Caruana Galizia was killed in 2017, she was fighting 47 SLAPPs in different courts, including the High Court in London. Caruana Galizia was an investigative journalist famous for her blog 'Running Commentary', which exposed corruption in Malta's political and business sectors. Her brave work earned her both supporters and enemies. Despite threats and lawsuits, she continued her mission to uncover the truth.

On October 16, 2017, Caruana Galizia was murdered in a car bombing near her home. This event shocked Malta and the international community, highlighting the dangers investigative journalists face. Her death brought attention to the critical role of investigative journalism in protecting democracy and holding those in power accountable.

Caruana Galizia's legacy lives on through a foundation in her name, inspiring journalists worldwide to seek the truth. Her dedication to exposing corruption and serving the public interest shows the significant risks journalists take, especially during times when investigative journalism is under threat.

With major media organisations closing their newsrooms, there is a growing reliance on freelancers (Hanitzsch *et al*, 2019). Their financial uncertainty, absence of a newsroom link and an increasing number of threats could lead, as evidence suggests, to self-censorship, which can eventually result in weakening democratic practices as the plurality of information will diminish (Žuffová and Carlini, 2021). In response to these challenges, investigative journalism has evolved by adopting new methods and forming international collaborations (Carson and Farhall, 2018). A notable example is the Panama Papers investigation, where more than 300 journalists from the International Consortium for Investigative Journalism worked together to uncover global tax evasion by prominent figures (Konow-Lund, 2019).

The last decade has also seen the rise of investigative journalism start-ups like The Centre for Investigative Journalism, The Bureau of Investigative Journalism, Open Democracy, and The Ferret Scotland. These initiatives emerged to counter the decline in traditional investigative reporting. However, Price (2017) noted that these digital journalism start-ups are economically fragile.

They often lack financial support and face high legal costs, particularly from libel lawsuits, which can lead to bankruptcy for small media organisations and freelance journalists. This economic vulnerability, combined with the increasing use of legal intimidation tactics, underscores the importance of understanding the dynamics of legal intimidation and SLAPPs, which will be explored in the following section.

Legal Intimidation vs SLAPPs

Public awareness of SLAPPs was relatively low until the onset of the war in Ukraine, which brought these issues to light due to the sanctions imposed on Russian oligarchs, considered the first deployers of SLAPPs. Few people knew that investigative journalists had long been targets of vexatious lawsuits, often filed in the High Court of London against both British and European reporters, many of whom had no connection to the UK (Coughtrie, 2022).

The primary goal of SLAPPs is not to secure financial compensation but to halt investigative efforts by personally targeting journalists and burdening them with exorbitant legal fees, which can amount to thousands of pounds (Borg-Barthet, Lobina and Zabrocka, 2021). These lawsuits, frequently based on weak or exaggerated claims, serve as a tool of intimidation against media freedom (Kerševan and Poler, 2023). They can drag on for years, inflicting severe psychological and physical stress on journalists (Papadopoulou and Maniou, 2024). Moreover, in several European countries, defamation is still considered a criminal offence, which adds the threat of criminal charges and imprisonment to the list of fears for journalists.

The distinction between legal intimidation and SLAPPs is often blurred in journalists' perception, for whom these terms are frequently synonymous (Hanna, 2024). They are commonly used interchangeably, as the term SLAPP is still open to interpretation, although it represents a de facto form of legal intimidation. As Hanna (2024) argues, an empirical assessment of SLAPP occurrences, such as documenting the number of claims identified as SLAPPs in formal proceedings over the past years, might provide clarity. However, the feasibility of such empirical measurements hinges on a universally accepted definition of SLAPPs; in addition, the subtle nature of SLAPPs means that they often do not manifest in formal records. The accurate scale of the problem usually emerges not through filed lawsuits but through more nuanced forms of intimidation, such as threatening calls from a claimant's lawyer or quiet warnings directed at potential defendants. Moreover, Borg-Barthet (2021) points out, SLAPPs tend to exert significant pressure in the pre-litigious phase, coercing respondents to comply with demands without resorting to the courts.

In this context, this chapter analyses the impact of SLAPPs through the hierarchy of influences model, originally developed by Shoemaker and Reese (1996). This model provides a comprehensive framework for understanding how various levels of influence – from the micro to the macro – shape journalistic work. It explains that news production is influenced by a range of factors, including (1) individual characteristics, (2) work routines, (3) organisational-level concerns, (4) institutional forces, and (5) broader social systems. These levels are not isolated; rather, they interact dynamically, meaning that influences at one level, such as legal pressures, can interact with or reinforce those at other levels, either enabling or inhibiting journalistic practices (Reese and Shoemaker, 2016).

The Worlds of Journalism Study (WJS) adds further complexity by distinguishing between objective and perceived influences (Hanitzsch *et al*, 2019, p. 113). Objective influences refer to tangible pressures, such as legal restrictions or economic conditions, while perceived influences reflect how journalists interpret and respond to these pressures. In the case of SLAPPs, the threat of legal action operates as both an objective and perceived influence, as we will observe later in this chapter. While SLAPPs represent a real legal risk, their power often lies in how journalists perceive the threat. Even the receipt of an intimidating legal letter can lead to self-censorship, as journalists anticipate potential lawsuits and the associated financial or reputational costs (Hanna, 2024).

According to data collected for this research, while 75% of journalists reported experiencing legal intimidation, only 15% identified these actions specifically as SLAPPs. This discrepancy highlights the interchangeable use of these terms for journalists.

This pattern is particularly evident in Italy, where SLAPPs are known as 'Querela Temeraria' (literally: reckless lawsuit). The Italian context exemplifies how local terminology and practices reflect the broader issue of legal intimidation aimed at journalists. Both SLAPPs and general legal intimidation's primary intent is to stop a public interest story, and there must be a significant economic imbalance, typically involving powerful individuals or entities suing journalists individually or small media organisations (Coughtrie and Ogier, 2020). European jurisprudence is leaning towards establishing a widely accepted definition of SLAPPs, which emphasises the presence of an act of public participation and the litigation tactics employed by the claimant rather than focusing on the claimant's motives (Borg-Barthet and Farrington, 2023). The UK government's policy paper on SLAPPs further states that these lawsuits aim to harass, intimidate, and financially or psychologically exhaust journalists through the misuse of legal systems (Dawson, 2024).

Journalists are often isolated through these lawsuits. A reporter might be personally sued for a tweet rather than a published article, making the individual more vulnerable (Posetti *et al*, 2021). It is crucial for journalists to remember that retweeting can be seen as repeating a defamatory statement, so they should carefully consider what they share on social media.

It's important to highlight that SLAPPs are not a means to cover up journalistic errors. When a lawsuit is meritorious, it can have severe repercussions, potentially costing journalists their jobs, careers, and even their homes. SLAPPs are not confined to defamation law; they can also arise from privacy law or General Data Protection Regulation (GDPR) violations. In some instances, claimants allege data protection breaches by journalists to take advantage of longer statutes of limitations. For example, while defamation claims typically have a 12-month limitation period, GDPR-related cases can extend up to 6 years.

Anti-SLAPPs Legislation: A Global Perspective

The proliferation of SLAPPs represents a significant threat to freedom of expression, democratic engagement, and the vital role of civil society in scrutinising public and corporate power (Kerševan and Poler, 2023). SLAPPs are legal actions used to intimidate, harass, and ultimately silence critics by overwhelming them with the costs and complexities of legal battles rather than aiming to win the case (Borg-Barthet and Farrington, 2023). This section examines the global landscape of Anti-SLAPP legislation, highlighting the varying degrees of legal protection available across different jurisdictions and emerging judicial responses to such cases.

United States

The United States has been at the forefront of implementing Anti-SLAPP legislation. Currently, at least 30 states have enacted laws specifically designed to protect against SLAPPs. These laws typically allow for early dismissal of cases that target individuals or entities for their participation in matters of public interest. For example, California's Code of Civil Procedure includes provisions enabling defendants to file special motions to strike a lawsuit if it arises from exercising free speech concerning a public issue. Successful defendants can also recover legal fees and court costs, reducing the financial burden these vexatious lawsuits impose (Shapiro, 2010).

California's Anti-SLAPP statute is particularly noteworthy for its comprehensive approach. The law defines SLAPPs as lawsuits intended to chill the valid exercise of the constitutional right to freedom of speech. The statute provides a mechanism for early dismissal, wherein the burden shifts to the plaintiff to demonstrate a probability of prevailing on the claim. This has been pivotal in protecting activists, journalists, and other public participants from meritless legal challenges aimed at silencing them.

In recent years, several states have adopted or amended their Anti-SLAPP laws. As of July 2024, 34 states and the District of Columbia have Anti-SLAPP laws, including Arizona, Arkansas, California, Colorado, Connecticut, Delaware, Florida, Georgia, Hawaii, Illinois, Indiana, Kansas, Kentucky, Louisiana, Maine, Maryland, Massachusetts, Minnesota, Missouri, Nebraska, Nevada, New Jersey,

New Mexico, New York, Oklahoma, Oregon, Pennsylvania, Rhode Island, Tennessee, Texas, Utah, Vermont, Virginia, and Washington (RCFP, 2024).

Additionally, the 2010 Securing the Protection of our Enduring and Established Constitutional Heritage (SPEECH) Act provides some federal protection by preventing the enforcement of foreign defamation judgements that conflict with US First Amendment principles. The Act was designed to stop libel tourism by allowing a different course of action if the claim involves a foreign claimant trying to stop an American citizen from exercising their freedom of expression (Toscano, 2021).

Canada

Canada has also made significant strides in adopting Anti-SLAPP legislation, particularly in the provinces of Ontario, British Columbia, and Quebec. Ontario's Protection of Public Participation Act (2015) is often cited as a robust model for Anti-SLAPP protection. It allows for the rapid dismissal of lawsuits intended to limit freedom of expression on matters of public interest, placing the burden on the plaintiff to demonstrate that their case has substantial merit. This legislation has served as an inspiration for other jurisdictions looking to implement similar protections.

British Columbia and Quebec have followed suit with their own Anti-SLAPP statutes. British Columbia's Protection of Public Participation Act, enacted in 2019, provides a framework for dismissing SLAPPs, emphasising the importance of protecting public discourse on matters of public interest. Quebec's Anti-SLAPP law, part of the province's Code of Civil Procedure, allows for the dismissal of clearly abusive actions, including those intended to silence public debate (Young, 2022).

Australia

Australia's approach to Anti-SLAPP legislation has been somewhat limited but notable. The Australian Capital Territory (ACT) was the first to introduce the Protection of Public Participation Act in 2008, following the high-profile case of Gunns Ltd v Marr, which involved defamation suits against environmental activists. Although this legislation marked a positive step, it has been critiqued for not providing as comprehensive protection as seen in the United States and Canada, focusing primarily on the improper purpose of discouraging public participation.

The ACT's law defines SLAPPs in a way that emphasises the intent behind the litigation, aiming to protect activities related to public participation. However, other Australian states and territories have yet to adopt similar legislation, resulting in inconsistent protections across the country. This highlights a significant gap in Australia's legislative framework for protecting public interest speech (Ogle, 2010).

Europe

The movement towards Anti-SLAPP legislation has gained momentum in Europe in recent years. It has been represented by several NGOs, including Daphne Caruana Galizia's foundations, led by her three sons. Additionally, the Council of Europe has established a committee of experts tasked with drafting and updating recommendations on the issue.

In February 2024, the European Parliament plenary session formally adopted at first reading a directive on protecting 'persons who engage in public participation from manifestly unfounded or abusive court proceedings.' State members have two years to adopt the directive called 'Daphne's Law' and strengthen their legal frameworks against SLAPPs. The directive outlines mechanisms for early dismissal, burden-shifting to plaintiffs, and awarding costs and damages to defendants. It also emphasises the need for member states to provide training for judges and legal professionals on SLAPPs, ensuring that the judiciary is well-equipped to handle such cases effectively.

Latin America and Other Regions

In Latin America, SLAPPs are a pervasive issue, with numerous cases reported in countries such as Mexico and Colombia. However, dedicated Anti-SLAPP legislation remains sparse. The judicial responses in these regions often rely on existing legal frameworks, such as abuse of process provisions, to dismiss SLAPP cases. The Inter-American Court of Human Rights has begun to address the problem, recognising the abusive nature of SLAPPs in its rulings and calling for legislative reforms to protect freedom of expression better.

International Initiatives

On the international stage, various human rights bodies have highlighted the dangers of SLAPPs and the need for stronger protections. The United Nations, through its Human Rights Council, adopted a resolution in 2022 expressing concern over the rise of SLAPPs and urging member states to implement laws and policies to protect journalists and human rights defenders. Similarly, regional human rights mechanisms, such as the Inter-American Commission on Human Rights and the Organisation for Security and Co-operation in Europe (OSCE), have underscored the importance of combating SLAPPs to safeguard democratic freedoms.

UK

Although this chapter refers to UK legislation, it is important to note that the UK comprises three distinct legal systems: England and Wales, Scotland, and Northern Ireland. Each system has its own defamation laws, which can be weaponised against journalists. Since none of these devolved countries currently have Anti-SLAPP legislation in place, they will all be collectively referred to as the UK.

In October 2023, the Economic Crime and Corporate Transparency Act (ECCTA) received Royal Assent. The Act constitutes the first Anti-SLAPP legislation introduced in UK law, providing judges with new powers to strike out SLAPP claims relating to economic crime and introducing the concepts of 'early dismissal' and 'power imbalance' if the journalists were sued individually. Limitations have been highlighted by the UK Anti-SLAPP Coalition (CASE). First, the Act would only protect journalists investigating economic crimes, failing to protect those investigating, for example, medical malpractice or sexual abuse. Moreover, the ECCTA introduces the concept of 'claimant motivation', expecting the court to establish the state of mind of the filer in order to recognise and define the legal action as a SLAPP (CASE Coalition, 2023).

A Call for Evidence in 2022 was followed by a proposed SLAPP Bill to establish a more general statute applicable to various legal actions. Critics, however, argue that the existing measures under defamation law and the proposed Anti-SLAPP provisions are insufficiently comprehensive. They contend that the laws lack precise definitions and robust mechanisms to effectively deter and dismiss SLAPPs promptly, highlighting the need for further refinement to ensure these laws can balance free speech interests with adequate defamation protection effectively (CASE Coalition, 2023)

In the meantime, pressed by media organisations and NGOs, the Solicitors Regulation Authority (SRA) has warned law firms about their conduct when drafting threatening letters on behalf of clients (SRA, 2022). The SRA has cautioned against using aggressive, intimidating language that could prevent recipients from seeking independent legal advice. Additionally, it has highlighted concerns about the excessive and disproportionate frequency of such letters. The authority also clarified the misuse of labels such as 'Not for Publication', 'Strictly Private and Confidential', and 'Without Prejudice' on correspondence. The SRA emphasised that these labels cannot enforce privacy or confidentiality unless these conditions already exist, warning that such correspondence might be lawfully published if it does not adhere to these pre-existing conditions.

Italy

Italy presents a significant challenge for journalists due to the widespread use of SLAPPs. A 2023 study commissioned by the Committee on Civil Liberties, Justice and Home Affairs (LIBE) of the European Parliament reported that Italy has the highest rate of SLAPPs, constituting 25.5% of the total cases examined (Borg-Barthet and Farrington, 2023). Italy continues to enforce criminal defamation laws, with Article 595 of the Italian Criminal Code prescribing penalties of up to three years. This legal provision has resulted in 42% of the criminal defamation actions noted in the LIBE study originating from

Italy. Additionally, there is an observed escalation in civil defamation actions, representing 74.5% of the total cases.

A trend confirmed by the participants in this research is that they are highly concerned about the now common tactics employed by claimants who increasingly resort to civil courts to seek substantial damages, potentially amounting to millions of euros. Such a shift is particularly alarming because the burden of proof in civil proceedings – on the balance of probabilities – is significantly lower than in criminal lawsuits – beyond reasonable doubt. Moreover, the protracted nature of the Italian justice system exposes journalists to a prolonged state of uncertainty, with some civil trials extending over a decade. As described by one participant, this scenario leaves journalists living a 'life in limbo', undermining their ability to function effectively and chilling journalistic freedom.

The Order and the Union of Journalists, with press freedom organisations and civil society, have advocated legislative reforms, asking for measures that would allow for the early dismissal of meritless lawsuits and provide protections and compensations for journalists. The last attempt to introduce a robust Anti-SLAPP legislation was the De Nicola Bill in 2018. The proposed legislation was never converted into law.

The Impact on Journalism Practice

A survey was initially conducted with 52 investigative journalists (31 from Italy and 21 from the UK) to assess the impact of abuse and intimidation on journalistic practices. This survey examined the relationships between journalists and their employers and analysed differences in journalistic principles and practices across these cultural contexts. The choice of these two countries is particularly pertinent: while Italian journalistic culture typically reflects the lesser degree of professionalism common in other Mediterranean nations, a stronger sense of professionalism characterises the UK (Hallin and Mancini, 2000). In addition, the UK, with its Anglo-Saxon solid tradition of investigative journalism, contrasts sharply with Italy, where such a tradition is less established (Gerli *et al*, 2018). However, the recent development of data journalism in Italy has sparked a significant increase in investigative reporting (Porlezza and Splendore, 2019).

Following the quantitative phase, semi-structured interviews were conducted with 16 journalists to validate the survey findings and add personal nuances, particularly concerning the emotional impacts. These insights will be further explored in the next section. These interviews were anonymised to provide journalists the freedom to discuss their experiences and to establish if abuse and intimidation, particularly legal intimidation, had a detrimental effect on their journalistic autonomy. All actual names, locations, organisations, and other potentially identifying details were removed and replaced with pseudonyms or descriptor codes (Saunders, Kitzinger and Kitzinger, 2015).

To determine whether journalists were censored or self-censored, the first step was to design the survey to assess the extent of the problem. This involved identifying at which stage of the editorial process these pressures influenced their decisions, such as whether stories were not pitched or withheld following advice from editors or media lawyers. Respondents were asked if they had ever redacted or abandoned 'accurate' public interest stories due to abuse and intimidation. The term 'accurate' was emphasised, as the research aimed to explore the emotional and professional toll on journalists forced to abandon or modify stories that were thoroughly researched and conducted with due diligence and the decision to abandon or redact such stories stemmed directly from the legal and personal pressures exerted through abusive intimidation tactics, as highlighted from Participant 01UK:

> You've just got to realise that when you are very small, it can be too risky. But you know we've got to let some of these go because we don't have the legal means to defend it. So, if we were sued, it could end the project completely, so we've got to err on the side of caution, which can be annoying, but that's what it is.

The impact of SLAPPs on journalistic practices was particularly evident in the responses gathered with the survey. In the UK, 57% of journalists reported having redacted stories, and 48% ultimately abandoned them, largely due to legal threats, particularly defamation claims. In contrast, in Italy, only 32% of respondents had redacted stories, and 23% abandoned them. This disparity can be attributed to the differences in legal and journalistic practices in the two countries. In Italy, journalists are generally required to offer the right to reply post-publication, as prescribed by law, meaning that many SLAPPs are filed after a story has been published. This was confirmed during the interviews, where Italian journalists noted that the right of reply is often treated more as a right to rectify after publication. Some respondents even reported being sued despite being offered the right to reply, highlighting how legal threats can persist regardless of adherence to pre- and post-publication protocols.

In the UK, however, legal challenges more commonly arise during the pre-publication phase, often influencing journalists to modify or drop stories entirely before they are made public. This pre-publication phase is particularly fraught with legal risks, especially for publications that deal with sensitive or controversial content.

Ian Hislop, the editor of Private Eye, noted that his publication does not automatically offer the right of reply before publication. Hislop (Turvill, 2015) explained that providing the opportunity for a response often led to injunctions being filed, which would prevent the story from being published altogether. He stated:

> We found that if you put your story to people, they'd then take out an injunction against you, and then you couldn't run the story.

Hislop also downplayed the potential for reducing mistakes by offering the right of reply, noting that:

> I don't think we make a huge amount of mistakes at the moment, and the mistakes we make I'm very happy to put my hands up to. But I don't think they come from failing to put the story to people.

When asked about the stage in the editorial process at which stories were either abandoned or redacted, survey data revealed that most UK respondents from mainstream media organisations indicated they acted on the advice of in-house media lawyers. Conversely, in smaller media organisations and in Italy, where most media lawyers are private practitioners, the editor typically makes the decision. Additionally, the survey showed that 19% of UK and 16% of Italian journalists chose not to pitch their stories after experiencing intimidation.

The findings from the research further reveal the dilemma journalists face when deciding how much of a story to publish, particularly when legal threats target specific details that may not seem central to the main narrative. As highlighted by one UK respondent, journalists sometimes omit the names of secondary characters to reduce risks. However, such omissions can withhold important information about individuals or organisations that could lead to further investigations or stories. This practice contributes to a broader culture of self-censorship within journalism, where the fear of legal repercussions creates a chain reaction of underreported stories, as explained by Participant 06UK:

> Coming closer to publication, you might publish 70% of your story and not 100%, you might have written it all and then receive some particularly nasty threats, and then maybe they're not central factors in the story that you're receiving threats from. So then you decide, we still get the message across without including these people's names and don't publish the names of these secondary characters, but that has a knock-on effect because somebody else could have read that and know a little bit more about what they've been doing.

As findings from this research highlight, the use of legal intimidation in the UK is broader than considered by previous studies (Coughtrie, 2020). To have a dimension of the phenomenon, a small organisation specialised in investigative work deals with over 70 intimidating letters a year, mostly requiring hours to prepare for any possible scenario, as Participant 07UK highlights:

> We probably spent 40 or 60 hours before publication [.] I probably spent that much time afterwards as well. Another 60 hours afterwards still, but probably more than 100 hours, and in a small organisation where you're

the editor you essentially can't do that your job in a 40-hour week. It means that you're working massive hours and massive stress.

Moreover, in Italy, SLAPPs are frequently employed by political figures and business leaders as a method to suppress journalists who seek to uncover corruption or misconduct. It is not unusual to observe high-profile politicians initiating lawsuits against reporters to obstruct investigative reporting. Politicians also engage in 'announcement strategies', where they publicly declare their intent to sue a journalist or a media organisation via television channels and social media, as reported by Participant 06ITA:

> We are assisting this new phenomenon with entrepreneurs and politicians, but mainly politicians, which announce to other media that they will sue us so that they can achieve two results: to intimidate us and to discourage others from pursuing the same story.

The Impacts on Journalists' Mental Health

While a substantial body of research shows that journalists can be affected emotionally by their work (Šimunjak, 2023), the impact of abuse and intimidation, particularly legal intimidation, on investigative journalists has not been deeply examined with empirical research. Research has mainly been conducted on journalists covering war (Feinstein, Osmann and Patel, 2018), natural disasters (Buchanan and Keats, 2011), or local news with traumatic crime or accident content (Pyevich, Newman and Daleiden, 2003).

Two recent studies have examined the impacts of SLAPPs on journalists: Papadopoulou and Maniou (2024) focus on Greece and Cyprus, while Kerševan and Poler (2023) investigate Slovenia. Both studies document the significant professional and personal toll these legal challenges take on journalists. Similarly, this study found that 63% of surveyed journalists reported that abuse and intimidation affected their mental health. Interviewees described in detail the psychological trauma of receiving threatening legal letters addressed to them personally, rather than to their organisations, and the fear of potentially losing everything they've built, both professionally and personally.

Anxiety was notably prevalent among journalists, with many attributing their stress to the potential legal repercussions of reporting on powerful entities. This fear is exacerbated by the direct and invasive nature of legal threats, often personally delivered to journalists' homes, disrupting their sense of safety and extending the emotional burden to their families.

The findings also highlight the substantial issue of isolation, where journalists facing legal challenges experience social withdrawal from the public and within their professional circles. This isolation often stems from colleagues' fears of association, which may lead to further professional and personal repercussions, as also reported by investigative journalist Tom Burgis during his oral evidence to the Foreign Affairs Committee (2023):

> You risk humiliation in the public square. The letters go to your editors, publishers, and lawyers, and you are cast as the most monstrous, scheming and corrupt version of yourself.

Burnout emerges as a critical concern, driven by the relentless demands of journalistic integrity and legal scrutiny. Journalists report extensive periods of stress due to the need for meticulous verification of facts before publication and the ongoing defence against potential lawsuits.

Additionally, the emotional toll profoundly affects journalists' personal lives, with many reporting fear for their family's safety as threats sometimes extend beyond the journalists to their loved ones. This fear can lead to significant psychological distress and a pervasive sense of vulnerability, as expressed by Participant 08UK:

> Because my family were involved as well, and because I was at that stage of life where you're suddenly thinking 'Oh my God, my career, I'm in the last 10 years of my career and this is happening.' I suppose I was worried about the effect it was having, not just that they were dragged in, but also the effect on my mental health and what that does to your children.

Another source of stress can be referred to as existential issues. These issues often include concerns about job security, income stability, and financial sustainability in an industry undergoing significant transformation and facing economic pressures (Carson, 2019). The freelance nature of investigative journalism exacerbates these concerns as journalists navigate the precariousness of freelance contracts, irregular income streams, and the absence of financial and psychological support (Žuffová and Carlini, 2021).

This was evident in both samples, with references not only to the difficulties experienced by freelancers, but also to how small media organisations face everyday battles to survive. In the context of abuse and intimidation, the scope of this research was to establish if economic instability impacts journalists' capacity to pursue stories, effectively leading to self-censorship, as explained clearly by many respondents.

The Italian participants, including those currently employed, mentioned the financial insecurity of freelancers as the main barrier to investigative journalism.

> If you think that a local newspaper pays you 4.71 euros per piece to write about mafia-ridden municipalities, and you risk your neck and the house your parents built for you. This is my context. For me, it's serious, and it's even more so because I live in this context. But actually, no one cares. It

doesn't matter to anyone if you don't have money to pay, and if the accusations don't stand.

(Participant 03ITA)

Participants from the UK sample added that small media organisations don't have enough human and financial resources to dedicate to legal issues, with huge constraints on editors who are obliged to work long hours. In addition, having to defend themselves in court could make a difference in the organisation's survival, as explained in the section about the nature of SLAPPs.

Conclusion: Building Resilience in the Face of Legal Intimidation

This chapter has revealed the significant challenges investigative journalists face under the persistent threat of legal intimidation, particularly through the misuse of SLAPPs. These lawsuits are weaponised by powerful entities to stifle public interest reporting, driving journalists toward self-censorship or forcing them to abandon critical stories. The findings demonstrate that a majority of UK journalists have either amended or abandoned stories due to fears of litigation, while in Italy, legal threats arise post-publication, creating different, yet equally challenging, pressures on journalistic practices.

The empirical data from both the UK and Italy highlights the urgent need for stronger legal protections that can shield journalists from litigation being used as a tool of censorship. While progress has been made in regions like the United States, Canada, and Australia through Anti-SLAPP legislation, a broader global consensus is required to ensure journalists everywhere are protected.

The personal toll of these legal threats is clear, with many journalists experiencing anxiety, isolation, and burnout as they face the possibility of legal battles. The interviews conducted during this research revealed the emotional strain of receiving personal legal threats, with journalists often feeling as though their livelihoods, careers, and personal lives were under attack. This highlights the critical need for legal reforms and the creation of support systems within media organisations, including access to mental health resources.

Despite these obstacles, investigative journalists remain committed to their work. Moral courage is a key trait that drives them to continue, as Feinstein (2023) suggests. One journalist explained how this courage can be discovered over time through collaboration and experience:

There were journalists who would come to me from other parts of our media organisation with a story and say, well, I don't have the experience to do this, but can I do it with you, can we do this? Some of those having done that for the first time would then go, 'Oh, I really like the feel of this. The buzz of doing this.' So I think you can discover that moral courage, you probably had it all along. You just didn't know, really.

(Participant 07UK)

However, courage alone is not enough. Journalists must also equip themselves with legal knowledge and resilience to face the unique challenges posed by defamation claims, privacy laws, and GDPR-related lawsuits. Defamation, as noted by Harrison and Hanna (2022), is often a consequence of failing to uphold standards of accuracy and fairness, making due diligence a critical part of the investigative process.

Journalists working internationally face even greater challenges, as defamation laws differ across jurisdictions, and they can be sued in countries other than their own. This adds another layer of complexity, as transnational legal battles involve language barriers and significantly higher legal costs. Therefore, meticulous record-keeping and strategic planning are essential to protecting themselves against these risks.

Beyond legal knowledge, resilience also depends on institutional support. Journalists – especially those working freelance or for smaller outlets – need access to legal advice, liability insurance, and mental health resources to withstand the pressures of legal intimidation. NGOs and press freedom organisations play a crucial role in providing journalists with these protections and ensuring that they are not isolated when facing legal threats.

Moving forward, it is crucial to recognise the resilience and adaptability of investigative journalists, whose dedication to uncovering hidden truths is vital for democratic accountability. Despite the increasing threats of legal intimidation, their work serves as a testament to their commitment to holding power to account (Ettema and Glasser, 1998).

CLASSROOM EXERCISE

Scenario

You are an investigative journalist for a small regional news outlet. After months of research, you have gathered strong evidence of corruption involving a local government official and a developer. Just before publishing your story, you receive a legal letter from the official's lawyers threatening defamation action if you proceed. Your editor is worried about the risks, given your outlet's limited resources.

Question

How would you respond to this legal threat? Would you proceed with the story, revise it, or drop it altogether? Consider the ethical and practical challenges, and think about the potential impact of your decision on press freedom.

References

Borg-Barthet, J. and Farrington, F. (2023) 'Open SLAPP Cases in 2022 and 2023'. European Parliament. Available at: https://www.europarl.europa.eu/RegData/etudes/STUD/2023/756468/IPOL_STU(2023)756468_EN.pdf.

Borg-Barthet, J., Lobina, B. and Zabrocka, M. (2021) 'The Use of SLAPPs to Silence Journalists, NGOs and Civil Society'. European Parliament. Available at: https://www.europarl.europa.eu/RegData/etudes/STUD/2021/694782/IPOL_STU(2021)694782_EN.pdf.

Buchanan, M. and Keats, P. (2011) 'Coping with traumatic stress in journalism: A critical ethnographic study', *International Journal of Psychology*, 46(2), pp. 127–135. Available at: https://doi.org/10.1080/00207594.2010.532799.

Carson, A. (2019) *Investigative journalism, democracy and the digital age*. Routledge: New York.

Carson, A. and Farhall, K. (2018) 'Understanding collaborative investigative journalism in a "Post-truth" age', *Journalism Studies*, 19(13), pp. 1899–1911. Available at: https://doi.org/10.1080/1461670x.2018.1494515.

CASE Coalition (2023) 'Governments' agreed stance on EU anti-SLAPP directive – a disappointing failure to support the adoption of robust safeguards for public watchdogs – CASE', 12 June. Available at: https://www.the-case.eu/latest/governments-agreed-stance-on-eu-anti-slapp-directive-a-disappointing-failure-to-support-the-adoption-of-robust-safeguards-for-public-watchdogs/

Coughtrie, S. (2020) *Unsafe for Scrutiny: How the misuse of the UK's financial and legal systems to facilitate corruption undermines the freedom and safety of investigative journalists around the world*. Available at: https://fpc.org.uk/publications/unsafe-for-scrutiny-12-2020-publication/

Coughtrie, S. (2022) '"London Calling": The issue of legal intimidation and SLAPPs against media emanating from the United Kingdom'. Available at: https://fpc.org.uk/publications/london-calling-the-issue-of-legal-intimidation-and-slapps-against-media-emanating-from-the-united-kingdom/

Coughtrie, S. and Ogier, P. (2020) *Unsafe for Scrutiny: Examining the pressures faced by journalists uncovering financial crime and corruption around the world*. Available at: https://fpc.org.uk/publications/unsafe-for-scrutiny/

Dawson, J. (2024) *SLAPPs: Strategic litigation against public participation*. 9962. House of Commons. Available at: https://researchbriefings.files.parliament.uk/documents/CBP-9962/CBP-9962.pdf.

Ettema, J.S. and Glasser, T.L. (1998) *Custodians of conscience: Investigative journalism and public virtue*. New York: Columbia University Press.

Feinstein, A. (2023) *Moral courage: 19 profiles of investigative journalists*. G Editions LLC.

Feinstein, A., Osmann, J. and Patel, V. (2018) 'Symptoms of PTSD in frontline journalists: A retrospective examination of 18 years of war and conflict', *The Canadian Journal of Psychiatry*, 63(9), pp. 629–635. Available at: https://doi.org/10.1177/0706743718777396.

Foreign Affairs Committee (2023) 'Oral evidence: Use of Strategic Lawsuits Against Public Participation'. Available at: https://committees.parliament.uk/oralevidence/9907/pdf/.

Gerli, M. *et al.* (2018) 'Constraints and limitations of investigative journalism in Hungary, Italy, Latvia and Romania':, *European Journal of Communication*, 33(1), pp. 22–36. Available at: https://doi.org/10.1177/0267323117750672.

Hallin, D.C. and Mancini, P. (2000) *Comparing media systems: Three models of media and politics*. Cambridge; New York: Cambridge University Press.

Hanitzsch, T. *et al.* (eds) (2019) *Worlds of journalism: Journalistic cultures around the globe*. Columbia University Press.

Hanna, M. (2024) 'SLAPPs: What are they? And how should defamation law be re-formed to address them?', *Journal of Media Law*, 16(1), pp. 118–145. Available at: https://doi.org/10.1080/17577632.2024.2345982.

Harrison, S. and Hanna, M. (2022) *McNae's essential law for journalists*. 26th edn. New York: OUP Oxford.

Kerševan, T. and Poler, M. (2023) 'Silencing journalists in matters of public inter-est: Journalists and editors assessments of the impact of SLAPPs on journalism', *Journalism*, 25(12), pp. 2485–2503 Available at: https://doi.org/10.1177/14648849231210695.

Konow-Lund, M. (2019) 'Negotiating roles and routines in collaborative investigative journalism', *Media and Communication*, 7(4), pp. 103–111. Available at: https://doi.org/10.17645/mac.v7i4.2401.

Ogle, G. (2010) 'Anti-SLAPP law reform in Australia', *Review of European Community & International Environmental Law*, 19(1), pp. 35–44. Available at: https://doi.org/10.1111/j.1467-9388.2010.00662.x.

Papadopoulou, L. and Maniou, T.A. (2024) *"SLAPPed" and censored? Legal threats and challenges to press freedom and investigative reporting*. Available at: https://journals.sagepub.com/doi/abs/10.1177/14648849241242181

Porlezza, C. and Splendore, S. (2019) 'From open journalism to closed data: Data journalism in Italy', *Digital Journalism*, 7(9), pp. 1230–1252. Available at: https://doi.org/10.1080/21670811.2019.1657778.

Posetti *et al.* (2021) *The Chilling: global trends in online violence against women jour-nalists; research discussion paper – UNESCO Digital Library*. Available at: https://unesdoc.unesco.org/ark:/48223/pf0000377223.

Price, J. (2017) 'Can the ferret be a watchdog?', *Digital Journalism*, 5(10), pp. 1336–1350. Available at: https://doi.org/10.1080/21670811.2017.1288582.

Pyevich, C.M., Newman, E. and Daleiden, E. (2003) 'The relationship among cogni-tive schemas, job-related traumatic exposure, and posttraumatic stress disorder in journalists', *Journal of Traumatic Stress*, 16(4), pp. 325–328. Available at: https://doi.org/10.1023/A:1024405716529.

Reese, S.D. and Shoemaker, P.J. (2016) 'A media sociology for the networked pub-lic sphere: The hierarchy of influences model', *Mass Communication and Society*, 19(4), pp. 389–410. Available at: https://doi.org/10.1080/15205436.2016.1174268.

Saunders, B., Kitzinger, J. and Kitzinger, C. (2015) 'Anonymising interview data: Challenges and compromise in practice', *Qualitative Research*, 15(5), pp. 616–632. Available at: https://doi.org/10.1177/1468794114550439.

Shapiro, P. (2010) 'SLAPPs: Intent or content? Anti-SLAPP legislation goes in-ternational', *Review of European Community and International Environmental Law*, 19(1), pp. 14–27. Available at: https://doi.org/10.1111/j.1467-9388.2010.00661.x.

Shoemaker, P.J. and Reese, S.D. (1996) *Mediating the message: Theories of influences on mass media content*. 2nd edn. White Plains, NY: Longman.

Šimunjak, M. (2023) *Managing emotions in journalism: A guide to enhancing resil-ience*. Palgrave Macmillan.

SRA (2022) *Strategic Lawsuits against Public Participation (SLAPPs) – Warning no-tice*. Available at: https://www.sra.org.uk/solicitors/guidance/slapps-warning-notice/

Toscano, J. (2021) 'SLAPPS across America', *Touro Law Review*, 37, p. 1703. Available at: https://heinonline.org/HOL/LandingPage?handle=hein.journals/touro37&div=59&id=&page=https://heinonline.org/HOL/Page?handle=hein.journals/touro37&id=1727&div=&collection=

Turvill, W. (2015) 'Ian Hislop declined to sign pro-BBC "luvvies" letter' because he would have looked an "overpaid wanker"', *Press Gazette*, 18 September. Available at:

https://pressgazette.co.uk/publishers/magazines/ian-hislop-declined-sign-pro-bbc-luvvies-letter-because-he-would-have-looked-overaid-wanker/

Young, H. (2022) 'Canadian anti-SLAPP laws in action', *Canadian Bar Review*, 100, p. 186. Available at: https://heinonline.org/HOL/LandingPage?handle=hein.journals/canbarev100&div=11&id=&page=

Žuffová, M. and Carlini, R. (2021) 'Safety of journalists in Europe: Threats and best practices to tackle them', *Social Science Research Network*. [Preprint]. Available at: https://doi.org/10.2139/ssrn.3829514.

6

HOW DID JOURNALISM PROFESSIONS AND THE PUBLIC RESPOND TO CHALLENGES IN INVESTIGATIVE JOURNALISM?

Introducing Nonprofit Newsrooms

Michelle Park[1]

Journalism has undergone severe challenges, particularly since the beginning of the 21st century. Over the last two decades, it has been well-documented how the working environment for journalists in implementing in-depth investigative journalism at a significant number of mainstream media worldwide has deteriorated (Freedman, 2019; Shin, 2016). Pressures from external political and economic forces are identified as critical aspects of the working condition (Benson and Powers, 2011; Cagé, 2016; Freedman, 2019; McQueen, 2008; Starkman, 2014). The political pressures and economic instability faced by mainstream newsrooms caused a decrease in diversifying perspectives, threatening pluralism in liberal democratic societies. In response to this, where a large portion of legacy media struggle to play a role as the Fourth Estate of their societies, a new form of a nonprofit media organisation for investigative journalism has sharply emerged, with an aim of holding power accountable for making healthy democratic societies (Roseman, McLellan and Holcomb, 2021). This chapter aims to contribute to an under-researched nonprofit journalism area by examining and interpreting the phenomenon from a case study of two nonprofit investigative journalism organisations in South Korea and the United Kingdom.

Nonprofit Investigative Journalism Organisations

A nonprofit investigative journalism organisation is a philanthropically funded newsroom (foundations and/or individual donations), and, in many cases, with the aim of publishing in-depth investigative news in the public interest. Some newsrooms subsidise their funding through advertising revenues or events, but they can be considered nonprofits in journalism if they do not

DOI: 10.4324/9781003478157-10

seek profit (Shaver, 2010). Although nonprofits have been sharply emerging since 2008 (Roseman, McLellan and Holcomb, 2021), there is a long history of nonprofit investigative journalism organisations, especially in the United States. Prominent examples are the *Center for Investigative Reporting*, established in 1977, and the *Center for Public Integrity*, established in 1989, which are considered pioneers in the nonprofit news sector (Konieczna, 2018). These pioneers are viewed as expanding an opportunity to use the internet for journalism, facing crises in the digital era (Walton, 2010).

With the early start of the nonprofit sector, American journalism experienced rapid growth in nonprofit newsrooms. For instance, the Institute for Nonprofit News (INN) has been tracking the development of an American network for nonprofit news organisations. Initially launched as the Investigative News Network in 2009, the INN observed growth in the number of members from 27 to roughly 450 as of September 2024 (INN, 2024). Since the INN includes all types of nonprofit media organisations, the number might not be equal to investigative journalism organisations. However, it shows the sharp growth of the nonprofit news sector, expanding its role in the wider media ecosystem.

The number of nonprofit investigative journalism newsrooms has increased across the globe despite the unfavourable media environment for investigative journalism. According to scholars, the increased need for in-depth news from the journalism practitioners and members of the public, in tandem with the affordances of advanced new technologies, has contributed to the rapid growth of nonprofit newsrooms (Birnbauer, 2019; Colbran, 2022; Konieczna, 2018; Tofel, 2013). Colbran (2022, p. 115) identified that journalism practitioners "seemed disillusioned with mainstream media and talked about how newsrooms no longer had the time or the money to fund investigative journalism and how, instead, editors were focused on how many 'hits' a story received online". Some journalists headed to the nonprofit sector, where newsroom independence allows newsworkers to report issues based on journalistic values (Colbran, 2022, p. 115). Moreover, Carson (2020, p. 89) argues that "Sales of quality newspapers and donations to investigative outlets in the United States hit new highs after the 2016 presidential election", with an example of the surge in support for *ProPublica,* a nonprofit investigative journalism organisation in the United States. Carson (2020, p. 89) also reveals that challenges in mainstream media, to some extent, helped to boost support for in-depth quality news from members of the public in the United States.

Nonprofit newsrooms are increasingly playing a role in promoting in-depth investigations within their respective societies (Konieczna, 2018; Tofel, 2013; Townend, 2016). In the United States, it is also noted that American nonprofit organisations are purposed to "improve on journalism *from within,*[2] by producing quality content to be disseminated by existing news organizations as well as collaborating with and training other reporters" (Konieczna, 2018, p. 63). This scholar aptly terms their approach as "field repair" (Konieczna, 2018, p. 63); a collaborative effort that aims to enhance the journalism sector. Research about the history and origin of nonprofit news in the United States has been well-conducted, while far less attention has been paid to nonprofit organisations outside the United States, which are also proliferating.

For instance, my case studies, the *Korea Center for Investigative Journalism* in South Korea, and the *Bureau of Investigative Journalism* in the United Kingdom were established in the early 2010s. Price (2017) also highlights news start-ups with sustainable financial models for journalism in the United Kingdom, such as Ferret, and beyond. Hence, this chapter focuses on the birth of nonprofit investigative journalism organisations beyond the United States for broadening the geographical scope of what we know about this type of newsroom.

Methodology

This chapter draws on my PhD research, encompassing ethnographic methodology conducted at two case study newsrooms in South Korea and the United Kingdom during Spring–Summer 2018. Ethnographic approaches in journalism studies have significantly contributed to advancing our knowledge owing to their unique approach to proximity to informants (see Anderson, 2013; Tuchman, 1978; Usher, 2014). Nevertheless, ethnography in newsrooms has rarely been used due to the practical challenges researchers face, particularly regarding access. Ethnography in investigative journalism is even more scarce due to the high level of confidentiality of the work. I persevered in my attempts to obtain the opportunity for ethnographic methodology for many years and ultimately was given access to these two nonprofit investigative journalism organisations.

I engaged journalists and editors in multiple phases, combining about 330 hours of participant observation and 47 semi-structured in-depth interviews lasting from 60 to 120 minutes. My observation helped me to customise interview questions for individual journalists and editors and to verify what they said they did in the interviews. The data from both participant observation and in-depth interviews was used to verify each result, thereby enhancing the reliability and validity of the research.

This chapter mainly inquires (1) how the newsrooms were established and funded, and (2) what the working conditions for investigative journalism were when the nonprofit was initiated. Both South Korean and British newsrooms have developed their funding models to shape what they are now since their foundation in the early 2010s. Because the media environment in which the news industry posits is different in South Korea and the United Kingdom, the analysis from each newsroom will be presented separately.

The Korea Center for Investigative Journalism in South Korea

The *Korea Center for Investigative Journalism* (KCIJ, https://www.newstapa.org/) in Seoul, South Korea, was founded in 2013 and is funded by individual citizen donations. The KCIJ has evolved from a "*Newstapa*" investigative newsroom project in 2012. The newsroom covers local, national, and international news, the most prominent of which is its collaboration with the *International Consortium of Investigative Journalists* as the only South Korean partner.

Need for an Independent Newsroom

Through my newsroom ethnography, it became clear that the foundation of the Newstapa project was the response of certain journalists and editors to the perceived decline in investigative reporting in the South Korean journalism sector. Their passionate eagerness to be independent of external political and commercial power motivated them to initiate the project.

One journalist, who had extensive experience at one of the publicly funded media organisations in South Korea, had to make a decision to leave the organisation due to its relationship with the government (personal communication, 22 March 2018). The system for appointing Director Generals of publicly funded media, for instance, has faced severe criticism for its government association, a concern shared across many countries (Benson and Powers, 2011; Freedman, 2019). The informant described the continually challenging situation of their organisation at that time:

> In my mind, it was the last hope for the organisation to be normalised. We thought we should establish a sturdy system preventing it from being swayed by any governmental and political changes because severe organisational changes were usually triggered by political decisions.
> *(Personal communication, 22 March 2018)*

The journalist above presents how the staff struggled to establish a better-governing system and to take the newsroom's independence back from the undue political considerations of those in senior positions within the organisation. However, the interviewee adds that none of the improved systems and policies they asked for was achieved, so the informant left the organisation.

Another journalist illustrates the media environment around the initiative of the Newstapa project:

> The political situation significantly affected the media industry. The media environment was closely interrelated with the politics. As mainstream newsrooms were unable to inform the public, there arose a need for an

independent news media outlet to provide information which the public had to know concerning how the government and society operate.

(Personal communication, 08 March 2018)

The journalist, who has experienced the challenging time of important news being under-reported at mainstream media organisations due to political influence, emphasises the need for more independent newsrooms. This struggle underscores the importance of editorial autonomy for journalists' freedom to report the informant notes. As inferred from both interview quotes above, practitioners of the time observed that such editorial decisions were swayed by political influence. They became more eager for a secure place for independent news, which led them to join the KCIJ.

The difficulties journalists face in being independent of external forces are not limited to political aspects but are related to commercial aspects. One journalist argues, "The company [a previous workplace] was obsessed with advertising" (personal communication, 19 March 2018). The journalist, whose previous company was operated by an advertising-based funding model, continues:

The newspaper company asked staff to find any critical news, an exposé, in order to pressure advertisers so they cannot help placing advertisements in the newspaper [...] The financial incentives for journalists were granted not based on the quality of journalism a journalist had produced but based on the number of advertisements a journalist had obtained.

(Personal communication, 19 March 2018)

The interview mentions that the purpose of an exposé was not driven by social justice or public interest but rather by the desire to use the story as a bargaining chip for advertising from the targeted company. The journalist also highlights a concerning imbalance in the appraisal of the journalist's performance at the informant's previous workplace, where advertising sales achievements were given more weight than journalistic outcomes. It can be inferred that journalists at some of the commercial companies continually deal with such challenging working conditions where journalistic norms and values are undermined.

Several informants above emphasise a lack of journalistic autonomy arising from undue political and economic considerations and influence on editorial decision-making. People left their workplaces for several reasons, such as being fired after protests in the workplace, disciplinary action, or voluntarily quitting their jobs (Shin, 2015). A collective spirit arising from individual needs for an independent newsroom led to the start of a journalism project, "Newstapa", in 2012. This was the journalism profession's response to overcoming the challenges in investigative journalism. Approximately eight people, a combination of professionals who used to work for South Korean legacy media outlets and volunteering university students, launched the project with some financial support from the National Union of Media Workers, according to interviews. As of Summer 2024, the KCIJ has approximately 65 staff of investigative reporters, data journalists, editors, and management officers (KCIJ, 2024a).

Responses from Members of the Public to Challenges in the News Industry

From its launch, Newstapa's investigative news reporting was broadcast through YouTube with free access, some of which became popular and hit one million views (personal communication, 09 March 2018). Members of the public responded to their efforts in producing investigative journalism. Many citizens, satisfied with the news, expressed interest in contributing to the project, reaching out to the Newstapa team to enquire about donations, according to many interviews at the KCIJ. Thanks to citizen support, in Summer 2012, the team opened an official bank account to receive donations from the public (personal communication, 09 March 2018). The Newstapa team continued to receive praise from the public. The total number of members had increased from roughly 8,000 to approximately 27,000[3] by the end of 2012, which motivated the official establishment of the KCIJ, according to several interviews. The KCIJ was established in February 2013[4] with more investigative journalists, including data journalists. According to one informant (personal communication, 29 March 2018), as of my field research in 2018, the average donation was $10 per member a month, making it $4.5 million a year.[5]

Nonprofit organisations have been burgeoning worldwide since 2008, but it is still rare that the membership funding model is a main funding stream (Price, 2017). It is more likely to be used as a part of diverse funding streams (Roseman, McLellan and Holcomb, 2021). Hence, it is also useful to examine the citizens who donate to the KCIJ in advancing our knowledge of the membership funding model (see Price, 2017). It is evident that the public increasingly supports the KCIJ in that the KCIJ has expanded its staff number since 2012, which proves its long-term success. It seems that the KCIJ's different and rare approach to funding has been favourably accepted by civil society.

This chapter also attempts to address the perspectives of donors through analysing reasons for donation. Donors can write reasons for their support for the KCIJ when they donate. I obtained an extensive list of the reasons from August 2017 to March 2018 from the newsroom.

Motivations mentioned by many donors indicate their desire to see investigative news reporting on the truth. Public members are eager to see investigative journalism that can inform citizens, shed light on hidden truths and report vital issues that other organisations cannot (or do not) publish. For instance:

- The KCIJ is the only media organisation that can report the truth.
- I wish you would be a force to shed light on the truth.

- I want to support because you do fact-checks and in-depth reporting on issues that other newsrooms don't deal with.
- Because the KCIJ informs citizens by exposing the dark side of our society.

Moreover, citizen donors want to see an independent newsroom that can be free of undue external influences such as commercial funders:

- Freedom of the press liberates all our liberty.
- I want to see journalism that is independent of the advertisers' influence.

It is also identified that the donors' link supporting investigative journalism in creating a better society:

- For a better society.
- I wish my children can live in a better society.
- For justice in the society.

Overall, the reasons listed represent how the public acts in response to the perceived decline in independent news that can provide thoroughly researched reporting to expose hidden truths. Similar to the desire of journalists who established and joined the KCIJ for an independent newsroom, the citizens' wish to see independent news and to bring about a better society through the KCIJ seems to be the key motivation to join the membership.

Mission

The KCIJ expresses their organisational mission on their website. It works for the public interest and wants to be a non-partisan and non-commercial newsroom:

> The Korea Center for Investigative Journalism (KCIJ) is the first nonprofit investigative reporting organization in the Republic of Korea. We reveal wrongdoing of power and bring about changes in laws or policies for public interest. Our journalistic work is published on Newstapa, an online news outlet.
>
> 'Newstapa' is a combination of 'news' and 'tapa (타파, 打破),' which means 'abolition' in Korean. As the name implies, KCIJ-Newstapa strives against partisanship and commercialism in journalism.
>
> *(KCIJ, 2024b)*

One informant encapsulates the objective of their initiative to be a nonprofit:

Nonprofit journalism means we won't earn money from journalism. In South Korea, advertising revenues or sponsorship could be the main funding streams, but if you rely on these, news media cannot help publishing news stories that are palatable to the advertisers or sponsors. [...] Therefore, we need an independent newsroom that is free from such organisational structure, and we pioneered to do so.

(Personal communication, 08 March 2018)

The informant highlights how the KCIJ differentiates itself from other media organisations that are operated by advertising revenues, sponsorship, or ownership by shareholders or a particular family. According to the interview, the KCIJ opens a new and alternative pathway for funding to be independent.

A majority of the KCIJ staff emphasise that the KCIJ aims to be an independent newsroom. One informant says: "Being free from capital and authority. The aim is absolutely clear" (personal communication, 21 March 2018). It is vital for the KCIJ to be nonprofit so that the newsroom does not have to seek to generate profits. Instead, the newsroom could be independent of such external non-editorial pressures.

Investigations

The KCIJ has consistently produced in-depth investigative journalism, some of which has received prestigious journalism awards (KCIJ, 2024c). It has also participated in cross-border collaborations with international organisations, notably serving as South Korea's only partner of the International Consortium of Investigative Journalists (see Park and Konow-Lund, 2024a).

Under the category titled "Change" on its website, the KCIJ documents the impact of its investigations. Since its establishment in 2013, the KCIJ has instigated a large number of political, economic, and societal changes. For instance, the National Assembly issued a new report recommending improvements to regulating politicians' budget spending for legislative and policy development within a month of KCIJ's investigation (Park, 2018). In response to a series of KCIJ investigations about document fabrication by academic associations, universities imposed disciplinary measures on the implicated academics (Hong, 2023).

The Bureau of Investigative Journalism in the United Kingdom

The Bureau of Investigative Journalism (BIJ, https://www.thebureauinvestigates. com/) in London, the United Kingdom, was established in 2010 and is philanthropically funded. It reports a wide range of political, economic, and social issues on a local, national, and global level. One of the most prominent projects is "intra-national local collaboration" (Park, 2022) with local media organisations led by the Bureau Local, a local unit of the BIJ.

Boosting Investigative Journalism in the British Journalism Sector

The BIJ was prompted by the perceived worrisome crisis in investigative journalism, a vital pillar of supporting democracy, and the subsequent damage to democracy in the United Kingdom, according to my observation at the BIJ.

One interview with a veteran journalist with a wealth of experience spanning several decades expresses the concern about the challenges:

> I mean I think it is definitely true that over the last 10 years, we saw the collapse of investigative journalism in the UK because of funding. […] So, the Bureau is definitely there to plug the gap in investigative journalism and is part of the change we want to see happening in journalism in the UK.
>
> *(Personal communication, 25 July 2018)*

According to the interview, the decline in investigative journalism was perceived among practitioners to be particularly caused by precarious business models of many media outlets. The journalist also argues that the BIJ becomes one of the possible opportunities for professional reporters to be independent in conducting investigative journalism and fills the void left by the scarcity of the type of news.

Another journalist, who used to work for a commercial media organisation, explains the differences between what they had done at the previous workplace and what they do at the BIJ now:

> So, in Company A,[6] you didn't spend lots of time finding stories as such. We didn't. Stories kind of came to us and we publish them whereas, here, you find all your stories they have to be kind of a new piece of information. […] bringing new information to the public.
>
> *(Personal communication, 27 July 2018)*

The interviewee's observation brings to light the contrasting priorities of different media organisations. It is widely acknowledged that many bodies, such as PR professions, provide newsrooms with news sources (Moloney and McGrath, 2020). In contrast, the journalist above also highlights the BIJ as a beacon of hope where journalists can enjoy a conducive working environment that encourages them to actively generate new information for the public.

One informant states a story of a commercially funded media organisation:

> At one newspaper, there was a big exposé of [Company B].[7] And then [Company B] pulled quite a lot of advertising with the paper. But it came back eventually.
>
> *(Personal communication, 27 July 2018)*

The interview underscores a well-known scenario in the news industry, where advertisers sometimes try to influence newsroom independence by withdrawing their advertising. Although the informant notes that the company advertised with the newspaper again, the story of news reporting that could potentially displease advertisers could raise a crucial question here. In a situation like this, where financial damage is a direct consequence, can a journalist maintain complete autonomy in reporting what they believe matters to society? (see Oborne, 2015). Through my ethnography research, it became apparent that there was a need among journalism professions for increasing the volume and quality of investigative journalism in the British journalism sector.

Need for a Watchdog of the British Society

The David and Elaine Potter Foundation acknowledged the significance of investigative journalism and founded the BIJ in 2010. Its mission on the website is as below:

> We provide grants that contribute to economic development and well-being in a plural, rational and tolerant society. Our purpose is to support projects promoting reason, accountability and education that will improve understanding, human rights, good governance and a stronger civil society.
> *(David and Elaine Potter Foundation, 2024)*

According to the statement, the Foundation supports Britain and other societies worldwide and highlights its aims to make society better.

Understanding the backgrounds of the founders can shed light on their support of investigative journalism. Elaine Potter was a former investigative journalist at the Insight Team, the legendary investigative journalism unit at *The Sunday Times*, a British broadsheet. She participated in many hard-hitting, high-profile investigations, and David Potter was from the IT industry. De Burgh (2008, p. 215) argues that "The 1970s are widely regarded as the great days of UK investigative journalism, and where this is so it is because of Insight". Elaine Potter is a co-author of several books from *The Sunday Times* projects, including *Suffer the Children: The Story of Thalidomide*, which is a decade-long investigation by the Insight Team on how victims of thalidomide in the United Kingdom were treated by the government and the drug company.

A driving force behind the establishment of the BIJ can be seen clearly from the message from Elaine Potter, who wrote a statement on the BIJ website:

> When we launched the Bureau, I wrote: "Democracy itself is imperilled in the absence of honest information and a robust watchdog to hold government and the powerful to account. Without that we all become susceptible to the

manipulation and deceptions orchestrated by governments, industry or even the media". In the eight years since then, things have got much worse.

(Potter n.d.)

Elaine's note, written eight years after the establishment, emphasises the pivotal role of the BIJ as a watchdog of society. She points out that democracy could be endangered without such a societal guardian. Her message serves as a reminder of the ongoing need for the BIJ to continue its vital work in investigative journalism.

The BIJ, initially launched with the David and Elaine Potter Foundation, has diversified its funders. It has secured core funding for the entire newsroom and project-based funding for individual investigations. Notably, the BIJ's revenue "rose from £490,000 in 2014 to over £1 million in 2017" (Leigh, 2019, p. 200). The number of funders is around 30 as of September 2024 (BIJ, 2024a).

The Trust for the BIJ gained charity status during my fieldwork in 2018. It was meaningful to observe that the BIJ staff were so happy about their achievement. I asked the reason behind this excitement. One informant noted, "it's much easier to persuade someone to give you money or encourage them to give you money if you've got charitable status" (personal communication, 23 August 2018).

Although such foundation funding has been supporting nonprofit newsrooms across the world, some scholars raise a concern about foundation funders' influence on news content (Birnbauer, 2019; Townend, 2016). One of the ways the BIJ insulates newsroom independence is by excluding any third party, including funders, from designing their investigative journalism projects. One journalist describes how a project-based funding application process works:

> We outline what the project would look like; who would work on it; what the wages would be; and the outputs. And not in terms of what we will write as such, but what areas we will cover as part of the project and how many stories we will produce. For example, in the proposal to the donor, you have normally committed to publishing a certain number of articles, and you should meet that goal. We have to write the donor some kind of closing report at the end of the project, alongside occasional reports on the project's progress.
>
> *(Personal communication, 23 July 2018)*

According to the interview above, any external influence is prohibited from engaging in the process of developing a project. Only journalists who are involved in the project can decide details in investigations, which serves to protect the newsroom's editorial autonomy.

When I first started researching the BIJ in 2014, there were about 8 staff members, but it has grown over time from 19 at the time of my field research in 2018 to more than 30 in 2024, including reporters, editors, producers, and admin officers. Investigative stories from the BIJ are available online free of charge on its website and co-publishing partners' platforms.

Mission

The BIJ's mission statement highlights its dedication to investigative journalism and its impact on society:

Our Mission: Journalism Driving Change

We believe investigative journalism plays a key role in keeping democracy strong, power accountable and societies more just. That is why we focus on in-depth, rigorous investigations that can make a real difference at a global, national or local level.

We look beyond the short term news agenda, and the need to generate clicks. Instead we take time to dig deep, led by the facts not by political or corporate agendas. We do not cower from difficult stories and we seek to listen to voices that are often overlooked.

(BIJ, 2024b)

The mission illustrates that the BIJ aims not to be beholden to any political or commercial factors. It also aims to contribute to democracy by investigating under-reported issues and allowing marginalised voices to be heard. Its mission can be observed through interviews as well. When asked about their aim, a journalist answers:

To produce public interest investigations. So, news is to hold power to account and highlights certain areas and have some kind of impact and lead to change whether that is raising awareness or more concrete changes.
(Personal communication, 27 July 2018)

Similar to the journalist above, a majority of the BIJ staff highlighted their mission of publishing investigative journalism in the public interest, illustrating the shared organisational mission among the staff.

Investigations

The BIJ has been publishing in-depth investigations, some of which won journalism awards (BIJ, 2024c), including an investigation titled "The drug was meant to save children's lives. Instead, they're dying" (Furneaux and Margottini, 2023). The Bureau Local, a new initiative of the BIJ, plays a crucial role in orchestrating journalistic collaborations between local newsrooms, one of which led to about 40 investigative stories (see Park and Konow-Lund, 2024b).

The BIJ publishes the impact of their investigations on their websites. Their investigations have sparked changes in public regulation and private companies' policy within and beyond the British society (Davies and Stockton, 2018; Murray, 2024; Nash, 2023) and have been used in court cases (McIntyre, 2023). For instance, their investigation into the use of antibiotics in India ultimately led to the regulatory changes in the country (Davies and Stockton, 2018). Similarly, the UK's House of Lords published a report on seasonal workers, following the Bureau's investigation into the welfare issues affecting migrant workers (Nash, 2023). Changes have also been observed within the private sector. It is demonstrated by the British supermarket chains dropping their supplier of pineapple products after the revelation brought to light by the BIJ (Murray, 2024).

Conclusion

This chapter has explored how journalism professions and the public have responded to political and economic challenges in investigative journalism through a case study on two nonprofit investigative journalism organisations in South Korea and the United Kingdom. In the cases of the KCIJ and BIJ, it is clear that journalists were eager to act against the perceived decline in investigative journalism in their respective countries. Also, it was the public, as individual citizens or foundations, playing a crucial and indispensable role in establishing these nonprofits as philanthropic funders.

Important to note is that more and more organisations pay attention to nonprofit models for journalism. The Charitable Journalism Project (CJP) is another crucial body that studies the nonprofit sector to support journalism. They aim to "research, analyse, and advance public understanding of public benefit journalism" (CJP, 2024).

In all, the KCIJ and BIJ broke through a pathway towards innovative nonprofit funding models for investigative journalism. With the citizens' help, they offer significant insights to the rest of the journalism sector in reconceptualising the traditional concept of "funders" for media organisations in the digital era.

CLASSROOM EXERCISE

1 Find out if any nonprofit investigative organisations in your area contribute to your society by publishing in-depth news in the public interest.
2 Examine if any of these newsrooms are looking for help. For example, the Bureau Local runs a network to facilitate collaboration among volunteers such as local journalists, students, bloggers, and so on. You can sign up for the Bureau Local Project here – https://www.thebureauinvestigates.com/local/.

Notes

1 This chapter is from my Ph.D. thesis (Park 2022), which was self-funded without any external funding.
2 Emphasis in the original text.
3 This data is based on rough numbers given by the interviewees in the verbal interviews, rather than written statistical data. Therefore, differences might exist between the actual numbers and the approximately given numbers.
4 https://kcij.org/history
5 This data is based on rough numbers given by the interviewees in the verbal interviews, rather than written statistical data. Therefore, differences might exist between the actual numbers and the approximately given numbers.
6 The interviewee's previous workplace is anonymised for the confidentiality of identity of interviewee.
7 This company is anonymised for the confidentiality of identity of interviewee.

References

Anderson, C. (2013) *Rebuilding the news: Metropolitan journalism in the digital age.* Philadelphia: Temple University Press.
Benson, R. and Powers, M. (2011) Public media and political independence: Lessons for the future of journalism from around the world. *Free Press*, pp. 1–88. Available at: http://rodneybenson.org/wp-content/uploads/Benson-Powers-2011-public-media-and-political-independence-1-1.pdf [Accessed: 27 May 2024].
BIJ. (2024a) *Our Funding.* Available at: https://www.thebureauinvestigates.com/about-us/our-funding/ [Accessed: 1 September 2024].
BIJ. (2024b) *About Us.* Available at: https://www.thebureauinvestigates.com/about-us/ [Accessed: 1 September 2024].
BIJ. (2024c) *Awards.* Available at: https://www.thebureauinvestigates.com/about-us/our-news/ [Accessed: 1 September 2024].
Birnbauer, B. (2019) *The rise of nonprofit investigative journalism in the United States.* New York: Routledge.
Cagé, J. (2016) *Saving the media: Capitalism, crowdfunding, and democracy.* Cambridge: Harvard University Press.
Carson, A. (2020) *Investigative journalism, democracy and the digital age, investigative journalism, democracy and the digital age.* New York: Routledge.
CJP. (2024) Who we are. *Charitable Journalism Project.* Available at: https://cjproject.org/about/who-we-are/ [Accessed: 27 May 2024].
Colbran, M. (2022) *Crime and investigative reporting in the UK.* Bristol: Policy Press.
Davies, M. and Stockton, B. (2018) India Set to ban use of "last hope" antibiotics to fatten livestock after bureau story. *BIJ*, 5. December 2018. Available at: https://www.thebureauinvestigates.com/stories/2018-12-05/indian-government-colistin-ban-bureau-story/ [Accessed: 3 December 2024].
David and Elaine Potter Foundation. (2024) *About the Foundation.* Available at: https://potterfoundation.com/about_the_foundation.html [Accessed: 27 May 2024].
De Burgh, H. (2008) *Investigative journalism.* 2nd edn. Oxon and New York: Routledge.
Freedman, D. (2019) "Public service" and the journalism crisis: Is the BBC the answer?, *Television & New Media*, 23(3), pp. 203–218.
Furneaux, R. and Margottini, L. (2023) The drug was meant to save children's lives. Instead, they're dying. *The BIJ* 25 January. Available at: https://www.thebureauinvestigates.com/stories/2023-01-25/the-drug-was-meant-to-save-childrens-lives-instead-theyre-dying/ [Accessed: 2 August 2024].

Hong, Y. (2023) [Byonwha] Gwangwang hakheo 'nonmun jojak' gyosudeal, 'imyong chuiso', 'jungjik' deang mudeogi jungjinggye [변화] 관광학회 '논문 조작' 교수들, '임용 취소', '정직' 등 무더기 중징계]. *The KCIJ* 22 December. Available at: https://www.newstapa.org/article/c-NiQ [Accessed: 2 August 2024].

INN. (2024) INN Mission & History. *Institute for Nonprofit Network*. Available at: https://inn.org/about/ [Accessed: 2 September 2024].

KCIJ. (2024a) *Jejakjin*. Available at: https://kcij.org/crew [Accessed: 1 September 2024].

KCIJ. (2024b) *About us*. Available at: https://newstapa.org/eng_about [Accessed: 1 September 2024].

KCIJ. (2024c) *Susang Naeyeok*. Available at: https://kcij.org/awards [Accessed: 1 September 2024].

Konieczna, M. (2018) *Journalism without profit*. New York: Oxford University Press.

Leigh, D. (2019) *Investigative journalism: A survival guide*. Cham: Palgrave Macmillan.

McIntyre, N. (2023) 'Class action suit launched over teleperformance working conditions', *BIJ*. Available at: https://www.thebureauinvestigates.com/stories/2023-06-28/class-action-suit-launched-over-teleperformance-working-conditions/ [Accessed: 3 December 2024].

McQueen (2008) 'BBC's panorama, war coverage and the 'Westminster consensus', *Westminster Papers in Communication and Culture*, 5(3), pp. 47–68.

Moloney, K. and McGrath, C. (2020) *Rethinking public relations: Persuasion, democracy and society*. 3rd ed. Oxon and New York: Routledge.

Murray, G. (2024) 'Morrisons drop pineapple supplier over violence at del Monte farm', *The BIJ*. Available at: https://www.thebureauinvestigates.com/stories/2024-06-27/morrisons-drop-pineapple-supplier-over-violence-at-del-monte-farm/ [Accessed: 2 August 2024].

Nash, L. (2023) 'New report urges stronger protections for UK's seasonal workers', *BIJ*. Available at: https://www.thebureauinvestigates.com/stories/2023-11-06/new-report-urges-stronger-protections-for-uks-seasonal-workers/ [Accessed: 3 December 2024].

Oborne, P. (2015) Why I Have Resigned from the Telegraph. *OpenDemocracy* 17 February. Available at: https://www.opendemocracy.net/en/opendemocracyuk/why-i-have-resigned-from-telegraph/ [Accessed: 2 August 2024].

Park, J. (2018) Gookhwoieouwon ibbubjungchaekgyaebalbi gaesunan balpyo… jungchaekbogoseo gonggyaeneaun geoboo [국회의원 입법정책개발비 개선안 발표…정책보고서 공개는 거부]. *The KCIJ* 30 November. Available at: https://www.newstapa.org/article/a-9C9 [Accessed: 7 December 2024].

Park, M. (2022) *Rejuvenating investigative journalism at nonprofit news organisations in South Korea and the United Kingdom*. Ph.D. Thesis. Cardiff University.

Park, M. and Konow-Lund, M. (2024a) 'Chapter 5 the Korea center for investigative journalism: A hybrid nonprofit funding model', in Konow-Lund, M., Park, M. and Bebawi, S. (eds.) *Hybrid investigative journalism*. Cham: Palgrave Macmillan, pp. 71–86.

Park, M. and Konow-Lund, M. (2024b) 'Chapter 4 the bureau local: A hybrid network for local collaborative investigative journalism', in Konow-Lund, M., Park, M. and Bebawi, S. (eds.) *Hybrid investigative journalism*. Cham: Palgrave Macmillan, pp. 57–70.

Potter, E. (n.d.) About us: From our founder. *The Bureau of Investigative Journalism*. Available at: https://www.thebureauinvestigates.com/about-us/ [Accessed: 27 May 2024].

Price, J. (2017) 'How to feed the ferret: Understanding subscribers in the search for a sustainable model of investigative journalism', *Journalism*, 21(9), pp. 1320–1337.

Roseman, E., McLellan, M. and Holcomb, J. (2021) *INN Index 2021: The state of nonprofit news, rising to new challenges and public needs in a crisis year*. Institute for

Nonprofit News. Available at: https://inn.org/wp-content/uploads/2021/06/INN-Index-2021-Report.pdf [Accessed: 27 May 2024].

Shaver, D. (2010) 'Online non-profits provide model for added local news', *Newspaper Research Journal*, 31(4), pp. 16–28.

Shin, W. (2015) 'Being a truth-teller who serves only the citizens: A case study of Newstapa', *Journalism*, 16(5), pp. 688–704.

Shin, W. (2016) *Being A "truth-teller" in the unsettled period of Korean journalism: A case study of Newstapa and its boundary work*. Ph.D. Thesis. University of Minnesota.

Starkman, D. (2014) *The watchdog that didn't bark: The financial crisis and the disappearance of investigative journalism*. New York: Columbia University Press.

Tofel, R. (2013) *Non-profit journalism: Issues around impact*. New York: Propublica. Available at: https://s3.amazonaws.com/propublica/assets/about/LFA_ProPublica-white-paper_2.1.pdf?_ga=1.204933332.53842270.1475860330 [Accessed: 27 May 2024].

Townend, J. (2016) 'Charitable journalism: Oxymoron or opportunity?', *Ethical Space: The International Journal of Communication Ethics*, 13(2/3), pp. 81–87.

Tuchman, G. (1978) *Making news*. New York: The Free Press.

Usher, N. (2014) *Making news at the new York times*. Ann Arbor: The University of Michigan Press.

Walton, M. (2010) 'Investigative shortfall', *American Journalism Review*, Fall, pp. 18–30.

7

IN CONVERSATION WITH DAVID CONN

Award-Winning Investigative Sports Journalist

Neil Farrington and John Price

While the sports desk was once viewed by some as the *Toy Department* of the newsroom, sports has become an increasingly important subject for work by investigative journalists. Sporting issues cut across many "hard" news subjects such as politics, economics, and health. The more that money is ploughed into sport by nations and corporations, and the more difficult it becomes for sporting authorities to be held accountable by national Governments, the more important it is for journalists to attempt to hold sport, and those who run and fund it, to account. Recent topics for important investigations have included corruption, fraud, human rights abuses, match-fixing and doping. In one of the most notable examples, Irish journalist David Walsh spent more than 13 years exposing a drug-taking scandal at the heart of professional cycling, which led to the downfall of sporting icon Lance Armstrong.

In this chapter, journalist and academic Neil Farrington discusses investigative sports journalism with David Conn, Investigations Correspondent for The Guardian. Among the topics discussed is the Hillsborough stadium disaster of 1989, which caused 97 deaths. At the time, The Sun newspaper ran a story headlined *The Truth,* based on false police accounts, in which they blamed the disaster on the drunken behaviour of Liverpool supporters. Conn and others have since spent years trying to tell the real truth of what happened that day and hold to account those responsible for the disaster and subsequent cover-up. His reporting on the bereaved Hillsborough families' continuing campaign for justice, including a 2009 article for The Guardian which prompted then Labour Government ministers Andy Burnham and Maria Eagle to press for all official documents relating to the disaster to be released, continues today.

DOI: 10.4324/9781003478157-11

Conn is a three-time winner of both the Sports Journalists' Association's Sports News Reporter of the Year award and the Football Supporters' Federation's Football Writer of the Year award, and was named Sports Journalist of the Year at the 2013 Press Gazette British Journalism Awards. He has written four acclaimed books on football – three of them, beginning with "The Football Business: Fair Game in the '90s?", focusing on the commercialisation and monetisation of English football, and "The Fall of the House of FIFA" (2017) exposing corruption within world football's governing body. In 2023, he won Private Eye magazine's Paul Foot Award for investigative journalism for exposing Conservative peer Michelle Mone's use of a government "VIP lane" to win hugely lucrative personal protective equipment (PPE) contracts during the COVID-19 pandemic.

*

Farrington: You've taken charge, whether as a solo journalist or, increasingly, as part of a team, of numerous investigations. How do such investigations come about?

Conn: I'd say that it's a mixture of self-generated leads and tip-offs. To some extent, you're always following your own nose and instincts on pretty much every story. But, working on a specific investigations team, there will always be stories that require team effort simply to ascertain whether there's a story there at all.

What you're looking for as an author and sports columnist, and what began to happen to me after I'd written for a while, is for people to come to you with stories or leads.

I think that's a rite of passage for any journalist looking to be genuinely investigative; to become a respected enough figure for people to trust and share with you the information that leads to unknown, unacknowledged or falsely denied facts.

How did you come to be an investigative journalist?

I think the key to my path into it was a combination of my legal training and good timing. I qualified as a solicitor but had always wanted to write. So, basically, I just did that. I started writing from scratch, and writing about my passion, which was football. When I started writing about the game, it was at that particular time in the early to mid-1990s when it was being commercially carved up probably for the first time.

A lot of football clubs were being bought and sold, or even floated on the Stock Exchange, and a lot of the football writers at that time didn't really understand what that involved. So, having studied some corporate law, I had a level of insight that, generally, they didn't.

I also had what I'd describe as a healthy level of cynicism, especially when we were being told, via so much Public relations (PR) and hype from the Premier League and Sky Sports, that this was a whole new ball game and all just 100% for the benefit of supporters.

Yes, what arrived in the 90s was generally an improvement – and a revival of sorts – after the disasters and the grim times of the 1980s. But while it was most obviously true that they'd made the stadiums safe, I had that gut feeling that, well, actually, this isn't quite what it says on the tin.

My instinct was that this was a well-packaged, well-sold commercial carve-up by not just the clubs at the top of the game, but by individual people who owned those clubs. So, while the focus of the vast majority of sports journalists remained on events on the pitch, my legal training allowed me to look at what was happening off it.

I could read accounts. I could understand corporate structures. I could understand how businesses should be run. And the more I looked at what was actually happening in boardrooms, particularly given the new TV revenue that was flooding into the Premier League, the more I understood how the game was quickly moving away from the common fan.

So, yes, that legal knowledge that I had was a trigger for it, and then there was also the fact that I was a huge football fan and relished the prospect of being involved in it professionally. So, by the time I came to conceive and start researching my first book, I was already writing about football in a professional sense – i.e. doing match reports.

However, I've also reflected over time that it must just also be my way of thinking and my way of looking at things that got me drawn into investigative work. I do have a strong sense of justice and a natural curiosity, and when people tell me things, my first instinct has always been to want to know more.

I wouldn't quite say I'm naturally cynical. But maybe a natural scepticism is critical. I'd say I have a critical eye for things that don't feel quite right and that I need to know more about. I just get drawn into things because of that, but it's not the reason I went into sports journalism. I did think it would be a dream job compared to being a lawyer; that it would be a dream to be writing about football. I was inspired by and thinking of the great descriptive sportswriters that I grew up reading, and by the thought of how amazing it would be to be writing about our beautiful game alongside them. So, I started doing match reports. But then my curiosity and scepticism took me in a slightly different direction, and I was quite quickly drawn into this huge investigative journey and writing a whole book about the business of football.

I still didn't think of myself as an investigative journalist, though. I think there's this kind of aura about investigative journalists. It's only now, or in more recent years anyway, that people have started calling me that, and that now, as my actual job title is investigations correspondent and I lead an investigative team, I regard myself as an investigative journalist – i.e. because people are calling me an investigative journalist, I must be an investigative journalist. But I am sometimes uncertain about that title because I actually think that there can be a bit of an artificial separation between investigative journalists and "normal" journalists. After all, all you're doing as an investigative reporter is researching, making inquiries, asking questions and trying to get to the facts. And I think a lot of general news reporting is investigative, but it's just they're called news reporters, not investigative reporters. But I think there is this aura about that job title. And so, for me, just the idea that I've become an investigative journalist is actually still a little surreal because the truly great investigative journalists – and great investigative journalism – still has that aura, for me.

Now, almost 30 years on, would you agree there's an irony that the thing which first drew you to investigative journalism – the rampant commercialisation of sport – has helped sustain you in career terms? Things have certainly come a long way since the days when the sports desk at a newspaper was traditionally referred to as the toy department.

I think absolutely that's the case. And it's really valid. But first of all, I think it always was unfair to classify sports desks as toy departments. I'm very emphatic about that. If anyone ever suggests to me "oh, you're doing the type of work that other football journalists don't", I always push back on that and support the football journalists. Firstly, because I know just what the role of covering sport, not least live sport, involves, and in that respect alone, they are doing an incredible and difficult job. But also, people seem to think that sports journalists aren't news journalists, or are failed news journalists, when the reality is that a lot of sports news reporting is both hugely important but also performed under intense pressure. Many sports reporters are doing investigative reporting, but day to day, while meeting very strict daily deadlines.

Just using Hillsborough as an example – and this is a bit of an untold story, which I am hoping to tell one day in a book I plan to write about Hillsborough. There was incredible work that the sportswriters who were there on the day, to report on the match, did when they suddenly had to become news reporters. Take David Walker, a Manchester-based football writer working for the Daily Mail, who later became sports editor of the Sunday Mirror and chairman of the Sports Journalists' Association.

When I was covering the Hillsborough inquest, David Walker was called as a witness – as was fellow football writer Steve Curry.

The particular evidence that David was called to give concerned the fact that he had been at the 1987 FA Cup semi-final at Hillsborough between Leeds and

Coventry. That day, as there seemingly always had been in the Leppings Lane end at big games, there was a crush, and the kick-off of the game was delayed.

The particular issue that David gave evidence about, not only at the inquest but at the later trial of David Duckenfield (the police match commander on the day of the Hillsborough disaster) and, I think, also to the Taylor inquiry way back in the day, was that he had seen in 1987 the crowds outside Leppings Lane being managed by the police using filters or cordons. It was a huge issue that, in 1989, Duckenfield, totally inexperienced, didn't know that the approach to Leppings Lane was difficult, and so they didn't have cordons in use that day.

First of all, it was totally inspirational to me to see a football writer, not someone who's been given the title of investigative reporter, coming to give vital evidence about something really, really important on the safety issue that he'd seen. But what people don't know – and I want to include this in the book when I write it – is what David and the other football writers did in the immediate aftermath of the disaster, i.e. what they did as journalists on the scene.

So, as we now know, as it all started and the crush was actually happening, Duckenfield told a lie: that fans without tickets had forced the gate. And that was relayed to the media. So, the TV commentator John Motson and the radio commentator Alan Green relayed that message. I'm not saying they said it as fact, but they said that was what they were being told.

David and the other football reporters who were there – and there, ostensibly, only to cover a football match, remember – were told the same. So that story was put out there straight away by the authorities. But rather than simply report that, those journalists who were on the spot decided to go down to the pitch and to go around outside the ground to cover the story properly. They instinctively realised, as the trained journalists they were, that they were now reporting about a human disaster, not about football, and had an absolute duty to find out as much as they could about what had happened and was happening.

David told me that they had met Liverpool fans and said to them that they were being told that the gate had been forced by fans. So, they were taken by a group of Liverpool fans to meet other fans who all showed them their tickets. They were tickets which still had the tab intact because they hadn't been taken at the turnstiles, but it showed that they had had tickets.

But also, the fans took David to Gate C at the Leppings Lane End, and he and the other journalists were shown that there was no evidence of the gate being forced, and were told that the gate had been opened by the police.

And so, those reporters pushed back on that lie – the lie of ticketless fans forcing the gate. Obviously, they couldn't also push back on all the other lies which followed about drunkenness and everything. But they could speak out on what they had seen. And, so, at 7 pm that night, South Yorkshire Police had to confirm: "Yes, we did order the gate to be opened".

So to me, that is an outstanding example of amazing, on-the-spot news reporting on the most important thing they would ever find themselves reporting on: a disaster in a disaster zone. And actually, what people often overlook is that the news reporting of Hillsborough in the days immediately after the disaster was really good, and the local paper – the Sheffield Star – and loads of national newspapers basically worked out the cause of the disaster within a day or two. If you look at that initial reporting, it homes in on the chief in command being new, being totally inexperienced and having not done a "recce", having simply not understood the ground well enough. The newspapers pinpointed that the police opened the gate, they didn't close off the tunnel, and they created the crush outside the ground through bad management. There had been the use of cordons outside Leppings Lane at big games, where the football journalists themselves had been there, in previous years. That's before you even talk about them not delaying the kick-off. All of this was highlighted clearly and quickly by excellent news reporting, which, by its nature, was itself investigative.

But there was then the really notorious coverage in The Sun on the Wednesday, the 19th of April, and it started with "Police officers have hit back …" before delivering the lies that we all know too well. And people inevitably look back on that Sun report and think that the media was terrible over Hillsborough, and that journalists in general propagated the police lies. But in fact, the Sun stuff was a pushback by the police against very sound and deeply damning reporting by a lot of the media in the days afterwards.

So, this idea of sports desks being the toy department or playroom journalism was untrue then, and it's untrue now. These guys had been at Heysel, they'd been at Bradford. They were incredibly nimble, expert journalists and also very sceptical and critical of the ownership of football clubs. And they knew better than anyone what went on at certain clubs, were under no illusions over some of the people in the game that they were dealing with and did what they could to uncover so many things, So I feel in awe of the work that they were doing back then, and I just don't think there should ever have been a distinction made between what they did and what non-sports journalists who were given the title "investigative reporter" did. And yet, I think it continues even to this day that the sports department and sports journalists can be a bit underestimated by wider journalism. But the fact is that there isn't that neat division between what sports journalists do, in an investigative reporting sense, and what other investigative journalists do.

Yes, there is match reporting and there are post-match interviews, and that's obviously the "entertainment end" of sports journalism, for want of a better phrase. But let's be honest, that's what people want to read and what fans are most interested in. That's why most of them engage with us about sport. But alongside that, there's so much sports news reporting that gets done in such a good and investigative and versatile way.

In terms of my own work and the place I established in the world of investigative sports journalism, I think the point is that those sports reporters of previous eras didn't have the training in areas such as corporate structures or finances in the same way as I did, and they hadn't really needed it before because, for example, football clubs were run like local fiefdoms rather than corporations to make profits. So, I just came in from the outside with the different training that I'd had, and was able to carve a niche because, yes, the money in football got huge. That meant the issues that I was highlighting became accepted as issues of public concern. Governments have since had different goes at "cleaning up the game" – again, for want of a better phrase, and finally, after all these years, they are actually bringing in a football regulator. But, in essence, that's a reaction to a lot of the issues that not just me, but bodies such as the Football Supporters' Association and other people were highlighting – in an investigative way – all those years ago. So that agenda that we had way back in the earlyish 1990s had me thinking, "Am I right in thinking this? Am I right to feel like this? Am I right to feel like this isn't quite right for the game of football?" … that's been vindicated.

As it was, people back then, whom I greatly respected, were telling me, "You're definitely on the right lines here. We're all seeing this as well. We know there's something wrong here. But we're not quite sure how to go about getting to the heart of it, so you need to crack on".

Yes, in football, the investigative scope we had to go at grew bigger because the issues got bigger, because the money got bigger, because the division between rich and poor got bigger, and because the public concern about it got bigger. Loads of smaller clubs started to go bust, or there would be controversial takeovers at the bigger clubs, and, generally, the issue of the business of football grew as a subject.Still, it was almost that I was lucky enough to arrive at the party early, critiquing the situation and writing a book {"The Football Business …"} that arguably gave people an early reference point for it. And now, as you say, there's a lot more recognition of the topic as a sports journalism narrative. It's seen as much more bread-and-butter sports reporting for people to write about the money, the finances, the Financial Fair Play breaches, etc. Whatever it is, the football reporters themselves are doing this reporting, which for me is great to see. And there's also a serious investment in journalism focusing on the bigger developing issues within the landscape of sports, such as the Saudi state's involvement. So, I'd like to think that I, maybe, had a small hand in helping to encourage that kind of critical and investigative reporting on those issues.

In terms of methodology, how much have things changed, whether because of the birth of the digital age, or anything else, for an investigative reporter since your first book? Is the information you are looking for more accessible now?

It's hugely more accessible, which does mean that a lot of information is more transparent. It's at everybody's fingertips.

In terms of comparing now with the era when I wrote the first book, accessing a company's financial accounts is a very simple but good example of the change. Company accounts are very basic public information, and they were back then too, in that, by law, a company has to publish its accounts. And yet, it was almost like an investigative endeavour back then to get the relevant documents and – again, because they hadn't ever looked for it before – a lot of football journalists didn't really know that information was out there.

So, back in the day, you had to literally physically go to a building – i.e. Companies House – or you would call organisations to ask them to send you documents. And you'd finally get these documents, and it was like, not quite finding gold dust, but it was such a relief, and there was so much solid information within them that it felt like a big discovery. So just getting basic facts back then felt like an investigative challenge, and a lot of that first book was essentially based on critiquing that simple information in football clubs' accounts – which barely anyone other than club officials and their accountants had seen – putting it all together and showing how not only was almost all the money in English football being taken by the Premier League, because the Premier League had been a breakaway by the clubs from the rest of the domestic game, but also showing that the people who we used to call chairmen back then – and often regarded fondly as benefactors of sorts – were actually club owners, and many of them were taking big money out of the game.

Yes, these people might well have held shares in their clubs, but those shares had never really been worth anything. So, to be fair to these people, money hadn't previously been the motive for their involvement in the game. That motive generally had been the local kudos of being involved in a town's football club. But now, with the Premier League, the commercial revenue, all the other money coming into the top end of the game and the way these guys had carved things up when breaking away from the Football League, those shares become tremendously valuable to them personally, and floating their club on the stock market was a way for them to cash in on that.

This all seems quite obvious now. But back then, because it was such a new development – and probably because the new product – i.e. Premier League football – itself was so entertaining, putting together this information and presenting it to people was quite revelatory, and made for a strong critique.

And I think now, despite this information being much more easily accessible now, a big part of the work of an investigative sports journalist is still putting it together for people, i.e. presenting the basic, factual situation, but in a way that is a critique or just an analysis that's very factual because many people still don't normally think about the business side of football, because they're so increasingly captivated by what's happening on the pitch.

It's funny because you could argue that the easier access to information now almost makes the investigative journalist's job harder because everyone acknowledges now that we can all see information such as company accounts. But I suppose that makes the ability to critique and analyse that information a more valuable skill still for the investigative journalist today.

That said, I'd reiterate there isn't a magic to the job – it's not like you cross over into investigative journalism, and you somehow develop new powers and can find things out that nobody else can. The absolute essence of the job is still looking – but REALLY looking – at all the information that is publicly available – and that now includes material obtained from other, newer means such as Freedom of Information requests. Yes, from there, your instincts as a journalist can help you decide what that information means and where the story is. You do a close reading of everything, and you never know what you might find if you follow your nose.

I think a key element of being a successful investigative journalist is combining that deep, detailed reading of information with what, as I mentioned before, are staples of journalism in general: good contacts and good contact information. Sometimes, those contacts will simply start your process by directing you to look at certain, openly accessible information that others haven't looked at. At other times, those contacts will come in later in your process by providing the knowledge, perhaps the inside knowledge, to be able to help you analyse and interpret that type of information in a way that leads to revelatory content.

So, contacts, in this digital age where accessing information almost becomes bread and butter rather than a serious endeavour, are probably more valuable now than they've ever been.

When the digital age first kicked in, and you could suddenly get information such as company accounts at the click of a mouse, I started panicking about how I was going to fill my time! That's how painstaking the effort to get that information had been, to the extent that, when I was based near Manchester, I used to get so frustrated waiting for documents to arrive with me in the post that I'd sometimes travel to Manchester to physically go to Companies House, which was a building near Piccadilly, and sit there for hours going through documents.

So, it's now that the information itself has generally become such common currency – with far more people reporting on it now that accounts come out online, football clubs themselves now make statements about their own accounts and the likes of the Press Association will report on them and send something out to all the newspapers – that the investigative element to it has become that analysis (i.e. what do the figures actually mean), contacts who either alert you to something not being right in that information or are so well-informed and well-connected that they can join up the dots within that information in a way that you can't.

People now tend to speak about "sources" rather than "contacts", but I don't particularly like the term "source". You know, these are still people; people with whom you've probably built a relationship over time. Often, they will become whistleblowers. It's very rare in a genuinely revelatory, investigative story that someone who is involved in a situation or a company where they see something so seriously wrong that makes them unhappy is prepared to come out publicly by name on the record. But they can become whistleblowers who give you something very serious and significant that sets you down the investigative path or helps you further along it.

Of course, whistleblowers have long been a traditional source of information for investigations in journalism. But the fact that it is still the case today shows that human relationships are just as important now for investigative journalists as they've ever been, despite the far, far easier methodology of accessing information.

And in terms of the actual methodology, there's still always a lot of work for the journalist to do. Even if you've got someone who is telling you a lot of information and prepared to be a whistleblower, all the evidence they give you has to be checked and corroborated – or "stood up", in old money. And however much you trust the person giving you the information, and however sure you are that it's true, you'll always have an instinct as a journalist that you need more to go on. You still ask yourself, "Is there any documentary proof? Is there any evidentiary proof I can get hold of?" And the bigger the story and the higher the stakes involved – and Hillsborough is a classic example of this – you know you have a big duty of care to speak to all or as many of the people involved, rather than just your initial contact or contacts, and to speak to them in a thorough and professional way that makes them feel that dealing with you was a worthwhile, happy experience.

In that respect, the work that you're most widely known for, Hillsborough, and its role in securing some measure of justice for the victims and their families, must have posed the ultimate test of balancing human relationships with a professional investigative perspective? For example, as you uncovered more and more evidence that was so damning of the authorities and such a vindication of the families, how difficult was it to

still perform the basic investigative task of checking and questioning that evidence?

I think that what happened with starting to write about Hillsborough was similar to how I started to work on "The Football Business …" book, in that my legal training was a strong starting point, and I actually began writing about the disaster as early as that book.

For the 35th anniversary of the disaster, the Liverpool Echo actually did an interview with me and asked how long I'd been looking into the disaster. I made the point that I'd written about Hillsborough for the first time in that book, in 1997, because it had been such a key event, as the last in a series of stadium disasters, in the chronology of how football changed in the 1990s.

The Taylor Report ordered huge changes to stadiums, clubs were given public money to help make those changes, and then you had the Premier League breakaway, all the money coming from Sky, and football was revived and reborn. But it all came from the game's worst moment: Hillsborough. Alongside that, Jimmy McGovern's TV docu-drama in 1996 had woken us up to the fact that there had been this terrible miscarriage of justice which, very sadly, hadn't really been covered much in the media. So, for my book, I went to see some of the Hillsborough families, and ended up basing that chapter on the terrible contrast between football clubs being able to physically rebuild their grounds while the families couldn't rebuild their lives because of the cover-up and fight for justice.

The first family I went to see were the Hammonds, whose 14-year-old son, Philip, had died. And yes, that was very, very emotional. But while I was always intent on reflecting that emotion – nobody can deny the importance of a journalist reporting on the human story; on its human impact – I think, again, my legal training was crucial in that as they started to explain the detail of Philip's and their story, I could just 100% understand it straight away from that dispassionate legal perspective as an astonishing miscarriage of justice. I first wrote about some of the different detailed elements of that injustice in the book.

The point of a miscarriage of justice isn't just that it's wrong in legal terms, and that the system has come to the wrong conclusion. It's that injustice inflicts terrible suffering and trauma on people. In the case of the Hammonds and the other families, you're talking about the loss of their loved ones, and for many of them, the loss of their children, at a football match – something unthinkable but which causes utter devastation. So, the task of a journalist in that context is to create content which investigates and encapsulates that injustice, measures how terrible that injustice is and underlines how important justice is to people. And, to do that, you have to understand both facts and people.

So, on the one hand, there's the intellectual job of getting the factual – in this case, legal – details correct, but also the task of getting the emotional details correct. To do both, you need to have empathy. But the challenge of reporting Hillsborough was to guard against your reporting straying completely from empathy to sympathy because – ultimately, given the scale of the miscarriage of justice involved – there was an absolute responsibility on me not to stray too far from the cold, very harsh and disturbing facts that we were looking to uncover.

Ultimately and tragically, it's the families that have had the terrible experience, not you. You're there to do a professional job. In the case of Hillsborough, that job was to uncover the truth.

Having realised that there had been a complete and total miscarriage of justice, you had to have an absolute commitment as an investigative reporter to expose that.

I think that the attempt to maintain some sort of detachment – to remain professional – when dealing with such a hugely emotive set of issues and circumstances is appreciated by the families, many of whom I've got to know very well over the years.

And, of course, as investigative stories go, this one – sadly – goes on and on…

It still feels very, very current. There's an ongoing injustice. Nobody has been held truly to account.

I still feel really committed to it. I covered the panel report in 2012, the quashing of the original inquest's finding in 2012 and the new inquest over a period of two years – I didn't attend it every day. But I went a lot and did major coverage for The Guardian. Then I covered the criminal trials in November 2019, after a retrial, David Duckenfield was acquitted of gross negligence manslaughter, and in May 2021, two retired police officers and an ex-solicitor accused of altering police statements after the disaster were also acquitted. And what those trials have exposed to me are what I consider to be major flaws in our legal system.

From what I've seen, the very basis of the system is flawed. I've seen the adversarial system between prosecution and defence, in front of a jury who have to know nothing beforehand about the issues being argued, fail – and fail miserably.

I think that failure is really, really serious – not just, obviously, in the context of Hillsborough, the victims, the families and 35 years of pain, but in the wider context of the place our justice system holds in the fabric of our society.

As things stand, the outcome of all those years of fighting re Hillsborough, and of the investigative work that has been done, sadly includes all sorts of unanswered questions. Like, just how could South Yorkshire Police succeed in that cover-up? Like, how could Sheffield Wednesday's ground be in such a terrible state? Like, how can no one ultimately be held accountable for a disaster, the nature of which is still barely conceivable, and that subsequent cover-up?

The broad answer to those questions is that the legal system completely failed, and that there's no accountability for that either. But, more specifically, I feel ever more passionate about journalism's responsibility to continue to press for answers – and justice – on behalf of those families and for other victims of miscarriages of justice, through investigative work.

And yet, there seems to be growing antipathy towards Liverpool supporters – and an apparent indifference to the Hillsborough story – among many other football fans?

That's a symptom of a toxic narrative that, sadly, seems exclusive to football club rivalry in this country, which is something I think is worth investigation and exposure in itself.

I appreciate this story has run for a long time, and that can engender a certain level of fatigue in an audience, but why do the people who deal in this toxicity not understand the truth? Why do they not understand that the Hillsborough inquest vindicated Liverpool fans? It's a particularly tough question for me when placed in the context of the almost universal reaction I've recently seen to The Guardian's investigations into government PPE contracts.

Having been very much involved with the Hillsborough inquest and watched and read all the coverage, my instinct is to think that everyone must know the true story now. But then you consider that people generally will have been busy that day. They might have heard a bit of the news on the radio or seen it on the TV, but not taken all that much notice because the story had been going on for such a long time. Then there was the nonsense of the criminal trials, despite us assuming, after the inquest, that the families would be vindicated and delivered justice by the courts.

But, rather than dissuade me from getting involved in new investigations, the frustration of reporting Hillsborough actually inspires me more because it reminds me that the time when a story gets properly imprinted on the public consciousness is when the event in question is actually happening and in the few days afterwards – i.e. when it's top of the news agenda and is all encompassing. And Hillsborough is a classic case of the authorities getting their story in early – that story being that the fans were drunk and/or ticketless – and getting it seen and heard so widely and loudly that their original version of events, no matter what truths are so clearly and comprehensively uncovered further forwards, is what sticks for many people.

Well, what we should be striving to do, given all the tools, techniques, and platforms – the powers of immediacy – that we now have as investigative journalists to find, corroborate and publish information, is to try to ensure that, in future, the first version of events that people see, hear or read is the truth. That brings its own challenges, in that I still absolutely love the writing side of my job – when you've amassed all the detail, when you've done all the hard yards, research-wise, and when you've gathered all the facts, to then be able to sit down and write an in-depth, investigative article – and to take some time over it – is a pure joy. But one of the values of working in a team, as I am now, is that you can pool your resources to ensure that the story gets told not only properly but also as promptly as possible.

I think that balance – between getting an important investigative story out there soon enough for it to have an impact and making sure it's the best story possible – is particularly crucial in sports journalism, where clickbait has arguably caused as much damage, in credibility terms, as anywhere else in the media landscape, and particularly in local journalism, which is awful to see and a really serious issue to a democratic society.

What I'm hoping is that the natural aversion that people have developed over recent years to clickbait will be the death of it, and that they are already being almost compelled to find and engage with platforms such as The Guardian and The Athletic, where they're not beset by pop-up ads.

The Guardian's financial model is now based on supporter contributions, and those supporters' reading habits are what is ensuring that investigative journalism is at the forefront of The Guardian's mission.

Then you look at The Athletic being probably the big sports journalism success story of recent years, and it's almost all long reads. But that should be no surprise, as the fact is that there is a particularly passionate, sometimes even captive, audience out there for investigative sports content, and, if done well, it can have a transformative impact on sport itself. Cycling alone is a great example of that, when you consider work such as David Walsh's incredibly dogged and courageous pursuit of Lance Armstrong, and Matt Lawton's investigation of Team Sky. Sports journalism is rich with investigative reporting talent – the emergence of The Athletic is another happy symptom of that. So, I'm hopeful for the future of the industry in that sense.

Another reason for optimism is that the internet offers an infinite amount of publishing opportunities, and one way in which sports platforms and publications have found that they can stand out is through investigative journalism because it means they're doing and offering something different and potentially unique, day in, day out. Again, The Athletic shows there is an audience in our country and worldwide for really good, revelatory, investigative sports journalism.

Do you have any advice for budding investigative sports journalists?

Work hard, speak to the right people, and get your facts straight … but get the first draft of your story done, and done quickly. Doing that allows you to lay out all the key information in front of you, and from there, you can shape it more effectively and quickly into the end product that you and, hopefully, your audience want.

CLASSROOM EXERCISE

You plan to write a feature about investigative sports journalism, aimed at giving advice to journalism students. As part of this, you have arranged to interview David Conn. Do the following:

1 Conduct background research into some recent investigative sports stories. Identify and provide a short summary of three "good" examples, identifying the techniques and sources used.
2 Plan five interview questions to ask David Conn about the advice he would give young sports journalists interested in doing investigative reporting.

Suggested Reading

Domeneghetti, R.(ed.) (2021) *Insights on reporting sports in the digital age*. London: Routledge.

English, P. (2022) Investigative journalism in sport in Coatney, C (ed.s) *Investigative journalism in changing times*. Routledge.

Rojas-Torrijos, J.L. and Nölleke, D. (2023) 'Rethinking sports journalism', *Journalism and Media*, 4(3), pp. 853–860.

Rowe, D. (2007) 'Sports journalism: Still the 'toy department' of the news media?', *Journalism*, 8, pp. 385–405.

Shafiu Ahmad, S. and Singh, P. (2024) 'Investigative and interpretative reporting in the digital age: Tools and techniques', *Journal of Communication and Management*, 3(01), pp. 44–50.

PART IV

The Impact of AI on Investigative Journalism

8

ENVIRONMENT, TECHNOLOGY, AND JOURNALISM

Tackling Environmental Issues Using Data and AI in Latin America

Mathias-Felipe de-Lima-Santos

Introduction

The climate emergency, which is widespread, rapid, and intensifying (IPCC, 2022), has globally driven news media to incorporate editorial brands covering environmental journalism. Investigative environmental journalism, however, has a longer history. For example, environmental reporting has sparked public awareness about the dangers of pesticides, the Bhopal disaster in India, and the Exxon Valdez oil spill, highlighting the devastating impact of industrial negligence on the environment (Kahn, 2007). Since 2019, many news outlets have responded to the climate crisis by creating climate reporting sections, such as the BBC, Bloomberg, The Guardian, and The Independent (Kunova, 2020). However, these organizations are largely based in Western countries, which often sidelines crucial debates on environmental issues affecting the Global South. Investigative journalism from regions such as Latin America, Southeast Asia, and Africa remains underrepresented, despite these areas being disproportionately impacted by climate change and environmental exploitation.

Media outlets have increasingly recognized the urgency of climate issues; for instance, in 1989, *TIME* made history by featuring "Endangered Earth" on its cover in place of the traditional Person of the Year, drawing attention to global environmental threats. In 2019, *TIME* revisited this focus with "2050: The Fight for Earth," devoting an entire issue to the climate crisis—one of only five times the magazine has dedicated its coverage entirely to a single topic (McGinn, 2019). Since 2019, many news outlets have created dedicated climate reporting sections, such as the BBC, Bloomberg, The Guardian, and *The Independent* (Kunova, 2020). Since 2019, many news outlets have created

DOI: 10.4324/9781003478157-13

climate reporting sections, such as BBC, Bloomberg, *The Guardian*, and *The Independent* (Kunova, 2020). However, these organizations are based in Western countries, undermining much of the debate on Global South issues.

To make themselves heard in this increasing market, two organizations in Latin America have driven their efforts to influence the environmental agenda by using data as their primary tool. InfoAmazonia, a small data-driven investigative outlet, relies on geo-visualization and information mapping to enhance public awareness about the Amazon rainforest (Salovaara, 2016). Similarly, *La Nación* (Argentina) has leveraged its report on environmental issues by launching a new editorial brand: "LN Naturaleza" (de-Lima-Santos, 2022).

Both news outlets have a solid international reputation and recognition due to the exceptional standards of their news products and a high level of innovation, which has brought them to an award-winning position. *La Nación* relies on its data team, LN Data, to develop data stories and build interactive tools to communicate effectively. Founded in 2011, the team has experimented with open data, civic journalism, and automated journalism since its foundation (Palomo, Teruel and Blanco-Castilla, 2019). Likewise, InfoAmazonia has contributed to the debate on more sustainable development in the Amazon region by devoting to geojournalism, i.e., news reporting techniques that combine data journalism and geodata, using particular features, such as geo-tagging, custom mapping, and interactive graphics (de-Lima-Santos and Mesquita, 2021a; Salovaara, 2016).

Under the lens of environmental journalism and data journalism, this chapter proposes a practice-reflection based on the two case studies mentioned above. It discusses the use of environmental data journalism (Appelgren and Jönsson, 2020) and also sheds light on the application of artificial intelligence (AI) techniques in environmental journalism (Marconi et al., 2017). Both news media organizations developed novel ways to produce environmental content by adopting these skills. Consequently, they also brought new possibilities to effectively communicate environmental problems and their solutions to the public. Thus, this chapter aims to answer the following question: How do data journalism and AI work as modes of production for environmental reporting in these organizations?

This chapter embraces a practical approach by bringing examples of AI solutions and data-driven stories on environmental journalism to achieve this goal. It relies on a qualitative approach drawing on a multi-method design that includes a devised document analysis, such as published stories, reports, journals, and websites (Bryman, 2016). This data is then triangulated with participant observation—three months of fieldwork in Q1 2020 at *La Nación*—and in-depth interviews with *La Nación*'s and InfoAmazonia's leading teams conducted in Q1 2020. Data is analyzed under thematic content analysis (Braun & Clarke, 2014), a traditional method to systematically analyze qualitative data and distinguish themes that emerge from it.

Environmental Journalism in Latin America

Viewed as a Western practice, environmental journalism was perceived as an exclusive preoccupation of the wealthy countries, as the Global South was "too poor to be green." Likewise, environmentalists were seen as "agents of Western influence," reporting to foreign governments about the Global South's issues, while trying to interfere in national matters. However, the nature issues are permanent in any society, even in the countries which seem to have a lower priority in the public debate (Guha & Martínez-Alier, 1997).

Environmental issues are an essential topic in Latin America. This concern emerged only after the 20th century, when many Latin American countries lived under an economic dependency on Western countries (Kovarik, 2020). Thus, this neocolonialism model of exploitation and abuse was first seen in the Amazonian rubber-growing industry in the early 1990s. It gave impetus to creating the first newspaper dedicated to covering environmental issues, *La Sanción*. Founded by the Peruvian businessman Benjamin Saldaña Rocca, it made the exposés of genocidal exploitation across the Amazon, having significant repercussions in the international media.

However, the first small foray into environmental journalism in Latin America suffered several challenges, such as the low interest from editors and readers, imprisonment of journalists, and censorship. For example, the Brazilian journalist Randau Marques was imprisoned and tortured after publishing a news story about lead poisoning among cobblers in the city of Franca. Even after his imprisonment, Marques made other exposés, such as the "valley of death" in the town of Cubatão, where industrial pollution was causing cancers and congenital disabilities. Similarly, the Brazilian rubber tapper leader Chico Mendes was an important actor, fighting to preserve the Amazon rainforest and advocating for the human rights of local and indigenous people. However, he was murdered in 1988. This episode has generated much concern from the international media about the "murders of native people, environmentalists, and human rights advocates" (Kovarik, 2020, p. 5467).

The region still attracts foreign investments, particularly from the drilling and mining industries, which draws the attention of environmentalists and human rights defenders. Hence, the region ranks at the top of people killed because of fighting against a dam, oil drilling, or mining projects (Raftopoulos, 2017). However, these professionals had to deal with the lack of editorial interest in reporting climate and environmental information, as the media landscape in the region is highly concentrated and located in the main urban centers of the countries. Consequently, a homogeneity on the editorial line exists, neglecting many issues and voices not in metropolitan areas (Koop, 2020). Even in this degraded environment, journalists demonstrated their resilience in reporting these issues.

These ongoing conflicts in the region helped to boost projects done by individuals and small organizations, such as ConexiónCOP (Peru), La Mula Verde (Peru), LatinClima (Costa Rica), Periodistas por el Planeta (Argentina), O Eco (Brazil), and InfoAmazonia (Brazil). In this context, Claves21 (Argentina) acted on "growing awareness in Latin American media outlets regarding the importance of environmental issues" (Koop, 2020, p. 385) by promoting training and courses for journalists.

However, these projects generally depicted the climate and environmental issues for niches, such as scientists, experts, governments, and NGOs, leaving out the views of the public. To overcome this, ConexiónCOP concentrated on the positive actions done by organizations or individuals to engage the audience in environmental journalism. InfoAmazonia has brought new ways to assess, plan, and implement journalistic products that attract public attention, using data along with geo-tagging, custom mapping, and interactive graphics. By relying on a data-driven approach to tell its stories, InfoAmazonia was able to engage in forward-looking discussions about the conservation and threats of the Amazon rainforest in the nine countries that it spans across: Brazil, Bolivia, Colombia, Ecuador, French Guiana, Guyana, Peru, Suriname, and Venezuela.

The Upsurge of Data Journalism in Environmental Reporting

As the Intergovernmental Panel on Climate Change (IPCC, 2022) described, our current society is living under a generated rhetoric and misinformation that undermine "climate science and disregards risk and urgency" (pp. 14–13), resulting in "public misperception of climate risks and polarised public support for climate actions" (pp. 14–13). Consequently, it requires new approaches to improve the public's perceptions of the environmental crisis. Scholars defended that encouraging public engagement and mobilization about climate and nature concerns is necessary. It can be done by finding new journalistic approaches, developing different business models, challenging news delivery, and seeking new ways to tell stories (Hackett et al., 2017).

However, environmental journalism brings some challenges because it is closely related to scientific communication, which may reduce the public's interest and understanding (Wormer, 2018). Thus, data journalism emerged as an essential endeavor to convert academic knowledge into news products that may be easier to comprehend and more appealing to audiences (Hermida and Young, 2019).

Additionally, data-driven storytelling can help to "balance the dependency on the public as both a subject of analysis and a source of professional legitimation" (Appelgren & Jönsson, 2020, p. 3). Historically, environmental journalists have been judged by their roles advocating for nature and science instead of producing "objective" journalism. It has generated much criticism as this unbalanced reporting did not stimulate a response to environmental and climate emergencies as expected (Howarth, 2012; Moser and Dilling, 2007). Therefore, data journalism's promises of objectivity, transparency, and trustworthiness to the news media industry are also valuable to environmental coverage.

However, this "objective" evidence, which would involve fewer human sources, is illusory. Technology is a byproduct of humans, whose limited capacity to grasp complex, multidimensional issues is echoed in these systems. Tong and Zuo (2019) contended three reasons why objectivity is inapplicable to data journalism and, consecutively, to environmental data journalism: (i) the impossibility to verify data along with the imbalance in its representation and access; (ii) the uncertainty about data contexts and algorithms; and (iii) the "design subjectivity" on the part of practitioners in transforming information into visuals.

In this respect, the journalistic choices in design and presentation can be associated with adverse effects, such as "controlling, non-transparent or intrusive" (Appelgren, 2018, p. 308). Alternatively, digital technology can be used to unlock the potential of new levels of interactivity, allowing data journalists to tell stories that frame the narrative of life that involves a combination of cognitive, emotional, and behavioral features that can enhance public engagement. Thus, data journalism could shed light on environmental concerns that would instigate the public to care about it and take action (Appelgren & Jönsson, 2020). By association, environmental data journalism becomes an evidence-based mechanism contributing to the burgeoning cognizance of environmental topics to foster nature's protection.

Mercado (2012) also found that environmental journalism in Argentina usually evades instituted editorial boundaries, such as politics, business, technology, and culture, helping to penetrate a diverse audience. This point brings another strong connection between data and environmental journalism. In general, data journalism can be applied to different news beats, mainly the ones that are data-rich domains, such as finance and sports (Segel & Heer, 2010).

Our environment is full of data waiting to be captured and used. As technology evolves, sensors and satellites are becoming more commonly used as recurring services for safeguarding and protecting the environment. These technologies applied to nature conservation and environmental defense all produce different forms of information, including basic data, indicators, and metadata. For example, satellite imagery and aerial photographs are primary data sources for illegal deforestation and bushfires. Likewise, sensors help measure emissions, pollution, and global warming (Szeliski, 2011).

The Upheaval of Environmental Data Journalism: Data to Drive Positive Change

Despite the volume of data available, it is not always well understood by the public, as reporting on the environment is complex and challenging. Journalists see data-driven reporting as a way to translate complex technical concepts into easy-to-understand stories. Prior studies have identified that the barriers for the public to take actions toward environmental protection and conservation are drawn not only on the lack of information and understanding, but also on how the topics are framed concerning personal-level values and experiences (Hacket & Gunster, 2017).

Data journalism can assist journalists in creating better links with environmental concerns and citizenship so that the public can relate to these topics better. Using data to illustrate real-life characters, or personalizing stories based on local context information rather than global, helps audiences see better the relationships between the data and their reality by the law of proximity (Kostelnick, 2019). This is evidenced by translating data into a plain and non-complex story with inherent simplicity that any audience can understand, which can be seen by using people's stories to illustrate figures (de-Lima-Santos and Mesquita, 2021b).

Appelgren and Jönsson (2020) studied environmental data journalism in two Swedish public service organizations. They found that, although not a priority area of coverage, these journalists had the intention to educate and make people aware of environmental problems. According to their interviewees, stories were restricted to low and moderate levels of interactivity to keep the audience interested. In this respect, the two Latin American cases discussed here bring more levels of interactivity and different approaches to environmental data journalism that are of broad interest to practitioners and scholars, indicating the potential pathways toward theme-data journalism (de-Lima-Santos, 2022).

InfoAmazonia: From Data Journalism to Geojournalism

Founded in 2012, InfoAmazonia is a nonprofit organization dedicated to raising awareness of the Amazon region, relying on geojournalism to report on natural and man-made disasters in nine countries that the Amazon spans across. InfoAmazonia contributed to the debate on more sustainable development in the Amazon region by working with scholars and locals who have a better idea of what is happening in their locality (de-Lima-Santos and Mesquita, 2021a).

This idea arose in 2008 while one of the co-founders, Gustavo Faleiros, was editor of the news portal O Eco, a non-governmental organization dedicated to covering environmental projects. He found on "Google Earth a possibility to use satellite imagery to create layers that could improve environmental storytelling" (Faleiros, April 2020). In this first data product, Faleiros created a map to monitor the fires in the Amazon, using open data from IBAMA (Brazilian Institute of Environment and Renewable Natural Resources) and INPE (National Institute for Space Research). According to Faleiros, this product inspired him to propose a large-scale project. Thus, he started to design what would be InfoAmazonia between 2008 and 2011. Meanwhile, he established alliances with communities dedicated to covering the environmental issues across the globe, such as the Earth Journalism Network and a network of journalists from the Amazon forest, which were fundamental to the organization's success.

This exchange of knowledge helped him design the basic idea of InfoAmazonia: a platform composed of three layers of information—deforestation, mining concessions, and bushfires—telling data stories of the Amazon region. From this initial idea, Faleiros found a different perspective on the geojournalism narrative structure to represent spatial and open data, highlighting the resolution and scale aspects of the storytelling. Using this view, the organization developed its own open-source plugin for CMS (Content Management System), called JEO, which was adopted by other environmental reporting outlets worldwide, such as Ekuatorial, InfoCongo, InfoNile, and InfoPacific. This plugin allows organizations to geo-tag the content according to its location. Additionally, it can be used in association with out-of-the-box solutions for data journalism (see de-Lima-Santos, Schapals and Bruns, 2021), such as Carto and Mapbox, expanding its use. It became one of the first revenue streams, as Faleiros gave consultancy to news organizations implementing JEO.

Another crucial chapter of InfoAmazonia's history was the Google Social Impact Awards prize. This was fundamental to support the company's activities in its first years, sharing its environmental data-driven reporting. Today, a significant part of the revenue comes from donations, mainly from philanthropic foundations. These resources are essential to performing data-driven investigations in the Amazon region, including those recognized regionally and internationally in recent years.

Award-Winning Investigations

As a small news outlet, InfoAmazonia saw the collaboration with journalistic organizations and nonprofit sectors as an essential endeavor to undertake investigative data journalism. An example was the story "Digging into the Mining Arc," published in collaboration with the Venezuelan newspaper *Correo del Caroní*[1] in 2018. This story investigated the destruction of 110 thousand square kilometers within the limits of the Amazon rainforest by one of the largest mining projects in the region. The news story showed that the undertaking is putting at risk the environment and dozens of indigenous communities, exposed to a high increase in malaria disease and mercury contamination.

To elucidate to the reader, the story uses multimedia features, such as photos, videos, and scrollytelling, associated with data and scientific information to explain how the rudimentary methods operating outside the law were hazardous for the environment and the population. According to Faleiros, the investigation was only possible due to a grant received from the Pulitzer Center on Crisis Reporting, as a local journalist needed to travel across the region to investigate it. After featuring in major news outlets "from more than five countries" (Faleiros, April 2020), this news story led to investigations from the highest Dutch government echelons about mineral trafficking from Venezuela to the Dutch Caribbean. Due to its high quality and importance, this story gained international recognition and prizes, such as the Online News Association (ONA) Awards, an honorable mention at the 40th Vladimir Herzog Award for Amnesty and Human Rights, and was shortlisted in the 2020 Brazilian data journalism awards.

"The Smugglers' Paradise"[2] was also widely acclaimed. Published in 2020 in partnership with *Correo del Caroní* (Venezuela), De Correspondent (Netherlands), *Miami Herald* (USA), and RunRunes (Venezuela), this year-long investigation described the damage caused by mining conflicts, gold trafficking, and illicit money flows in the Venezuelan Amazon rainforest. Using the Mapbox tool, the story was developed in a way that helps readers understand how corrupt military forces, Venezuelan gangs, and Colombian guerrilla groups were benefiting from illegal gold mining and illicit trade in the Orinoco Mining Arc and Yapacana National Park. Through scrollytelling and geojournalism, InfoAmazonia traced the route of this tragic story that starts in the Amazon, with gold being sent to the Colombian border and later dispatched to Caribbean islands. The gold was then exported, without inspections, to the Netherlands. Once in Europe, it was sold throughout the continent and the Middle East. Based on their data analysis, Colombia exported in 2019 more gold than it could produce locally, revealing discrepancies in the official reported information. This allowed the news outlets to identify stakeholders in the conflict-ridden mines and link them with international gold buyers.

This collaborative project—funded by the Human Rights Foundation and the Dutch Fund for Journalism Projects—has also received broad international recognition, culminating in winning the ONA awards and the Gabo Awards. Another environmental data journalism product created with philanthropic money from the Pulitzer Center was "Amazônia Minada."[3] In this project, InfoAmazonia combines daily information extracted from the mining requests with the indigenous lands and strict-use protected areas in the Amazon to generate a map with these areas and uses a Twitter bot to alert users. Equally, InfoAmazonia deployed another Twitter bot, "Amazônia Sufocada," dedicated to warning about the fires in the Amazon.[4] These examples show the relevance and dependency of foundations' money to produce investigative and data-driven products in Latin America (Requejo-Alemán & Lugo-Ocando, 2014). More recently, the "Inhaling Smoke" project investigated the effects of air pollution caused by forest fires on the health of the Amazonian population, which was awarded the 2022 King of Spain International Journalism Prize for environmental coverage.[5]

According to Faleiros, the bushfires in the Amazon in 2019 were one of the events that enjoyed better visibility and generated significant traffic online for

InfoAmazonia. This is partly explained because they build products that other organizations can use. For instance, InfoAmazonia's real-time wildfire map was readily embeddable in other news portals, such as Página 12 (Argentina) and La Vanguardia (Spain). Consequently, it resulted in massive traffic for InfoAmazonia's news products, which caught the attention of Mapbox, the tool used to deploy this map. As the business models of these out-of-the-box platforms are built on different access levels (de-Lima-Santos, Schapals and Bruns, 2021), InfoAmazonia's version was limited to a certain number of user accesses, which was exceeded in the case of the bushfires. Due to the importance of the event and the long-term partnership, Mapbox decided to concede a better license that allows unlimited simultaneous user access.

These tools are of great utility in producing improved visuals for a broad range of stories, requiring less time commitment and skills. During the COVID-19 outbreak, InfoAmazonia reported on the distance of indigenous villages to the closest beds in the Intensive Care Unit (ICU).[6] Using the mapping tool Carto, the data story highlighted the distances between hospitals and these villages, which could reach more than 1000 km. This innovative visualization made the team shortlisted in the visualization category of the 2020 Brazilian data journalism award. Faleiros explained a need to balance the production of long-term investigations and simple analyses that bring relevant information. "The challenge is to counter-balance both," added Faleiros.

Cooperation with other institutions is also a central strategy for InfoAmazonia. Beyond these temporary collaborations, InfoAmazonia has an alliance with *El Espectador*, one of the leading newspapers in Colombia. According to Faleiros, a person sits at *El Espectador*, dedicated exclusively to reporting on the Colombian Amazon. These news stories are usually published in both news portals, giving "recognition to InfoAmazonia's brand and work in Colombia," explained Falleiros. More recently, InfoAmazonia launched in collaboration with MapaBiomas and Natura, PlenaMata, a platform that brings data and stories about deforestation in the Amazon.[7]

However, this is not enough to engage people and raise awareness of the broader issues surrounding climate and environmental matters. According to Faleiros, they are planting a seed to reap a conscience in the future. Thus, people can understand what is "the Amazon, which regulates the climate, the Amazon of the flying rivers, the Amazon of the greatest biodiversity," he concluded.

La Nación: A Distinguished Position in the Data Journalism Industry

Born as print media in 1870, *La Nación* helped nurture the political power of its founder, Bartolomé Mitre, former President of Argentina (Mercado, 2012). Since then, the newspaper has become a leading national daily newspaper, turning into an agenda-setter and disruptor of innovation in the local media ecosystem. In particular, *La Nación* succeeded in adopting offline-online convergence, becoming the first newspaper to launch a digital version at the national level in 1995. This allowed the organization to gain a solid online presence through its lanacion.com.ar. Another effort in the digital environment is the data team, popularly referred to as LN Data. Founded in 2011, the data unit has always worked hard to provide new ways to produce and interact with news content.

In its endeavors in data journalism, *La Nación* became known for its efforts to engage the public in producing data stories. From analyzing data to transforming audiences into data for its stories, LN Data improved its overall skills, leading to a better relationship with the public. The team quickly achieved international recognition by offering new products to the audience, turning *La Nación* into a data journalism powerhouse in the region (Mazotte, 2017; Palomo, Teruel and Blanco-Castilla, 2019).

In 2019, LN Data was invited to join the alliance ClimateNow (Covering-ClimateNow.org). This cooperation arose from the results of the UN's IPCC, which proposed to increase the media's coverage of the climate crisis and raise awareness of limiting global warming to well below 2 °C (Hertsgaard, 2019). According to Angelica (Momi) Peralta, the organization was "the first in Argentina to join the Climate Now alliance" (February 2020). This experience was fundamental for the team to see the potential of environmental data journalism, which has led to the creation of "LN Naturaleza," a cross-sector editorial brand led by the data unit. It implies that the brand is neither a new team nor a new beat, but it produces content associated with other desks, which could be seen during the observation, as the team was always pitching journalists with ideas or vice versa.

LN Naturaleza produces content on three pillars: climate change, biodiversity, and participation (de-Lima-Santos, 2022). The team built an agenda of content that they want to create throughout the year in each pillar. However, this plan can be modified whenever necessary. For example, it was adjusted to breaking news stories concerning environmental themes, such as the bushfires in Australia[8] and Argentina.[9] In particular, special dates were taken into account in this agenda. The team focused on climate change concerning the ozone layer during September, as the International Day for Preservation of the Ozone Layer is held on the 16th.

On the second pillar, LN Data focuses on biodiversity themes. In August, due to the celebration of National Tree Day on the 29th, the team produced news articles about trees across Argentina. Among these stories, the team used data to explain the growth of Jacarandás—a species of flowering plant native to tropical and subtropical regions of Latin America and the Caribbean—in the city of Buenos Aires (Argentina)[10] and relied on historical data to show the loss of 2.7 million hectares of native forest in the last ten years.[11]

In its third pillar, LN Naturaleza promotes actions toward public participation on environmental topics, such as beach clean-up, plastics recycling, and reforestation. Several news projects have embodied this approach, such as the one in which the data team worked with La Nación Foundation, a newspaper sector dedicated to civic engagement, to plant 150 trees in the city of Buenos Aires that represent the age of the newspaper. This action was recorded using Instagram stories, which featured specialists who used data to talk about the benefits of planting trees. To include the public in this conversation, LN Data also created Instagram filters—one of the most popular augmented reality (AR) applications at present—called "SOS Planeta" (SOS Planet, in English) that was used by the public in the 6D movement. This filter generally had statements against climate change, such as "neither a degree above nor a species to a lesser extent" or "there is no planet B," explained Peralta. As previous studies note (Krøvel, 2012), the idea was to generate online community activism that could lead to real social change. Similarly, this pillar also includes collaboration with NGOs and civil society groups, which seek to defend and promote environmental awareness.

Another critical element of LN Naturaleza's endeavor is the development of cooperative efforts inside and outside of the newsroom. The team works "close to journalists from other desks to produce the stories, as LN Naturaleza is not properly a desk" (Peralta, February 2020). It means that there is a need to pitch other journalists with ideas and vice versa.

On the external level, the team holds meetings with individuals and institutions with environmental concerns, such as open data communities, NGOs, and scholars. During the sessions, I observed that the initial approach serves to understand more about the topic and see if there is a potential collaboration between the parties. In case positive, an agreement is reached by dividing the tasks. In general, these collaborations happen sporadically and involve a particular project or news product, echoing findings in the literature (Heft et al., 2019). For example, the organization invited the members of the Argentine B Corp chapter to understand more about this certification and its relation to environmental topics.

Similarly, the organization brought in former government members for an event called "A Data Day for Energy." During this meeting, the data unit, along with a journalist from the economy desk, spent half-day discussing the renewable energy production and the investments made by the Argentine government, known as RenovAr, an acronym for Argentina Renewable Energy Auctions, projecting to grow 20% renewables sources in the country's matrix by 2025 (IFC, 2018). By working with these professionals, LN Data saw the opportunity to monitor the deployment of solar energy within the framework of RenovAr.

From Data Journalism to AI

Driven by climate change concerns, RenovAr promised to use Argentina's abundant clean energy resources by promoting renewable energy generation. Composed of several phases, the project includes agreements between the state and the private sector. However, getting a bid on an item in an auction does not guarantee delivery within that timeframe. Furthermore, Latin America has historically become well-known for its high risk of corruption (see Lagunes and Svejnar, 2020).

Having that in mind, LN Data made a substantial effort to deploy its first AI project to map the deployment of solar farms in the country. The idea was inspired by other successful projects that used satellite imagery to map large objects on Earth. In 2019, the New Media Research and Training Manager, Florencia Coelho, spent about one year at Stanford to "research the AI-powered solutions in the news media and discovered many projects that were using satellite imagery to conduct investigations" (Coelho, March 2020), such as the "Leprosy of the land" produced by the Ukrainian organization TEXTY, which used satellite images from Microsoft's Bing to detect illegal amber mining in the north of the country.[12]

Similarly, other organizations used satellite imagery to identify solar panels, such as Google's Sunroof project, Stanford's Deep Solar in the US, OpenClimateFix's solar photovoltaic (PV) mapping, and a Polish study from Poznań University. Inspired by them, LN Data decided to use satellite imagery to map solar farms in Argentina. However, it required expertise in implementing computer vision (CV) algorithms that the team did not have. Moreover, the project demanded high computing power due to the size of the country (Argentina is the sixth-largest country per area in the world). To overcome these limitations, the team has contacted some organizations and researchers to better understand the issue and the challenges involved. In one of these conversations, the team met DymaxionLabs, a startup with experience in cloud computing and CV algorithms to identify objects on satellite images. The startup offered LN Data its know-how and computing power to process such a large amount of information. After signing a Memorandum of Understanding (MOU), where they established their roles and responsibilities in this project, LN Data and DymaxionLabs started to work together to conduct this investigation.

To place this in context, DymaxionLabs is a startup specialized in projects using CV, a subset of machine learning (see de-Lima-Santos & Ceron, 2022), which is a subfield of AI dedicated to deducing what is shown in the image. CV models cannot actually see the content of images like a human eye, but they use mathematical algorithms to infer it based on learning from the data provided (Szeliski, 2011). These methods are helpful in quickly classifying and organizing a large number of images and videos, enabling "journalists to source evidence for investigative pieces" (Marconi et al., 2017, p. 14). Until recently, AI had a limited capacity due to technological requirements or process characteristics, a bottleneck constraining its widespread use. In fact, this has changed in recent years due to the reduced costs and popularization of AI capabilities, resulting in better hardware, algorithms, and an abundance of storage and data availability (Castro and New, 2016; Hassaballah and Awad, 2020).

Although these resources are more popular, they are not deployed in newsrooms, as there is a lack of resources and infrastructure for technological innovation (Paulussen, 2016). In this investigation, the team identified 20 of 24 solar farms presented in the list provided by the government, which corroborated that, on average, RenovAr was delivering solar farms as expected.[13] Moreover, the algorithm detected two solar farms that were private installations. In this experiment, LN Data could "see the potential of technology to conduct large-scale investigations, which would not be possible without AI" (Coelho, March 2020).

Conclusion

This chapter discusses how these two organizations embrace data-driven storytelling in environmental reporting. InfoAmazonia, even with the lack of resources and funds, uncovers award-winning stories about the devastating rise in deforestation rates and investigates mining conflicts, gold trafficking, and illicit money flow in the Amazon region (Painter, 2019). By combining innovative approaches, collaboration, and out-of-the-box tools, InfoAmazonia overcomes its limited resources and staff shortages to produce investigative stories that engage in forward-looking discussions about the conservation and threats in the Amazon. Thus, data journalism is essential in this process to bring to light stories that otherwise would not have been told, transforming data into digestible, visual stories.

Similarly, *La Nación* showed how collaboration is vital for the team. LN Naturaleza is an editorial brand dedicated to covering environmental topics, which requires internal and external partners to generate insights. By combining data from different areas of knowledge, the team ensures the audience's engagement and interest in its stories. Furthermore, LN Naturaleza established an agenda that follows special environmental dates to shed more light on this matter as it gains attention. Differently, LN Data strongly invests in new ways to produce data stories, such as the AI-powered investigation using satellite images to detect and check the construction status of solar farms proposed by the government. Even with the challenges faced by LN Data, such as the lack of expertise in CV algorithms, the team resorted to collaborations to deploy a large-scale investigation, showing the potential that AI solutions have for environmental and investigative journalism.

By discussing these two cases, this chapter sheds light on the complexity of the task of raising concerns about the region's environmental threats and the lack of interest and funds necessary for its protection. In this respect, these two organizations present an alternative to traditional environmental reporting by proposing the reliance on environmental data journalism to produce stories that matter, reaching high impact in their societies. Furthermore, these news outlets created compelling and engaging narratives in various formats, such as Twitter bots and infographics.

Thus, this chapter argued that data journalism and AI increase technical capabilities for producing investigative environmental reporting in these organizations. It is not limited to technical relations of production, but also connections governing their productive assets, such as the cooperative work ties and forms of association between the public and data products, and innovative narrative models. To conclude, the intersection of journalism, data, and AI can contribute to this new trend in environmental journalism. Still, it is crucial to consider their dependencies and vulnerabilities, as data and technologies are artificial products subject to bias and error (Tong and Zuo, 2019).

CONDUCTING ENVIRONMENTAL INVESTIGATIONS USING DATA AND AI

If you are interested in conducting your own environmental investigations using data and AI, here's a step-by-step guide to help you get started:

1 **Define your focus**
Begin by identifying a specific environmental issue that you are passionate about. For example, you could focus on deforestation, water pollution, or the impact of climate change on local ecosystems. Choose a region or community that would benefit from greater visibility on the issue.

2 **Gather and understand data sources**

- **Identify reliable data sources**: Look for publicly available environmental datasets such as those from government agencies, NGOs, or academic institutions. Examples include satellite imagery, forest cover data, deforestation, pollution levels, or weather patterns.
- **Use open data platforms**: Governmental institutions provide geospatial data that can be used for environmental reporting, such as Brazil's INPE (National Institute for Space Research) or the USA's NASA (National Aeronautics and Space Administration) These institutions often provide open datasets on deforestation, bushfires, among others.

3 **Tools and software for data visualization**

- **Out-of-the-box tools**: Platforms like Mapbox, Tableau, or Flourish allow you to visualize geographical data and create interactive maps. InfoAmazonia created a similar tool to track and visualize geographic data, allowing storytellers to geo-tag content and make data-driven stories more accessible.

- **Data cleaning**: Tools like Microsoft Excel, Google Sheets, or OpenRefine help clean and organize large datasets. Before analyzing data, ensure it's consistent and free of errors.
- **AI Integration**: If you are working on larger-scale data (such as satellite imagery), look into using AI tools to automate data analysis. Basic AI tools like NotebookLM, PinPoint, AI Studio, Google Vision API, or Python libraries like OpenCV can help process images and extract relevant patterns.

4 **Conduct investigative research**

- **Form hypotheses**: Based on the gathered data, develop hypotheses or questions about the environmental issue or concern. For example, if you notice patterns in deforestation data, hypothesize about potential causes, such as illegal mining or logging.
- **Analyze data**: Use statistical methods to test your hypotheses or answer your questions. For instance, you can calculate the rate of deforestation over time or map out areas most affected by pollution.
- **Interview experts**: Contact local environmentalists, scientists, or journalists to gather insights and validate your findings. These interviews can provide context that raw data may not reveal.

5 **Tell a data-driven story**

- **Study successful projects**: Explore award-winning investigations like "Digging into the Mining Arc" to understand how data and storytelling can be combined. Analyze how they use multimedia elements and data-driven insights to create impactful stories.
- **Craft a narrative**: Use your data to build a compelling story. Environmental journalism benefits from visual storytelling, so think about how you can incorporate maps, infographics, or videos into your reporting.
- **Make it interactive**: Tools like scrollytelling can enhance the user experience. InfoAmazonia frequently uses this technique in its reports on environmental issues.
- **Engage your audience**: Include actionable insights in your story. Suggest ways for your audience to get involved, such as supporting local conservation efforts or advocating for policy changes.

6 **Publishing**

- **Collaborate with media outlets**: If possible, partner with local news organizations or environmental NGOs to publish and disseminate your story. This collaboration can help your work reach a wider audience.

Notes

1 Digging into the Mining Arc. 2018. https://arcominero.infoamazonia.org/?lang=en.
2 The Smugglers' Paradise. 2020. https://smugglersparadise.infoamazonia.org/?lang=en
3 Amazônia Minada. 2020. https://infoamazonia.org/project/amazonia-minada/. Twitter bot. https://twitter.com/amazonia_minada
4 Amazônia Sufocada. 2020. Twitter bot. https://twitter.com/botqueimadas
5 Inhaling Smoke. 2020. https://infoamazonia.org/en/project/inhaling-smoke/
6 Far from ICUs and ventilators, indigenous people from the Amazon try to shield themselves from the virus. 2020. https://infoamazonia.org/en/2020/05/11/distantes-de-utis-e-respiradores-indigenas-da-amazonia-tentam-se-blindar-do-virus/
7 PlenaMata. 2021. https://plenamata.eco/en/
8 The dramatic impact of bushfires in Australia. 2020. https://www.lanacion.com.ar/el-mundo/el-dramatico-impacto-incendios-australia-nid2324960/
9 The country is on fire: 175,000 hectares of forests and wetlands are burned. 2020. https://www.lanacion.com.ar/sociedad/el-pais-llamas-se-quema-area-bosques-nid2432281/
10 Jacarandás: Why are there more and more specimens in the city? 2020. https://www.lanacion.com.ar/buenos-aires/jacarandas-por-que-hay-cada-vez-mas-nid2512696/
11 Argentina lost 2.7 million hectares of native forest in the last ten years. 2020. https://www.lanacion.com.ar/sociedad/en-10-anos-se-deforesto-superficie-mayor-nid2432071/
12 Leprosy of the land. 2019. https://texty.org.ua/d/2018/amber_eng/
13 Artificial intelligence to map solar farms in Argentina. 2020. https://www.lanacion.com.ar/tecnologia/inteligencia-artificial-mapear-parques-solares-argentina-nid2370879/

References

Appelgren, E. (2018) 'An illusion of interactivity', *Journalism Practice*, 12(3), pp. 308–325. https://doi.org/10.1080/17512786.2017.1299032

Appelgren, E. and Jönsson, A.M. (2020) 'Engaging citizens for climate change—Challenges for journalism', *Digital Journalism*, 9(6), pp. 755–772. https://doi.org/10.1080/21670811.2020.1827965

Braun, V., & Clarke, V. (2014). What can "thematic analysis" offer health and wellbeing researchers? *International Journal of Qualitative Studies on Health and Well-Being*, 9(1). https://doi.org/10.3402/qhw.v9.26152

Bryman, A. (2016). *Social research methods*. 5th edn. Oxford: Oxford University Press.

Castro, D. and New, J. (2016) *The Promise of Artificial Intelligence*. Center for Data Innovation, https://www2.datainnovation.org/2016-promise-of-ai.pdf

de-Lima-Santos, M.F. (2022) 'Setting an agenda to tackle environmental issues with data and collaboration', *Journalism Practice*, 16(2–3), pp. 540–560. https://doi.org/10.1080/17512786.2022.2031256

de-Lima-Santos, M.-F., & Ceron, W. (2022). Artificial Intelligence in News Media: Current Perceptions and Future Outlook. *Journalism and Media*, 3(1), pp. 13–26. https://doi.org/10.3390/journalmedia3010002

de-Lima-Santos, M.-F. and Mesquita, L. (2021a) 'The strategic value of data journalism', In Salaverría, R. and de-Lima-Santos, M.-F. (eds.) *Journalism, data and technology in Latin America*. London: Palgrave Macmillan, pp. 97–136. https://doi.org/10.1007/978-3-030-65860-1_4

de-Lima-Santos, M.F. and Mesquita, L. (2021b) 'Data journalism beyond technological determinism', *Journalism Studies*, 22(11), pp. 1416–1435. https://doi.org/10.1080/1461670X.2021.1944279

de-Lima-Santos, M.-F., Schapals, A.K. and Bruns, A. (2021) 'Out-of-the-box versus in-house tools: How are they affecting data journalism in Australia?', *Media International Australia*, 181(1), pp. 152–166. https://doi.org/10.1177/1329878X20961569

Guha, R., & Martinez-Alier, J. (1997). Mahatma Gandhi and the environmental movement. In Rangaranjan, M. (ed.) *Environmental issues India: A reader*. London: Pearson Education.

Hackett, R. A., Forde, S., Gunster, S., & Foxwell-Norton, K. (2017). Introduction: Journalism(s) for climate crisis. In Hackett, R. A., Forde, S., Gunster, S., & Foxwell-Norton, K. (eds.) *Journalism and Climate Crisis*, pp. 1–19. London: Routledge. https://doi.org/10.4324/9781315668734-1

Hassaballah, M. and Awad, A.I. (2020) *Deep learning in computer vision*. 1st edn. Boca Raton, FL: CRC Press.

Heft, A., Alfter, B., & Pfetsch, B. (2019). Transnational journalism networks as drivers of Europeanisation. *Journalism*, 20(9), pp. 1183–1202. https://doi.org/10.1177/1464884917707675

Hermida, A. and Young, M.L. (2019) *Data journalism and the regeneration of news*. 1st edn. London: Routledge.

Hertsgaard, M. (2019) Covering climate change now signs on over 170 news outlets. Retrieved February 24th, 2021, Columbia Journalism Review, from https://www.cjr.org/covering_climate_now/covering-climate-now-170-outlets.php

Howarth, M. (2012) 'Participatory politics, environmental journalism and newspaper campaigns', *Journalism Studies*, 13(2), pp. 210–225.

IFC. (2018) *RenovAr (Argentina): Scaling 'Express Edition.'* Retrieved from https://www.ifc.org/wps/wcm/connect/industry_ext_content/ifc_external_corporate_site/infrastructure/resources/scaling+infra+-+renovar+-+argentina

Intergovernmental Panel on Climate Change (IPCC). (2022). *Climate change 2022: Impacts, adaptation, and vulnerability. Contribution of Working Group II to the Sixth Assessment Report of the Intergovernmental Panel on Climate Change* (Pörtner, H.-O., Roberts, D. C., Tignor, M., Poloczanska, E. S., Mintenbeck, K., Alegría, A., Craig, M., Langsdorf, S., Löschke, S., Möller, V., Okem, A., & Rama, B. (eds.). Cambridge University Press. https://doi.org/10.1017/9781009325844

Kahn, M.E. (2007) 'Environmental disasters as risk regulation catalysts? The role of Bhopal, Chernobyl, Exxon Valdez, love canal, and three Mile island in shaping U.S. environmental law', *Journal of Risk and Uncertainty*, 35(1), pp. 17–43. https://doi.org/10.1007/s11166-007-9016-7

Koop, F. (2020) Environmental journalism in Latin America. In Sachsman, D.B. and Valenti, J.M. (eds.) *Routledge handbook of environmental journalism*. 1st edn. pp. 383–391. London: Routledge. https://doi.org/10.4324/9781351068406-42

Kostelnick, C. (2019). *Humanizing visual design*. London: Routledge. https://doi.org/10.4324/9781315114620

Kovarik, B. (2020) The rise of environmental journalism in Asia, Africa, and Latin America. In Sachsman, D.B. and Valenti, J.M. (eds.) *Routledge handbook of environmental journalism*. 1st edn. pp. 52–69. London: Routledge. https://doi.org/10.4324/9781351068406-5

Krøvel, R. (2012). Setting the agenda on environmental news in Norway: NGOs and newspapers. *Journalism Studies*, 13(2), 259–276. https://doi.org/10.1080/1461670X.2011.646402

Kunova, M. (2020) Bloomberg Media invests in climate reporting, launches new brand. Retrieved May 29th, 2020, from https://www.journalism.co.uk/news/bloomberg-media-heavily-invests-in-climate-reporting-launches-new-brand/s2/a750852/

Lagunes, P. and Svejnar, J. (eds.) (2020) *Corruption and the Lava Jato scandal in Latin America*. Routledge.

Marconi, F., Siegman, A. and Machine Journalist. (2017) *The future of augmented journalism: A guide for newsrooms in the age of smart machines. AP insights.* New York. Retrieved from https://jeanetteabrahamsen.com/wp-content/uploads/2017/09/ap_insights_the_future_of_augmented_journalism.pdf

Mazotte, N. (2017). How the Argentinian daily La Nación became a data journalism powerhouse in Latin America. *Nieman Journalism Lab.* https://www.niemanlab.org/2017/04/how-the-argentinian-daily-la-nacion-became-a-data-journalism-powerhouse-in-latin-america/

McGinn, M. (2019, September 13) *Time magazine devoted an entire issue to climate change – again.* Grist. https://grist.org/article/time-magazine-devoted-an-entire-issue-to-climate-change-again/

Mercado, M.T. (2012) 'Media representations of climate change in the Argentinean press', *Journalism Studies*, 13(2), pp. 193–209. https://doi.org/10.1080/1461670X.2011.646397

Moser, S.C. and Dilling, L. (2007) Toward the social tipping point: Creating a climate for change. In Moser, S. C. and Dilling, L. (eds.) *Creating a climate for change.* 1st edn. pp. 491–516. Cambridge: Cambridge University Press.

Painter, J. (2019) 'Climate change journalism: Time to adapt', *Environmental Communication*, 13(3), pp. 424–429. https://doi.org/10.1080/17524032.2019.1573561

Palomo, B., Teruel, L. and Blanco-Castilla, E. (2019) 'Data journalism projects based on user-generated content. How *La Nacion* data transforms active audience into staff', *Digital Journalism*, 7(9), pp. 1270–1288. https://doi.org/10.1080/21670811.2019.1626257

Paulussen, S. (2016). Innovation in the newsroom. In T. Witschge, C. W. Anderson, D. Domingo, & A. Hermida (eds.), *The SAGE handbook of digital journalism* (1st edn), pp. 192–206. London: SAGE. https://doi.org/10.4135/9781473957909.n13

Raftopoulos, M. (2017) 'Contemporary debates on social-environmental conflicts, extractivism and human rights in Latin America', *International Journal of Human Rights*, 21(4), pp. 387–404. https://doi.org/10.1080/13642987.2017.1301035

Requejo-Alemán, J. L., & Lugo-Ocando, J. (2014). Assessing the sustainability of Latin American investigative non-profit journalism. *Journalism Studies*, 15(5), pp. 522–532. https://doi.org/10.1080/1461670X.2014.885269

Salovaara, I. (2016) 'Participatory maps: Digital cartographies and the new ecology of journalism', *Digital Journalism*, 4(7), pp. 827–837. https://doi.org/10.1080/21670811.2016.1173519

Segel, E., & Heer, J. (2010). Narrative visualization: Telling stories with data. *IEEE Transactions on Visualization and Computer Graphics*, 16(6), 1139–1148. https://doi.org/10.1109/tvcg.2010.179

Szeliski, R. (2011) *Computer vision.* London: Springer London.

Tong, J. and Zuo, L. (2019) 'The inapplicability of objectivity: Understanding the work of data journalism', *Journalism Practice*, 15(2), pp. 153–169. https://doi.org/10.1080/17512786.2019.1698974.

Wormer, H. (2018) Mind the statistics gap: Science journalism as a bridge between data and journalism. In Nguyen, A. (ed.) *News, numbers and public opinion in a data-driven world.* 1st edn. pp. 226–241. Bloomsbury Academic.

9

INVESTIGATIVE JOURNALISM AND AI

Paul Bradshaw

Introduction

Investigative journalists have been among the earliest adopters of artificial intelligence (AI) in the newsroom, and pioneered some of its most compelling—and award-winning—applications (Amponsah and Atianashie, 2024). Investigative journalism's close relationship with data journalism and open source intelligence (OSINT) provides fertile ground for experimentation with AI, and the explosion of *generative* AI has opened up further territory for innovation (Villa, 2023).

Although there is no widely accepted definition of the term (Russell, Norvig and Chang, 2022; Wang, 2019), within journalism "artificial intelligence" has been used to refer to a range of technologies whose functions range from classifying documents to the generation of video or images. But the technology has many branches, often with their own applications and challenges.

Tools such as ChatGPT and Google's Gemini, for example, use a form of AI known as *large language models* (LLMs). These are part of the wider field of *generative AI*, which includes image generation tools such as DALL-E and Midjourney, video generation tools such as OpenAI's Sora and audio tools including Meta's AudioCraft. These models are trained on large datasets of images, video or audio, to build media by essentially *predicting* each word, pixel, or sound as it writes, "draws" or composes. That prediction is what gives an appearance of intelligence, but it doesn't mean that the result is always going to be factually correct. Factual inaccuracies are such a recurring problem that a specific term has been coined to describe them: "hallucinations" (O'Brien, 2023).

Generative AI, in turn, is part of the branch of AI known as "deep learning", which is itself a branch of the wider field of *machine learning*. Machine

DOI: 10.4324/9781003478157-14

learning involves training an algorithm to predict, classify, or cluster inputs into associated groups. By 2018 this form of AI was already being used by three quarters of "digital leaders" in one survey for purposes ranging from content recommendation to fact-checking (Newman, 2018), and within investigative journalism specifically by 2024 machine learning was being used by two of the 15 winners of the Pulitzer Prize (Deck, 2024).

The two most common ways to train an algorithm are known as *supervised* and *unsupervised learning*. Unsupervised learning involves letting the algorithm cluster data into any patterns it identifies, and it needs very little information about that data, which makes it a powerful way of identifying groups of related documents or words, for example. Supervised learning, in contrast, requires training data which has been labelled in some way. This makes it more useful for classifying new data (based on how the training data was labelled) or making predictions (based on relationships it identifies between differently labelled data).

This chapter will outline a series of recurring investigative journalism scenarios within which AI technologies have been applied, before critically analysing the issues that those applications raise, from accuracy and bias to transparency, practicality and technical challenges. Conclusions and recommendations for further developments are then made.

The Use of AI in Investigative Journalism

AI's wide range of applications have been used in all stages of journalism, from idea generation and alerts, to story research, production, publication, distribution, feedback and archiving (Gibbs, 2024; Hanson et al, 2017). But within investigative journalism specifically, it has applications in at least nine scenarios. These include:

1 Establishing a problem—or its scale.
2 Finding the needles in the haystack: reducing the scale of an editorial project.
3 Modelling and predictions.
4 Algorithmic accountability: unmasking a system.
5 Text-as-data: natural language processing.
6 Extraction, matching and cleaning.
7 AI in the sky: satellite and other imagery.
8 Sensors and acoustic-based machine learning.
9 New storytelling forms and outputs.

Establishing the Scale of a Problem and Finding Needles in Haystacks

When the data journalism team at Swiss broadcaster Schweizer Radio und Fernsehen (SRF) decided to investigate the use of fake followers by social media influencers, they turned to machine learning. The team created a dataset of

Instagram accounts classified as either fake or real, and used this to train an algorithm that could be applied to millions of followers of Swiss influencers (Scurrell and Grossenbacher, 2017). The results established that the practice of buying fake followers was rife in the industry, and, for the first time, the scale of the problem empowered reporters to question those with the most fake followers.

A year earlier, BuzzFeed had used the same techniques to establish just how widespread "spy planes" were in US airspace (Aldhous, 2017) and how they behaved, including the fact that they seemed to be circling mosques and areas with large Muslim populations (Aldhous and Seife, 2016). The team had already reported on individual instances of spy planes, and machine learning provided a way to scale that up.

Machine learning's ability to classify can be especially useful for filtering: when the Atlanta Journal-Constitution wanted to establish the scale of doctors being allowed to continue to practise after being found guilty of sexual misconduct, for example, it used it to reduce a set of 100,000 documents to around 6,000 that were likely to relate to that offence (Atlanta Journal-Constitution, 2016).

The potential scale or location of future problems can be established by using machine learning's ability to predict future events. In the award-winning series *Waves of Abandonment,* reporters had compiled a wide-ranging database on oil in Texas and saw an opportunity to use it to identify potential problems. Senior data reporter Clayton Aldern says, "This was a classification problem: which wells might be abandoned in the next couple years. And it's a perfect question for machine learning" (Sengul-Jones, 2021)

The model allowed the reporters to write a story about the potential cost to taxpayers of the coming problem. Historically, this type of story would have relied on academics deciding to identify the same issue and conducting analysis over many years, but machine learning made it possible for reporters to take the initiative over a shorter timescale.

Similar techniques were used to investigate repossessions (Eye on Ohio, Crebs and Walinchus, 2021) and potentials Ebola outbreaks. In the latter, a model developed by ProPublica was able to identify deforestation as a major risk factor and highlight Nigeria as being particularly at risk (Chen, Shaw and Hwang, 2023).

Algorithmic Accountability

AI is often used to shine a spotlight on algorithms in wider society—what has become known as "algorithmic accountability" reporting:

> What we generally lack as a public is clarity about how algorithms exercise their power over us. With that clarity comes an increased ability to publicly debate and dialogue the merits of any particular algorithmic power
>
> *(Diakopoulos, 2014)*

ProPublica's series "Machine Bias" (propublica.org/series/machine-bias) is one of the longest-running and most high-profile examples of algorithmic accountability reporting: between 2015 and 2022, it investigated biases in software used to inform criminal sentencing, uncovered discrimination in insurance premiums, and revealed Amazon's bias towards its own products. Elsewhere, the collaborative journalism project Lighthouse Reports used similar techniques to investigate algorithmic profiling used by Dutch local government:

> The digital equivalent of fraud inspectors knocking on every door in a certain area and looking at every person's records in an attempt to identify cases of fraud, while no such scrutiny is applied to those living in better off areas
>
> *(Schot et al, 2024)*

While machine learning was used in all these projects, it is not essential: four approaches to investigating AI identified in one report on "Black Box Reporting" include the use of Freedom of Information requests, analysing the outputs of automated systems, and interviews and documents (BR AI + Automation Lab, 2023).

Text-as-data: Extraction, Matching and Cleaning

One branch of AI, which often uses machine learning, is Natural Language Processing (NLP), a technology that allows computers to appear to understand language. As well as facilitating translation, summarisation and optical character recognition (OCR)—which extracts text from images such as scanned PDFs—NLP includes a number of techniques that have applications within investigative journalism.

Sentiment analysis, for example, is a branch of NLP used to classify textual material as likely to be positive, negative, or neutral. A Washington Post investigation into audits of an international development agency used this technique to compare language that was removed from agency audits before publication, identifying that "more than 400 negative references were removed from the audits between the draft and final versions" (Higham and Rich, 2014).

Topic modelling is an NLP technique using unsupervised learning to take a text-based dataset and classify it into a specified number of "clusters" based on shared language. This technique was used by Jeff Kao to identify suspicious patterns within millions of submissions to a public consultation on net neutrality, providing evidence of an automated disinformation campaign (Kao, 2017), and also by AP journalists to identify accidents in schools involving law enforcement officers and educators' firearms, from 140,000 incident reports (Associated Press, 2018; Marconi, Siegman and Machine Journalist, 2017)

A more widely used application of NLP in investigations is *named entity recognition* or *entity extraction*. Journalists dealing with large document caches or leaks use this technology to generate lists of the people, places, organisations and key concepts within documents, and more quickly navigate between mentions of a target entity, saving large amounts of time in an investigation. Entity extraction is a feature of journalist tools, DocumentCloud (Ibrahimovic, 2024) and Google Pinpoint (Meyer, 2021), and is also built into the cuttings service Nexis. Many of these tools also use OCR to unlock text and data published in PDFs, facilitating quicker *knowledge base construction* by journalists (Stray, 2019a).

Matching separate datasets for knowledge base construction might also use AI technologies. One investigation into property tax evasion, for example, used Locality Sensitive Hashing (LSH)—a branch of unsupervised machine learning which groups together similar records—to match property data with utilities data (Roberts, 2019). And the Entity-Focused Data System project (Ernsthausen and Deng, 2015) uses a branch of NLP called *probabilistic parsing* (Manning and Schütze, 1999) to clean data on names and addresses so that they are easier to match across different datasets. Similar parsing and cleaning have been done with generative AI tools (Rocha, 2023).

Satellite Journalism, Object Detection and Sensors

A particular use for machine learning has been found in the growing field of satellite journalism: stories about illegal mining operations, human rights violations, sanctions breaches and war crimes have all drawn on this application of AI to find a different kind of "needle in the haystack".

In these cases, a separate branch of machine learning is involved: *object detection*. This involves training a machine learning algorithm to identify objects within images. In 2023, for example, the New York Times visual investigations team used this technique to look for evidence of Israel's use of 2,000-pound bombs in southern Gaza (Desk, 2024).

Audio is a relatively under-explored source for AI in investigative journalism. Environmental nonprofit Rainforest Connection, however, has pioneered the use of machine learning with acoustic monitoring in remote areas to detect illegal logging (Coldeway, 2018) and measure a number of different impacts of climate change (Johnson, Jumail and Salgado-Lynn, 2023).

Audio material can be used to train a machine learning algorithm in the same way as text or media, opening up the potential for using AI to trawl through audio recordings to identify a particular speaker or pick out certain categories of event. At Spanish language media group PRISA, these techniques were used to create VerificAudio, an experimental tool to detect audio deepfakes (Novoa, 2024).

New Forms and Sources of Engagement

While AI's most obvious uses may relate to handling large amounts of information, it has also made it possible to explore new ways of telling and distributing stories. The Brazilian watchdog project *Operation Serenata de Amor* (serenata.

ai), for example, uses machine learning to monitor politicians' expenses, but by linking it to an automated Twitter account, @RosieDaSerenata, the journalists also attempt to scale up the process of involving the audience and seeking a response from the politician involved when a suspicious claim is identified. "We are living in a time in which congresspeople argue with robots on Twitter," says one of the journalists involved in the project. "We made democracy more accessible. People can ask for information about public expenditures straight to the politician and get the answer in a tweet" (Vilanova, 2017).

Personalisation or "versioning" stories for different audiences, or from different inputs, is also made easier by AI technologies, including *Natural Language Generation* (NLG) (Diakapoulos, 2019, p. 126) and generative AI. More advanced NLG might involve a level of *Natural Language Understanding* (NLU), selecting and extracting information from source material based on an algorithmically-informed judgement about importance and relevance, or based on input from *computer vision* models, which can interpret images.

Analysis

Having outlined the range of ways in which AI has been applied to journalistic investigations, some clear challenges emerge. The most basic is practicality: not only do AI technologies such as machine learning require a certain combination of skill sets and the time and resources to bring those together, but also the availability of a sufficient quality and quantity of data to train models (Dörr, 2016; Stray, 2019b) and the computational infrastructure to run them (Sengul-Jones, 2021).

These practical challenges sometimes lead newsrooms to outsource part or all of the projects involving AI, or partner with external parties. The New York Times's investigation into bomb craters in Gaza, for example, used a third-party object detection platform, partly because of the computing power required. "Satellite images can easily surpass several hundred megabytes or even a couple gigabytes," reporter Ishaan Jhaveri explained. "Any local development work on satellite images would naturally be clunky and time-consuming" (Desk, 2024). And while the International Consortium of Investigative Journalists "doesn't outsource the work of training data to ensure accuracy" (Sengul-Jones, 2021), they did use a machine learning tool called Snorkel to help classify text and images, while the OSINT platform Bellingcat has used the Ship Detection Tool—a machine learning algorithm run on Google Earth Engine—in its investigations (Ballinger, 2023).

The use of third-party tools such as Google's Pinpoint, Cloud Document AI and Gemini, and OpenAI's ChatGPT, raises issues around independence and power (de-Lima-Santos, 2022; Whittaker, 2021), and—where editorial information is fed into such tools—information security, copyright, privacy and data protection (Cools and Diakopoulos, 2024). Many organisations' guidelines, for example, prohibit "entering confidential information, trade secrets, or personal data into AI tools" (de-Lima-Santos, Yeung and Dodds, 2024).

In some cases manual methods of classification may be quicker than an automated approach: most of the spy planes identified in Peter Aldhous's story for BuzzFeed, for example, could have been identified through data analysis while one analysis of investigative journalism projects concludes that "many document sets in journalism are simply too small to benefit from AI methods" (Stray, 2019b). Alternative, quicker, approaches to machine learning listed by the New York Times's Rachel Shorey include: "making a collection of text easily searchable; asking a subject area expert what they actually care about and building a simple filter or keyword alert; [and] using standard statistical sampling techniques" (Bouchart, 2018). In some projects, however, the time and cost of development might be amortised over multiple stories, such as the Norwegian fact-checking outlet Faktisk Verifiserbar, which worked with AI researchers to develop a language identification tool and a tank identification tool (Kahn, 2024).

Accuracy: Training Models and Human Oversight

The quality and quantity of data used to train AI models has a direct impact on the quality of the results obtained—a principle summed up in the mantra "Garbage In Garbage Out" (GIGO). This includes the classification of training data: in the Pulitzer-winning investigation "Missing in Chicago", a machine learning tool called Judy was trained on police misconduct records labelled by 200 volunteer workers from the community. Data director Trina Reynolds-Tyler emphasised the "lived experience" of the volunteers, which "an outsourced data labeler could not [have. Machine learning projects should] understand the value of embedding in the community they are reporting on, and [ground] their data work in real places and real people" (Deck, 2024).

A 100% accuracy is rarely achieved in a model. Indeed, an extremely high accuracy can be a sign of "*overfitting*" (whereby a model fits its training data too closely and so performs poorly when tested on other data). An "*underfit*" model, in contrast, performs poorly on both training data *and* testing data, often as a result of a simple model based on too little data and/or too little training. A successful algorithm will be neither (Russell, Norvig and Chang, 2022).

Feature engineering (choosing the facets of the data that the model will use) is key in shaping the accuracy of any machine learning model (Bouchart, 2018), and specialist knowledge of the field can be key to choosing the most relevant features, as demonstrated by ProPublica's consultation of scientists in their modelling of Ebola outbreaks (Chen, Shaw and Hwang, 2023).

The levels of accuracy needed can vary depending on the purpose of the model. 90% accuracy in extracting information from PDFs disclosing political advertising spending on TV and cable, for example, is described as "not high enough for production use" in one paper (Stray, 2019a), but a less accurate tool developed to identify claims on social media that needed fact-checking was seen as successful because it reduced the time spent monitoring tweets by 80% (Larraz, 2023).

Human oversight on this and the resulting data is key in accurate use of AI, and a recurring theme both in news organisations' guidelines on the use of AI (Becker, 2023; de-Lima-Santos, Yeung and Dodds, 2024), and in concerns expressed by journalists (Cools and Diakopoulos, 2024).

For those models used over a longer timescale, or those involving predictions, that oversight should include monitoring: when the Atlanta Journal-Constitution created a model in 2015 to forecast whether bills would pass the Georgia legislature, for example, the performance of the model was regularly reviewed in public (Ernsthausen, 2016).

Such transparency and accountability are encouraged in many guidelines, both as a further protection against errors and as a means of maintaining trust (Becker, 2023; de-Lima-Santos, Yeung and Dodds, 2024). But this is problematic: "Algorithms challenge this goal," guidance from the Catalan Press Council notes, "because of the opacity involved in the way they make automated decisions" (Ventura Pocino, 2021).

That opacity can present problems on two separate fronts: *explainability* and *interpretability* (Russell, Norvig and Chang, 2022): a model might be explainable (you can explain *what* it does and *why* it arrives at a certain output) but not interpretable (you do not know *how* it does that).

Explainability and interpretability can determine the choice of technology: many investigations opt for a "decision tree" or "random forest" algorithm over more powerful "neural network" or "deep learning" approaches because of interpretability (they also don't need as much data). One ProPublica investigation into political emails, for example, used a decision tree-based algorithm "because [they] produce a human-readable tree of partitions of the data" (Larson, 2012).

Regulations such as the European General Data Protection Regulation (GDPR) now require AI systems to include explanations, and so even less interpretable models might require an explanation. The audio deepfake detection tool VerificAudio, for example, indicates to journalists which audio attributes were a factor in the resulting score (Novoa, 2024).

A particular editorial challenge is presented by the fact that machine learning models produce estimates or likelihoods, rather than specific figures, analogous to reporting on predictions or surveys where there is a margin of error (Diakopoulos, 2022). Journalists can communicate the uncertainty in the data accurately in a number of ways: through qualifying language ("about a quarter", "estimated to be"), attribution ("according to the algorithm") (Bradshaw, 2019), or through further manual confirmation or investigation of the results. Even confirmation means that false negatives (matches that should have been identified but weren't) will be missed, and so qualified language will still be needed to report that the real figure is "likely to be higher".

Diversity, Bias and Fairness

Artificial intelligence's tendency towards bias and diversity issues is often the focus of algorithmic accountability reporting, but these also present a challenge for reporters using AI. Categories of bias identified in one paper include: biased labelling or features; a biased objective; homogenisation bias (where the output from one model is used for future models); active bias (where data is made up); and unanticipated machine decisions (where a lack of context leads to "untenable answers" (Das et al, 2021)).

Bias is also a consideration when collecting data: minorities are typically underrepresented in datasets, leading to selection bias and lower accuracy in relation to those groups (O'Brien et al, 2022) and in testing (if a model is not tested with diverse inputs or monitored for bias). LLMs, for example, have much poorer performance with regard to non-English languages and non-Western contexts (Kahn, 2024), as these represent a much smaller part of both the training data and of testing (OpenAI, 2023), as does material authored by women (Kuntz and Silva, 2023). For those creating their own models, there is a similar lower availability of labelled datasets and research in those languages and contexts (Adelani, 2022; de-Lima-Santos, Yeung and Dodds, 2024).

Identifying and measuring these biases is an important consideration in ensuring "*fairness*" in an algorithm. This concept can involve multiple criteria which may conflict with each other, from individual and group fairness (being treated similarly to other individuals and groups), to equal outcome (there should be parity in the outcomes for different demographic groups), opportunity (parity regardless of demographic) and impact (both positive and negative) (Russell, Norvig and Chang, 2022).

With third-party generative AI, journalists have no control over the training material that has been used or the way that the model was trained. Guidelines produced by Birmingham City University's Sir Lenny Henry Centre for Media Diversity therefore advise:

> Journalists should explicitly seek, through their prompts, for Generative AI to draw on source material written and/or owned by different demographics. Where this is not possible journalists should use prompts to obtain lists of experts and recognised commentators on specific issues from different backgrounds
>
> *(Sir Lenny Henry Centre for Media Diversity, 2023)*

Even when it comes to custom machine learning models, although some news organisation guidelines on AI specify that the development should involve a diversity of people and cultures, few make reference to the need for the same consideration with regard to models' training material (Gibbs, 2024). Exceptions include the Guardian's reference to "the dangers of bias embedded within generative tools and their underlying training sets" (Viner and Bateson, 2023) and Bayerischer Rundfunk (BR), which

> [Discusses] the "integrity and quality of the training data" as a matter of principle, even for internal developments … BR is the only organization to go further than addressing only the quality of the training data, also looking at the quality of the other data with which the model works
>
> *(Becker, 2023)*

A further issue related to diversity is raised by AI's potential to produce personalised content. Guidelines advise that such content "may clash with the mission of offering a diversity of information to the public" (Ventura Pocino, 2021), and that it "should respect information integrity and promote a shared understanding of relevant facts and viewpoints" (Reporters Without Borders, 2023)

Conclusion

What is striking from the exploration of AI in this chapter is both the range of technologies and the ways in which those have been used within investigative journalism. And this does not include the range of ways in which investigative journalists are using *generative* AI tools, in particular for more routine tasks, such as idea generation and research, planning, editorial feedback (e.g. identifying jargon and potential bias in story drafts), publication and distribution. Already, a "second generation" of generative AI tools and "custom GPTs" based on ChatGPT has emerged for journalistic use (Reilley, 2024). Examples include the document analysis tool EmbedAI; AI OSINT (investigating domains and emails); Fintool (company data); and AI Search Whisperer (for forming advanced search queries). Journalists who use programming languages in their investigations are also likely to accelerate their work through the use of generative AI tools that make coding easier (Cools and Diakopoulos, 2024).

While this chapter has identified a number of challenges for news organisations using AI in investigations, from accuracy and fairness to resources and explainability, one area which requires further research is the more subtle impact on the working process—and the new work created alongside the efficiencies: the work of finding specific AI tools and learning how to use them; breaking down tasks into AI-amenable steps, or preparing material for AI tools; effective prompt-writing; and editing and checking the results. Monitoring developments and changes in models is likely to become more important, as "the behavior of the 'same' LLM service can change substantially in a relatively short amount of time" (Chen, Zaharia and Zou, 2023). "AI can shape relationships between people as well," notes one report into the technology, describing one respondent as saying, "instead of asking a colleague for help with a heading, I always ask ChatGPT first" (Gibbs, 2024).

This wide range of applications and contexts suggests that the idea of "AI assisted journalism" will eventually come to be considered too vague a term to be useful, just as "computer assisted reporting" came to be seen as dated and redundant earlier this century (Howard, 2014). As literacy in the field increases, research and industry discussion may need to revolve around more specific fields and terms: "machine learning-based journalism", for example, or "investigating with NLP" or "custom GPTs in visual investigations". We should expect a deeper and more critical understanding of artificial intelligence in general as the power of AI is better scrutinised in all aspects of our lives—a process in which journalists will perform a central role.

CLASSROOM EXERCISE

One of the most common uses of AI is to find the "needle in the haystack" or to get an overview of a large set of documents. Generative AI (genAI) tools also provide an easy way to experiment with this application. This exercise allows you to see this in practice and assess potential problems and risks.

1 You will need a collection of documents that a journalist would use to find a story. One example would be financial reports for the UK's royal family: these can be downloaded from royal.uk/media-centre/financial-reports by going into each year—download files for multiple years, or you will find copies at github.com/paulbradshaw/genAI/tree/main/docsfornotebooklm/royalfinances.
2 Open Google's NotebookLM (notebooklm.google.com) and create a "new notebook".
3 Upload your documents to the notebook.
4 Try the following prompt in the chat box at the bottom: *"List the names of the ten people that appear most often in these documents, what their roles are, and where they appear".*
5 Evaluate the response:

   a How might this be useful journalistically? What steps will you need next as a journalist? What other information?
   b How can you check that the responses are accurate and truthful? (Generative AI sometimes "hallucinates" information that doesn't exist. Note that the page states, *"NotebookLM may still sometimes give inaccurate responses, so you may want to confirm any facts independently."*).
   c What is happening here is called "entity extraction": identifying parts of the text that meet the "pattern" of a person's name. Think of reasons why a person might not be identified by this process.

6 Prompt-writing is a skill that takes practice, reading, and experimentation to develop. Try the following follow-up prompts:

  a *"Format the results as a table"* (specifying the format of the output in your prompt can make it easier to explore the information).

  b *"You are a journalist for a national broadcaster in the UK. Make a bullet list of five potential news story leads from these documents."* (Specifying the role of the AI can make results more relevant to your needs. This prompt requires the model to "translate" the text into a list of leads—the quality and accuracy of each translation will vary.)

  c *"Your audience is particularly interested in environmental issues. Make a new bullet list of story leads"* (specifying audience and/or subject can help generate more focused results).

7 Read about the critical issues surrounding the use of generative AI tools in journalism, particularly bias, hallucinations, information security, and environmental impact. Identify practical steps you can take to address these for this project and others (including not using genAI in some circumstances).

8 Read about "prompt design", the skill of writing prompts. Try new prompts based on what you learn.

Note: If NotebookLM is not available, try uploading your documents to AI Studio (aistudio.google.com), Claude.ai or ChatGPT (or search for "NotebookLM replacements"), and compare the results.

References

Adelani, D.I. (2022) Natural language processing for African languages, dissertation, Universitat des Saarlandes. https://dx.doi.org/10.22028/D291-40305

Aldhous, P. (2017) BuzzFeed News Trained A Computer To Search For Hidden Spy Planes. This Is What We Found. GitHub, August 2017 https://buzzfeednews.github.io/2017-08-spy-plane-finder/

Aldhous, P. and Seife, C. (2016) See Maps Showing Where FBI Planes Are Watching From Above, BuzzFeed News, April 6 2016, https://www.buzzfeednews.com/article/peteraldhous/spies-in-the-skies

Amponsah, P.N. and Atianashie, A.M. (2024) 'Navigating the new frontier: A comprehensive review of AI in journalism', *Advances in Journalism and Communication*, 12, pp. 1–17. https://www.scirp.org/journal/paperinformation?paperid=130552

Associated Press. (2018) Correction: Guns in School-Accidents story, AP, May 7 2018, https://apnews.com/general-news-08659d568d7448a6b500f27d98a6c3a6

Atlanta Journal-Constitution. (2016) How the Doctors & Sex Abuse project came about, Atlanta Journal-Constitution, July 2016, https://doctors.ajc.com/about_this_investigation/

Ballinger, O. (2023) Grain Trail: Tracking Russia's Ghost Ships with Satellite Imagery, Bellingcat, May 11 2023, https://www.bellingcat.com/news/2023/05/11/grain-trail-tracking-russias-ghost-ships-with-satellite-imagery/

BBC. (n.d.) Guidance: The use of Artificial Intelligence, https://www.bbc.co.uk/editorialguidelines/guidance/use-of-artificial-intelligence/, no date. Accessed May 20 2024

Becker, K.B. (2023) 'New game, new rules: An investigation into editorial guidelines for dealing with artificial intelligence in the newsroom', *Journalism Research*, 6(2). https://journalistik.online/en/paper-en/new-game-new-rules/

Bouchart, M. (2018) Discussing the ethics, challenges, and best practices of machine learning in journalism, Data Journalism Awards, June 25 2018, https://medium.com/data-journalism-awards/discussing-the-ethics-challenges-and-best-practices-of-machine-learning-in-journalism-72af0ce40632

Bradshaw, P. (2019) If we are using AI in journalism we need better guidelines on reporting uncertainty, Online Journalism Blog, May 23 2019, https://onlinejournalismblog.com/2019/05/23/ai-in-journalism-guidelines-on-reporting-uncertainty/

BR AI + Automation Lab. (2023) Black Box Reporting - How Journalism Can Report on AI and Algorithms, BR AI + Automation Lab, 21 December 2023, https://interaktiv.br.de/paper/AI-Automation-Lab_Blackbox-Reporting_EN.pdf

Cools, H., & Diakopoulos, N. (2024). Uses of Generative AI in the newsroom: Mapping journalists' Perceptions of perils and possibilities. *Journalism Practice*, 1–19. https://doi.org/10.1080/17512786.2024.2394558

Chen, C., Shaw, A. and Hwang, I. (2023) How We Used Machine Learning to Investigate Where Ebola May Strike, ProPublica, August 8 2023, https://www.propublica.org/article/how-propublica-used-machine-learning-investigate-where-ebola

Chen, L., Zaharia, M. and Zou, J. (2023) How is ChatGPT's behavior changing over time? Arxiv preprint, October 31 2023, https://arxiv.org/abs/2307.09009

Coldeway, D. (2018) Rainforest Connection enlists machine learning to listen for loggers and jaguars in the Amazon, TechCrunch, March 23 2018, https://techcrunch.com/2018/03/23/rainforest-connection-enlists-machine-learning-to-listen-for-loggers-and-jaguars-in-the-amazon/

Das, S., Donini, M., Gelman, J., Haas, K., Hardt, M., Katzman, J., Kenthapadi, K., Larroy, P., Yilmaz, P. and Zafar, M.B. (2021) 'Fairness measures for machine learning in finance', *The Journal of Financial Data Science*, 3(4), pp. 33–64. https://doi.org/10.3905/jfds.2021.1.075

Deck, A. (2024) For the first time, two Pulitzer winners disclosed using AI in their reporting, NiemanLab, May 9, 2024, https://www.niemanlab.org/2024/05/for-the-first-time-two-pulitzer-winners-disclosed-using-ai-in-their-reporting/

de-Lima-Santos, M.F. (2022) 'Artificial intelligence in news media: Current perceptions and future outlook', *Journalism and Media*, 3(1), pp. 13–26. https://www.mdpi.com/2673-5172/3/1/2

de-Lima-Santos, M.F., Yeung, W.N. and Dodds, T. (2024) Guiding the Way: A Comprehensive Examination of AI Guidelines in Global Media, arXiv preprint, May 7 2024. https://doi.org/10.48550/arXiv.2405.04706

Desk, A. (2024) For the first time, two Pulitzer winners disclosed using AI in their reporting, NiemanLab, May 9 2024, https://www.niemanlab.org/2024/05/for-the-first-time-two-pulitzer-winners-disclosed-using-ai-in-their-reporting/

Diakopoulos, N. (2014) 'Algorithmic accountability reporting: On the investigation of black boxes', *Tow Center for Digital Journalism*. https://doi.org/10.7916/D8ZK5TW2

Diakopoulos, N. (2019) *Automating the news: How algorithms are rewriting the media*. Cambridge, Massachusetts: Harvard University Press.

Diakopoulos, N. (2022) 'Predictive journalism: On the role of computational prospection in news media', *Tow Center for Digital Journalism*. https://dx.doi.org/10.2139/ssrn.4092033

Dörr, K.N. (2016) 'Mapping the field of algorithmic journalism', *Digital Journalism*, 4(6), pp. 700–722. https://doi.org/10.1080/21670811.2015.1096748

Ernsthausen, J. (2016) Predict-a-bill in 2015: how'd we do? AJC News Apps, January 27 2016, https://ajcnewsapps.tumblr.com/post/138159247646/predict-a-bill-in-2015-howd-we-do

Ernsthausen, J. and Deng, C. (2015) Parse names and parse… anything, really, DataMade, March 3 2015, https://datamade.us/blog/parse-name-or-parse-anything-really/

Eye on Ohio, Crebs, E., Walinchus, L. (2021) How Do Public Officials Make Land Bank Decisions? Artificial Intelligence May Seek Patterns, WOSU, December 27 2021, https://www.wosu.org/news/2021-12-27/how-do-public-officials-make-land-bank-decisions-artificial-intelligence-may-seek-patterns

Gibbs, (2024) *Generative AI in journalism: The evolution of Newswork and ethics in a generative information ecosystem.* Associated Press. https://drive.google.com/file/d/1rXruz2wQLAXmUtzm1B7lJCpxdWbOHijS/view

Google News Initiative. (2024) Extract Structured Data Using Google's Pinpoint, Google News Initiative, April 15 2024, https://www.youtube.com/watch?v=Rqr6rker5V0,

Hanson, M., Roca-Sales, M., Keegan, J.M. and King, G. (2017) Artificial Intelligence: Practice and Implications for Journalism, Tow Center for Journalism, September 2017, https://doi.org/10.7916/D8X92PRD

Higham, S. and Rich, S. (2014) Whistleblowers say USAID's IG removed critical details from public reports, The Washington Post, October 22, 2014, https://www.washingtonpost.com/investigations/whistleblowers-say-usaids-ig-removed-critical-details-from-public-reports/2014/10/22/68fbc1a0-4031-11e4-b03f-de718edeb92f_story.html

Howard, A.B. (2014) *The art and science of data-driven journalism, tow center for digital journalism.* Columbia University. https://academiccommons.columbia.edu/doi/10.7916/D8Q531V1

Ibrahimovic, S. (2024) How Brazilian journalists tapped DocumentCloud's AI tools to analyze tens of thousands of social media posts, Muckrock, February 21 2024, https://www.muckrock.com/news/archives/2024/feb/21/how-brazilian-journalists-tapped-documentclouds-ai-tools-to-analyze-tens-of-thousands-of-social-media-posts/

Johnson, C.-C., Jumail, A.Y. and Salgado-Lynn, F. (2023) 'Applications and advances in acoustic monitoring for infectious disease epidemiology', *Trends in Parasitology*, 39(5), pp. 386–399. https://doi.org/10.1016/j.pt.2023.01.008

Kahn, G. (2024) *Generative AI is already helping fact-checkers. But it's proving less useful in small languages and outside the West.* April 29 Reuters Institute. https://reutersinstitute.politics.ox.ac.uk/news/generative-ai-already-helping-fact-checkers-its-proving-less-useful-small-languages-and

Kao, J. (2017) More than a Million Pro-Repeal Net Neutrality Comments were Likely Faked, Hackernoon, November 22 2017, https://hackernoon.com/more-than-a-million-pro-repeal-net-neutrality-comments-were-likely-faked-e9f0e3ed36a6

Kuntz, E. and Silva, J. (2023) *Who authors the internet? Analyzing gender diversity in ChatGPT-3 training material.* October 9 Tech Policy Press. https://www.techpolicy.press/who-authors-the-internet-analyzing-gender-diversity-in-chatgpt-3-training-material/

Larraz, I. (2023) *Friend or foe: Using AI as an investigative tool.* Mechelen, Belgium: DataHarvest. https://docs.google.com/presentation/d/19EQpiXbjWZsVVFfT56ZV8uwJ6yrNQ-MhwIOkeXyBOws/edit?usp=sharing

Larson, J. (2012) *How ProPublica's message machine reverse engineers political microtargeting.*, October 18 ProPublica. https://www.propublica.org/nerds/how-propublicas-message-machine-reverse-engineers-political-microtargeting

Manning, C. and Schütze, H. (1999) *Foundations of statistical natural language processing.* Cambridge, MA: MIT Press.

Marconi, F. (2020) *Newsmakers. Artificial intelligence and the future of journalism*, 2020. New York/Chichester: Columbia University Press.

Marconi, F., Siegman, A., Machine Journalist. (2017) *The future of augmented journalism: A guide for newsrooms in the age of smart machines.* February Associated Press. https://jeanetteabrahamsen.com/wp-content/uploads/2017/09/ap_insights_the_future_of_augmented_journalism.pdf

Meyer, G. (2021) 'A new tool by google puts the power of AI in the hands of reporters', *JournalismAI.* https://blogs.lse.ac.uk/polis/2021/04/05/a-new-tool-by-google-puts-the-power-of-ai-in-the-hands-of-reporters/

Newman, N. (2018) *Journalism, media, and technology trends and predictions 2018.* Reuters Institute. https://reutersinstitute.politics.ox.ac.uk/sites/default/files/2018-01/RISJ%20Trends%20and%20Predictions%202018%20NN.pdf

Novoa, O. (2024) *How a Spanish media group created an AI tool to detect audio deepfakes to help journalists in a big election year.* Reuters Institute. https://reutersinstitute.politics.ox.ac.uk/news/how-spanish-media-group-created-ai-tool-detect-audio-deepfakes-help-journalists-big-election

O'Brien, M. (2023) *Chatbots sometimes make things up. Is AI's hallucination problem fixable?.* Associated Press. https://apnews.com/article/artificial-intelligence-hallucination-chatbots-chatgpt-falsehoods-ac4672c5b06e6f91050aa46ee731bcf4

O'Brien, N., Van Dael, J., Clarke, J., Gardner, C., O'Shaughnessy, J., Darzi, A. and Ghafur, S. (2022) *Addressing racial and ethnic inequities in data-driven health technologies.* February 24 Institute of Global Health Innovation, Imperial College London. https://spiral.imperial.ac.uk/server/api/core/bitstreams/f1dd3e4d-1a51-462f-9a10-3e919d114057/content

OpenAI. (2023) GPT-4 System Card, OpenAI, March 23 2023, https://cdn.openai.com/papers/gpt-4-system-card.pdf

Reilley, M. (2024) Custom GPTs for Journalists, JournalistsToolbox.AI, May 28 2024, https://journaliststoolbox.substack.com/p/custom-gpts-for-journalists

Reporters Without Borders. (2023) Paris Charter on AI and Journalism, November 10th 2023, Reporters Without Borders, https://rsf.org/sites/default/files/medias/file/2023/11/Paris%20charter%20on%20AI%20in%20Journalism.pdf

Roberts, B. (2019) Dissecting a machine learning powered investigation, *Artificial Informer*, 1. https://artificialinformer.com/issue-one/dissecting-a-machine-learning-powered-investigation.html

Rocha, R. (2023) Using ChatGPT to clean data: An experiment, Roberto Rocha, April 2023, https://robertorocha.info/using-chatgpt-to-clean-data-an-experiment/

Russell, S.J., Norvig, P. and Chang, M.-W. (2022) *Artificial intelligence: A modern approach.* Prentice Hall.

Schot, E., Davidson, D., Minczeles, C., van Hulst, R., Heesterbeek, W., Klaassen, S., van Dijk, R., Geiger, G. and Bubbert, F. (2024) Automating Distrust, Lighthouse Reports, February 27 2024, https://www.lighthousereports.com/investigation/automating-distrust/

Scurrell, J.V. and Grossenbacher, T. (2017) Identifying a Large Number of Fake Followers on Instagram: A Statistical Learning Approach, SRF Data, October 2017, https://srfdata.github.io/2017-10-instagram-influencers

Sengul-Jones, M. (2021) Bring in the machines: AI-powered investigative journalism, DataJournalism.com, December 1 2021, https://datajournalism.com/read/longreads/machine-learning-investigative-journalism

Sir Lenny Henry Centre for Media Diversity. (2023) Generative AI Diversity Guidelines, Birmingham City University, June 2023, https://www.bcu.ac.uk/media/research/sir-lenny-henry-centre-for-media-diversity/blog/six-principles-for-responsible-journalistic-use-of-generative-ai-and-diversity-and-inclusion

Stray, J. (2019a) Extracting campaign finance data from gnarly PDFs using deep learning, June 13 2019, jonathanstray.com, http://jonathanstray.com/extracting-campaign-finance-data-from-gnarly-pdfs-using-deep-learning

Stray, J. (2019b) 'Making artificial intelligence work for investigative journalism', *Digital Journalism*, 7(8). https://doi.org/10.1080/21670811.2019.1630289

Ventura Pocino, P. (2021) *Algorithms in the newsrooms: Challenges and recommendations for artificial intelligence with the ethical values of journalism.* Catalan Press Council. https://fcic.periodistes.cat/wp-content/uploads/2022/03/venglishDIGITAL_ALGORITMES-A-LES-REDACCIONS_ENG-1.pdf

Vilanova, P. (2017) Brazilian group develops an AI to help in public expenditures monitoring. Rosie, the robot's name, found more than 8.000 suspicious reimbursements from Brazilian congresspeople, Medium, October 30 2017, https://medium.com/data-science-brigade/brazilian-group-develops-an-ai-to-help-in-public-expenditures-monitoring-757900c99552

Villa, S. (2023) Investigating—And Embracing—The AI Revolution, Global Investigative Journalism Network, September 20 2023, https://gijn.org/stories/ai-and-investigative-journalism-gijc23/

Viner, K. and Bateson, A. (2023) The Guardian's approach to generative AI, The Guardian, June 16, 2023. https://www.theguardian.com/help/insideguardian/2023/jun/16/the-guardians-approach-to-generative-ai

Wang, P. (2019) 'On defining artificial intelligence', *Journal of Artificial General Intelligence*, 10(2), pp. 1–37. https://doi.org/10.2478/jagi-2019-0002.

Whittaker, M. (2021) 'The steep cost of capture', *Interactions*, 28 (6), pp. 50–55. https://doi.org/10.1145/3488666

PART V

Two Crucial Strands

Teaching and Collaborative
Investigative Journalism

10

CROSS-BORDER INVESTIGATIVE JOURNALIST EDUCATION

The Process Towards Normalisation

Maria Konow-Lund, Lucia Mesquita, and Carolyne Lunga

Introduction

In recent years, several studies have focused on cross-border collaborative investigative journalism via watershed projects such as the Panama Papers.[1] Still, this area of practice remains largely under-researched, especially regarding journalism education and how students respond to and benefit from the type of teamwork required by cross-border collaborative journalism. In this context, an *exploratory* study was conducted to understand the teaching methods, the lessons learned, and the main characteristics of cross-border collaborative journalism education focused on developing cross-border collaboration skills and mindset. This study investigated the Erasmus+ pilot project "Crossborder Journalism Campus" (CJC), a collaboration among universities and journalism entities in different countries within Europe. This initiative enables students to work together on mutually determined topics, share ideas and research, and publish investigative stories both nationally and internationally. Approximately 150 students participated in joint projects over two consecutive academic years, with 75 students each year. According to CJC's website, "cross-border collaborative journalism is a relatively young practice. Teaching cross-border collaborative journalism in practice is in its earliest stages. However, pilot journalism education models are now under development."[2] Thus, an aspect of this study is to examine changes in journalism education aimed at integrating cross-border journalism into existing curricula, as outlined by the CJC model.[3] The project replicates real-world cross-border investigative practice as students are both supervised and supported by seasoned professional journalists.[4] The project collaborators include the University of Gothenburg, established in 1954, which boasts a long tradition of education in journalism with a special focus on sustainability

DOI: 10.4324/9781003478157-16

and international responsibility. Leipzig University was founded in 1409 and is among Europe's oldest universities; it excels in interdisciplinary research and privileges international cooperation. The Centre de Formation des Journalistes in Paris/Lyon is a private institution started in 1946 that specialises in media and journalism and offers a two-year master's programme with a high graduate employment rate.[5] Dutch NGO Arena is also an active and equal partner in the project; it has long promoted cross-border collaboration among reporters and with "scholars, scientists, and civil society."[6] The research for this article draws upon the spring 2023 phase of the CJC project. All students participating in the CJC project engage for one full academic year as part of existing master's programmes at their respective universities.

Konow-Lund, Park and Bebawi (2024) note that cross-border journalism fosters an international perspective, unlike journalism with exclusively national interests (Berglez, 2013). Its strength lies in enhancing story validity and reliability through diverse international sources. This form of journalism addresses various challenges today. As media intermediaries disrupt traditional business models, journalists and news organisations leverage collaboration to navigate these changes. Cross-border investigative journalism also helps media entities and journalists advance societal goals and hold power to account. Journalists worldwide see collaboration as a chance to reinforce professional standards and motivations (Graves and Konieczna, 2015). To this end, the CJC approach to cross-border investigative journalism aligns with Brigitte Alfter's summary (2019, p. 18):

1 journalists from different countries with
2 an idea of mutual interest
3 gathering and sharing material and
4 publishing to their own audiences.

And yet, as stated in the Erasmus+ announcement for the CJC project, "crossborder collaborative journalism is a competence that journalism educations need to provide their students with, in order to meet demand in the industry (European Commission, n.d.). How, then, can we normalise this practice within our existing educational frameworks (Baack, 2016)? As Wahl-Jorgensen has noted, professional journalists have a "tendency to 'absorb' practices that threaten to undermine their professional autonomy into conventional hierarchies of newsgathering" (Wahl-Jorgensen, 2014, p. 2588). Jane Singer (2005) refers to this process as "normalisation," and it has yet to take place in journalism education with regard to cross-border collaboration; according to Brigitte Alfter, "to our best knowledge there is no other European partnership offering a model like this" (University of Gothenburg, 2021). The CJC was specifically designed to normalise cross-border practices by enabling students to work in groups on real-world investigations.

In what follows, we will shed light upon the competencies required for such a project to succeed and its goal of catalysing best practices within the journalism profession. We contend that projects like the CJC will best equip the next generation of investigative reporters with the tools to tackle intricate, border-defying issues in the digital era and ultimately restore trust in journalism.

Cross-Border Collaborative Investigative Journalism: Navigating Its Affordances for Educational Practices

While cross-border investigative journalism is not new (Sambrook, 2018, p. 1), projects like the Panama and Paradise Papers marked a shift in its execution. Recent examples include investigations into deforestation in 12 Latin American countries (2023) [7], the Faith Transnationals' fundamentalist agenda involving 16 media outlets across 13 countries[8], and the Cyprus Confidential investigation revealing Cyprian firms assisting Putin's regime in hiding assets[9]. Since the 1990s, organisations like the International Consortium of Investigative Journalists (ICIJ) have promoted collaborative journalism (Lewis, 2018). Despite this landmark work, there remains a gap in journalism education's response to these changes (Crossborder Journalism Campus, n.d.).

Aside from notable exceptions at Columbia University, Sciences Po, and the Newsreel project, which involved Erich Brost Institute for international journalism (EBI) at Dortmund University, University of Pécs (Hungary), IS-CTE-University Institute Lisbon (Portugal), the University of Bucharest (Romania) and Masaryk University in Brno (Czech Republic), most journalism institutions and educational programmes remain underprepared to embrace the diversity intrinsic to this evolving practice (Alfter, Wiik and Deuze, 2019; Deuze and Witschge, 2020). Moreover, journalism education still perpetuates an industry-centric curriculum in a market that emphasises commercialisation over cooperation. It fails, in short, to reflect best practices in a globalised, multicultural world (Hanitzsch *et al*, 2019; Solkin, 2022).

To effectively teach cross-border investigative journalism, we must understand its origins and relationship to traditional investigative journalism. Among the many factors that have contributed to this investigative model's growth are the many affordances of digital technology (Konow-Lund, Park and Bebawi, 2024). Journalism has always been impacted by technological advancements (Örnebring, 2010), but cross-border collaborative journalism, which often works with datasets, requires specific tech expertise not normally found in the newsroom (Alfter, 2019, p. 4).

While information and communication technologies have long supported cross-border journalistic work, the study *Newsreel 1* (University of Pécs, 2018; Bettels-Schawabbauer, 2017, p. 90) found that the ongoing digitalisation of communication has presented challenges to journalism on many levels. These challenges range from the need to develop new revenue streams to managing the frenetic pace of an often-overwhelming flow of information. The report also noted that journalism educators believe there is no need to follow every trend; instead, they emphasise the importance of teaching core competencies. Research in the Global South, for example, indicates that collaborations across borders frequently emerge from the shared need to evade repression, safeguard newsrooms, and protect journalists (Mesquita, 2022). In many such contexts, navigating political challenges and constraints upon freedom of expression incentivise collaboration, whatever the technological circumstances (Lunga, 2022). Even under very challenging conditions, these journalists manage to uphold core professional standards (Hanitzsch *et al*, 2019).

In addition, cross-border investigative journalism typically emphasises non-commercial, public-focused reporting through a decentralised and horizontal approach (Coronel, 2016; Smyrnaios, Marty and Chauvet, 2019). This methodology enables journalists to address topics often overlooked by the mainstream media while engaging diverse community members and stakeholders in their critical investigative endeavours. While there are various models of collaborative investigative journalism, key attributes of the cross-border iteration include its networked structure, which facilitates decentralised information exchange, and its dependence upon a holistic understanding of global sociopolitical and socioeconomic challenges (Berglez, 2013; Hostwriter, 2019). It benefits from its practitioners' awareness of the power dynamics within networks, community realities, and the unconscious biases that can undermine journalism's defence of democracy (Grzeszyk, 2019).

An important concept that can greatly enhance the effectiveness of cross-border journalism in educational settings is the "common denominator." Brigitte Alfter (2018) emphasises the importance of finding common ground when journalists from different countries collaborate. Alfter and Ulla Sätereie, the initiators of the project, jointly developed and managed the CJC concept. They explain how their different backgrounds complemented each other, with both having extensive experience in traditional journalism careers. While Sätereie transitioned into journalism education, Alfter focused on developing collaborative practices and creating infrastructure for cross-border journalism at the European level. According to both Alfter and Sätereie, their combined competencies—Alfter's professional experience and Sätereie's academic background—along with their shared experiences and professional networks, were key to the successful development of the CJC project.

After all, this form of collaboration is different from cooperative arrangements such as shared resource access for individual purposes. It is a mode of interaction characterised by mutually engaged, direct partnerships among cooperating entities who share common interests and objectives (the common denominators) and interact with consideration and trust (Heft, 2021).

Insights from Real-World Collaborations and the CJC

Cross-border collaborative journalism is increasingly prevalent in addressing global challenges and networked societies, exemplified by high-profile investigations like the Panama Papers and local issues such as affordable housing. This method leverages digital opportunities to foster new journalism practices that transcend national boundaries. It is crucial for journalism education to incorporate cross-border collaboration skills to meet industry demands and support democratic societies. Future journalists need competencies in intercultural communication, transnational outlook, digital tools, and ethical considerations. The CJC project aims to create a flexible, transferable model for educating students in cross-border collaborative journalism[10]; thus, serving as a robust framework for future endeavours.

The CJC project transcends national boundaries by engaging approximately 150 students based in three countries, over two academic years, enabling them to collaborate on joint projects with a focus on European Union issues. These findings were published in partnership with prominent media outlets like *Le Monde* and *Mediapart* (France), *mdr* (Germany), *Svenska Dagbladet* and *Göteborgs-Posten* (Sweden), and *EUobserver* (Belgium) (Crossborder Journalism Campus, n.d).

The consortium consists of five partners. Three contribute students, while Arena and Oslo Met offer other essential competencies. The project collaborators include the University of Gothenburg, with a longstanding tradition in journalism education focused on sustainability and international responsibility, and Leipzig University, one of Europe's oldest institutions, known for interdisciplinary research and international cooperation. The Centre de Formation des Journalistes in Paris/Lyon offers specialised media and journalism programmes with high graduate employment rates. Arena, a Dutch NGO, actively promotes cross-border collaboration among journalists, scholars, scientists, and civil society.

The CJC is supported by the Erasmus+ programme but maintains full editorial independence. The educational team includes prominent lecturers and practitioners such as Brigitte Alfter, Ulla Sätereie, Sarah Pilz (Gothenburg University), Adriana Homolova (Arena), Edouard Perrin, Cédric Molle-Laurençon (CFJ), Uwe Krüger, Felix Irmer, Maria Hendrischke and Adrian Breda (LU) and from the participating institutions. The students participated in the start week in Brussels, engaging with guest speakers and European officials. Following a thorough evaluation, the CJC aims to share its insights and methodologies with other journalism programmes to shape the future of investigative journalism in Europe and beyond.[11]

Methodology

For this exploratory study, we first attended an introduction to the CJC over Zoom, and the first author also went to a seminar in Leipzig, Germany, where student feedback from the first phase of the CJC was presented. This feedback was later shared online as well. As we had limited resources, we focused on elaborating on the main points in the feedback and using it as inspiration for an interview guide.

The CJC project manager later informed all students and participants, encouraging them to contribute to our study. In the end, we received input from a group of students, as well as from Brigitte Alfter and Ulla Sätereie—the course's creators, who also served as supervisors and teachers. In this section, we also emphasise that the first author, Maria Konow-Lund, is a partner in the Erasmus+ project. However, her role is primarily as a scholar rather than being directly involved in cross-border teaching or supervision. Although OsloMet, her university, is formally a partner in Erasmus+, Konow-Lund has maintained a certain academic distance from the project's more practical aspects. We have remained mindful of the importance of maintaining objectivity while participating in the project (see, for example, Candea, 2020) and the ability to "navigate between the insider's perspective and that of an analyst" (Candea, 2020, p. 65).

We focused on the first cohort of the CJC, drawing upon informants' experiences from autumn 2022 through spring 2023. The interviews for this study were conducted between the end of April 2023 and the beginning of July 2023, during which data was collected. All participants were assured complete anonymity. The project was also reported to SIKT, the Norwegian Agency for Shared Services in Education and Research. One of the ethical conditions of this study is to provide full anonymity to informants, unless they explicitly request that their full names be used. Due to this, we have been careful not to add either direct or indirect information that might lead to identification in any way, such as gender and location. The feedback from students in summer 2023 was intended to impact the project in the following year, which would have required another round of data gathering that was beyond the scope of the study. The project ends with the calendar year 2024, and when "the programme is finalised, the findings, evaluation of the process as well as teaching material will be made public for other practice-oriented educators to see, be inspired by and develop further."[12] This article is therefore an analysis of mid-project experiences and feedback. We began by conducting semi-structured qualitative interviews with various informants selected through a multifaceted process. The CJC project manager actively solicited informants and shared emails with us so we could contact them directly. Despite limited time and numerous obligations, some participants eventually surfaced; ultimately, we interviewed 14 altogether for their insights into the CJC and its influence on their professional interests.

This study also employs a qualitative research methodology known as "elite" interviews that originated in studies conducted with top-ranking executives (Giddens, 1972), highly skilled professionals (McDowell, 1998), and experts with unique insight and knowledge (Richard,1996; Vaughan, 2013). While it is rarely used in journalism studies (Ustad Figenschou, 2010), it worked well here, given that the aforementioned project leaders, Brigitte Alfter and Ulla Sätereie, had such unique insight into their experiment. Our interviews lasted from 50 to 90 minutes, allowing us plenty of time for detailed discussion.

Rather than aiming for broad statistical representation, that is, we deliberately selected participants and materials with the most direct relevance to our research. Our goal was to delve into the complexities rather than reduce or simplify them by breaking them down into variables. In the interests of gauging the potential role of cross-border investigative journalism in master's-level journalism education, we concentrated on the following aspects of the practice: To understand the teaching methods, lessons learned, and key characteristics of cross-border collaborative journalism education, with a focus on developing skills and mindsets for cross-border collaboration.

For our analysis, we employed a hermeneutic methodology typical of ethnographic production studies (Gans, 1979/2004; Schlesinger, 1978; Tuchman, 1978). This approach generates knowledge by accessing the field through meetings, partnerships, and interviews, often combined with semi-structured qualitative interviews. In the case of the CJC, our observations were derived from both Zoom meetings with the management group and a three-day physical meeting at Leipzig University in February 2023. By then, the first semester of the CJC had been completed, and the project's managers, supervisors, and initiators were convening to evaluate the process. Our data gathering took place before the CJC ended the first year with synchronised publication in June. We conducted semi-structured interviews with these individuals as well as participating master's students residing in (though not necessarily originating from) Sweden, Germany, and France. The project organised various groups of students around story topics such as deforestation/biomass, fishing, agriculture, housing, social justice, right-wing movements, and taxonomy.

We have also drawn upon four interviews with journalists and editors with specific foreign correspondence experience conducted in May and June 2023. All interviews were recorded and subsequently transcribed in compliance with European data protection regulations.

Results and Findings

Mutual Topics as a Hub and a Main Common Denominator

The CJC student groups addressed environmental topics connected to the EU's future objectives for the Green Deal (informant interviews, spring 2023).

The CJC project was focused on both the results of their investigations and the experience they gained in cross-border collaboration and expanding their networks. The initial plan for the project was to hold a full physical meeting in Brussels in fall 2022 and evaluate the project or collect insights on lessons learned in spring and summer 2023. The evaluation process was implemented to inform the second pilot year (2023–2024) by introducing improvements derived from the insights gained during the first pilot year (2022–2023).

The choice of a broad, international issue, such as the Green Deal, was aimed at harnessing the strengths of cross-border journalism's international outlook and aligning the project with the lived experiences of its students. The global outlook concept, which is deeply rooted in journalism and especially cross-border investigative practices, captures the intricate interconnections and implications of the world's economies, businesses, cultures, and politics. It further supports the critical examination of nations and governments and the challenging of conventional national narratives (Berglez, 2013; Handley, 2014). It is a tool for understanding globalisation, alongside similar terms such as globalised knowledge, which, as "knowledge from everywhere," transcends geographical and cultural boundaries, eliminating distinctions and fostering a global perspective (Hulme, 2010). Together, these concepts advocate for a more interconnected, inclusive, and comprehensive approach to understanding and navigating our increasingly globalised world, encompassing both information dissemination and the lens through which we perceive it.

Understanding the intricacies of cross-border collaboration is crucial to the success of such initiatives. An academic article by Brigitte Alfter (2018), a pioneer in cross-border collaboration and a CJC initiator, advocates for the value of common denominators among journalists of different nationalities to enhance these investigations. In turn, the CJC project tried to simulate the practice by allowing participants to meet at "eye level" to develop a shared vision of the topic they were investigating (interview, Alfter, 5 May 2023).

Interestingly, the present study's findings indicate that a shared vision of topic, work practices or routines is particularly challenged in cross-border education due to different cultures and even organisation of work in various universities. In this case, Sweden, Germany and France. Through interviews, it became clear that while some students in one country have dedicated time to work on their master's, students in a different country might have internships. It should be mentioned that the CJC has specifically chosen a "flexible model, because it will be immediately applicable by other journalism educations without the need to adapt, integrate and nationally accredit new curricula"[13] (The Erasmus + announcement). Ultimately, while this benefits the naturalisation of the cross-border education, the institutional coordination is less strict. Some students, for example, lamented the tendency for their teaming peers to withdraw over time, which negatively impacted the cross-border nature of their work:

> In the beginning, we had students from the German campuses, and from the French campuses, as well. We ended up being five people from Gothenburg with different nationalities. And our French colleagues disappeared, and we tried to get hold of them. [...] So that was disappointing, of course. Today I don't know what happened to them either. We contacted them, and we contacted their lecturer as well. Don't know what happened. I know that they had—the schedules weren't syncing, really. So, they had some time in the beginning, then they had other projects, and I think they were working at the same time, so ... They were supposed to do this CJC project on the side of their internship, as I understood it, so it was a bad thing there. And then no answers. So, in our team, the cross-border campus aspect of it unfortunately didn't exist.
>
> *(Interview, informant, 26 May 2023)*

Still, experiences varied—the same informant said that another group had great success working with French students who were excellent in coding and scraping. Their cross-border collaboration revealed that the Sweden Democrats consistently distinguished themselves from other far-right parties by voting against all proposals related to environmental and climate change issues. The team analysed voting patterns in the European Parliament over several years, which was crucial in uncovering the Sweden Democrats' opposition to the Green Deal, a key focus of one of their ongoing investigations. This is one example of 27 international exposés published in national and international media outlets during the summer of 2023.

Ultimately, the Erasmus+ pilot CJC contributes to the naturalisation of a new form of journalism education, characterised by a willingness to experiment and refine over several years, paralleling similar naturalisation processes within professional cross-border journalistic practices. As a cross-border education project, it presents both challenges and benefits, yet it has already demonstrated a clear need for this innovative approach to journalism education. More research must be done to better understand the common denominators that enable these kinds of arrangements within both traditional and innovative professional and educational settings.

Intercultural Communication

Intercultural competence includes the development of skills, behaviours, knowledge, and personal and interpersonal abilities that are useful for individuals working in a transnational and transcultural environment (Deardorff, 2009; Kim, 2012). The CJC project aimed to provide students with a foundational understanding of intercultural communication terminology, accompanied by a reading list. While students in Gothenburg engaged deeply with this material, students in Leipzig and France were introduced to it through an online lecture. However, Alfter believes that intercultural communication extends far beyond just language, which is vital to journalism and especially cross-border investigative projects. Our study found that even when intercultural communication is part of a training curriculum, it remains a challenge.[14] As pointed out by Heft (2019), cross-border collaboration can take place between two individuals or among teams of various sizes and levels of diversity. Whatever the arrangement or cast of stakeholders, they will need common denominators to advance their work most productively, including, for example, language. At the CJC, students were asked to have an open mind when it came to English and practise what their lecturers called "bad English."

> I think intercultural communication works best by doing it. I'm not super sure if we *need* a course and a reading, or a seminar and the reading on it. However, I don't think it should be underestimated as much as other people maybe did. I mean the language obviously is always something that people are afraid of. At some point we got a mail where our lecturer said the working language is "bad school English." And I think everybody really took that to heart… And obviously sometimes things get lost in translation, but everybody was always very understanding of that. And in my group, you could tell that there was one person who really wasn't saying a word for the first month. And at some point, it was so much so that we thought, "Maybe they just don't speak English." But all of a sudden that person started speaking English, and it was very solid.
>
> *(Interview, CJC student, 15 May 2023)*

Clearly, some students confronted issues already very familiar to professional journalists in cross-border collaborations. One senior foreign correspondent and editor-in-chief (interview, 21 October 2023) recalled how, during the height of the COVID-19 pandemic, everyone wanted international sources. However, many were hesitant to reach out to their colleagues and informants in other countries due to their insecurity about communicating in English as a common language. Interestingly, this was an acknowledged challenge among the organisers of the Panama and Paradise Papers projects as well (see, for example, Obermayer and Obermaier, 2017). They mitigated it by communicating among their multicultural participants in a hybrid manner (Konow-Lund *et al*, 2024) involving both digital platforms and physical meetings. Drawing on Alfter's definition of cross-border collaborative journalism— where reporters from different countries, united by a shared interest, generate and share material before publishing to a targeted audience—the CJC project provides students with practical experience. This experience includes not only the use of technology and the organisation of work across time and space, but also training in intercultural communication. Interviews reveal that students particularly benefit from this training when meeting in person, as evidenced by the Brussels start-up meeting.

Moreover, by pioneering cross-border education, the project yields valuable insights and stories. For example, as the EU intensifies its commitment to environmental sustainability through the Green Deal, parallel initiatives like the CJC are contributing to the development of a more innovative and environmentally conscious European educational landscape.

Organising Work to Transcend Limitations in Time and Space with Digital Technology

Technology is a fundamental enabler of cross-cultural investigations, especially in terms of mitigating cultural and practical differences among participants. Soon after the Panama Papers project splashed across the world's front pages, Baack (2016) argued that such collaborations were not new and linked them to both WikiLeaks and the increasing use of SecureDrop, a system through which informers could drop off tips in a safe manner. According to Baack, the emergent technology surrounding the enabling of leaks to journalists "did not just provide (exclusive) access to the leak, but also developed tools and platforms that help journalists cooperate on a much larger scale." During the Panama Papers project, for example, the ICIJ created an internal wiki for reporters to sift through information as well as share their findings and perspectives with one another (Obermaier and Obermayer, 2017).

Initially, the CJC project utilised the open-source software Rocket Chat for communication, but it was later replaced with Signal due to issues with its chat function, as noted by our informants (interview with Ulla Sätereie, 22 May 2023). These technological tools highlight crucial concerns regarding safety and security in collaborative communications and data sharing, offering students practical experience in managing these challenges. By addressing these issues, the CJC project exemplifies good professional practice.

> The digital platform we used to store all the material of the investigation was Next Cloud because our teachers said that it was, you know, safer and for the privacy of the information. Every group had a folder on Next Cloud where you gather all the material like the wiki, the link to the source in the transcript of the interviews, the videos, and so on. But I consider Next Cloud a weakness of the [CJC] project. […] In my group, we had more than one member who wasn't able to access Next Cloud for the whole year. This led us to do a backup folder on Google Drive that was accessible to everyone. So basically, we had to duplicate all the documents. And, you know, to be sure that everyone was aware of how the investigation was

working because our teachers wanted us to keep the Next Cloud, but Next Cloud wasn't accessible to everyone. So, we had to use two digital platforms and that was, of course, tricky and time-consuming.

(Interview, informant, 22 May 2023)

CJC instructors listened to criticism and quickly responded with improvements along the way, planning, for example, to use Signal in the future rather than Rocket Chat[15] (interview, Ulla Sätereie, 22 May 2023).

Concluding Remarks

By using an open-ended, exploratory approach while interviewing the groups of master's students and the project initiators, we uncovered important challenges and benefits to the process of replicating real-world cross-border journalistic practice. Of course, the field of journalism has repeatedly undergone change or innovation and its subsequent normalisation, however slow it might be, via both training and reporter conduct. Stefan Baack (2016), for example, looked at how newsrooms adapted to leaks on their own terms in the wake of the WikiLeaks phenomenon. While practitioners can be hesitant or awkward about accommodating new routines and practices, journalism educators can be slower still—the Newsreel 1 report related this to the chronic lack of resources plaguing universities today in terms of the ability to offer certain courses or accelerate the impact of data journalism, for example, via expensive new technology (University of Pécs, 2018,).

Still, if no one is willing to experiment or respond to "disruption," the field will become stuck and, worse, lose relevance. The normalisation of new approaches to journalism education focuses less on individual outcomes and more on encouraging openness to new possibilities in education. These possibilities are strongly linked to intercultural communication, the use of alternative platforms, and communication through various technologies. Our study is small in scale and limited in time, yet it clearly demonstrates the need for educational pilot projects like the CJC to accelerate the normalisation of cross-border journalistic collaboration through the real-world conditions involved in *learning by doing*. This training must take place where the students are studying and allow for whatever resources and academic structure are available at the given institution. The Newsreel 1 study did caution journalism educators not to chase every trend (2018, p. 90) but rather to remain focused on core competencies. We would argue, however, that cross-border collaboration has become a core competency, and that it is best taught by enabling the students themselves to partake in it directly. Effective cross-border journalism education enhances decentralised information exchange, promotes cultural awareness, and addresses complex societal issues, but its effective implementation requires continual adaptation and consideration of a range of technological, cultural, and practical factors. This study contributes valuable insights into navigating these challenges and optimising the educational and professional outcomes of initiatives like the CJC. **Our findings can be summarised in a list of key best-practice recommendations for students and educators, as found below:**

1 **Mindset shift**: Investment for universities to embrace and support cross-border educational opportunities. Journalism schools offer opportunities for students to do collaborative projects, locally, nationally or internationally.
2 **Emphasise communication and cultural sensitivity**: Open and respectful communication across cultural boundaries is crucial. Students and educators should foster an environment of mutual understanding, especially when working with peers from different backgrounds.
3 **Leverage diverse technologies**: Encourage the use of secure, open-source technologies for cross-border collaboration, while staying adaptable to the diverse technological realities of participants, ensuring they are comfortable with a variety of tools.
4 **Encourage adaptability and flexibility**: Both students and educators must be open to changing plans and adapting to evolving challenges, whether technological, logistical, or cultural.
5 **Focus on collaboration over competition**: Promote a spirit of teamwork and shared goals, rather than competition, to achieve the best results in cross-border projects.
6 **Integrate real-world experience**: Provide hands-on, practical opportunities for students to apply their knowledge in real-world scenarios, fostering the skills needed for future journalistic work.
7 **Promote reflection and feedback**: Encourage ongoing reflection and peer feedback to ensure continuous improvement and a deeper understanding of the collaborative process.

By following these recommendations, students and educators can maximise the success and impact of cross-border journalistic collaborations, ensuring both educational enrichment and professional preparedness.

Acknowledgements

We extend our deepest gratitude to Brigitte Alfter and Ulla Sätereie for unwavering support throughout the development of this work. Their insightful feedback and thoughtful suggestions fostered significant growth and learning. We are sincerely grateful for their generosity with their time and expertise, as well as their continuous willingness to provide support, and we are profoundly thankful.

CLASSROOM EXERCISE (WOULD WORK BEST FOR GROUPS WITH THREE TO FOUR STUDENTS)

1 **Analyse common themes in investigated topics:**

- Explore the topics covered by well-known international investigative networks like ICIJ and The Forbidden Stories, and ask how these networks work and investigate possible commonalities. Start by discussing the networks themselves, how they are constituted, and what makes the network unique from traditional journalism with its lone-wolf approach.
- Discuss whether the topics share recurring themes or stand as unique investigations.

2 **Plan a cross-border collaborative investigation:**

- If you were to undertake a cross-border investigative project, outline how you would organise the collaboration.
- Consider the logistics, decision-making process, communication methods, division of tasks, and tools you would use.
- Provide a rationale for your proposed approach, explaining how it would support the investigation's success.
- How would you bring in the players? What factors will you consider?
- What possible challenges do you foresee, and how will you mitigate them?

Notes

1 "EU programme for education, training, youth and sport". Erasmus+, European Commission, 2021, https://erasmus-plus.ec.europa.eu/projects/search/details/2021-1-SE01-KA220-HED-000030315.

2 "About Cross-Border Journalism Campus," *Cross-Border Journalism Campus*, n.d., https://crossborderjournalismcampus.eu/about/.

3 "EU programme for education, training, youth and sport". Erasmus+, European Commission, 2021, https://erasmus-plus.ec.europa.eu/projects/search/details/2021-1-SE01-KA220-HED-000030315.

4 University of Gothenburg. (2024, October 14). *Crossborder Journalism Campus.* https://www.gu.se/en/study-gothenburg/crossborder-journalism-campus.

5 "EU programme for education, training, youth and sport". Erasmus+, European Commission, 2021, https://erasmus-plus.ec.europa.eu/projects/search/details/2021-1-SE01-KA220-HED-000030315.

6 Crossborder Journalism Campus. (n.d.). *About CJC.* https://crossborderjournalismcampus.eu/about/.

7 Distintas Latitudes. (n.d.). *Los bosques que perdimos.* https://bosqueslatam.distintaslatitudes.net/

8 Segnini, G., & Cordero, M. (2019, August 31). *Líderes evangélicos amparados por la Casa Blanca exportan agenda fundamentalista a América Latina.* El Clip. https://www.elclip.org/lideres-evangelicos-amparados-por-la-casa-blanca-exportan-agenda-fundamentalista-a-america-latina/?lang=enin

9 International Consortium of Investigative Journalists. (2023, November 14). *Cyprus Confidential.* https://www.icij.org/investigations/cyprus-confidential/

10 "EU programme for education, training, youth and sport". Erasmus+, European Commission, 2021, https://erasmus-plus.ec.europa.eu/projects/search/details/2021-1-SE01-KA220-HED-000030315.

11 "Cross-Border Journalism Education," Cross-Border Journalism Campus, n.d., https://crossborderjournalismcampus.eu/cross-border-journalism-education/.

12 "Cross-Border Journalism Education," Cross-Border Journalism Campus, n.d., https://crossborderjournalismcampus.eu/cross-border-journalism-education/.

13 "EU programme for education, training, youth and sport". Erasmus+, European Commission, 2021, https://erasmus-plus.ec.europa.eu/projects/search/details/2021-1-SE01-KA220-HED-000030315.

14 In the aftermath Brigitte Alfter (July 2024) added that the CJC project explicitly wished to provide students with the basics of intercultural communication terminology, including a reading list. The students in Gothenburg worked with this, while students in Leipzig and France were introduced to the same material via an online lecture, however without the connected exercises. Intercultural communication in our perception goes way beyond language.

15 The organizers of the CJC have resolved to migrate all materials to a more reliable server to ensure stability and accessibility.

References

Alfter, B. (2018) 'New method, new skill, new position? Editorial coordinators in crossborder collaborative teams', in Sambrook, R. (ed.) *Global teamwork: The rise of collaboration in investigative journalism.* Reuters Institute for the Study of Journalism, University of Oxford, pp. 41–58.

Alfter, B. (2019) *Cross-border collaborative journalism: A step-by-step guide.* Routledge.

Alfter, B., Wiik, J., & Deuze, M. (2019). Taking stock of cross-border journalism education in times of cross-border collaboration. In *Academic Track Reader. A Collection of Research Papers Submitted for the Global Investigative Journalism Conference September* (pp. 72–92).

Baack, S. (2016) ', July 26). What big data leaks tell us about the future of journalism— And its past [online publication]', *Internet Policy Review.* Retrieved from https://policyreview.info/articles/news/what-big-data-leaks-tell-us-about-future-journalism-and-its-past/413

Berglez, P. (2013) *Global journalism: Theory and practice.* Peter Lang.

Candea, S. (2020). Cross-border Investigative Journalism: a critical perspective. PhD thesis University of Westminster Westminster School of Media and Communication.

Coronel, S. (2016) *Coronel: A golden age of global muckraking at hand.* Global Investigative Journalism Network. https://gijn.org/2016/06/20/a-golden-age-of-global-muckraking/

Crossborder Journalism Campus. (n.d.). *About CJC.* https://crossborderjournalism campus.eu/about/

Deardorff, D.K. (2009) *The SAGE handbook of intercultural competence.* SAGE.

Deuze, M. and Witschge, T. (2020) *Beyond journalism.* John Wiley and Sons.

European Commission. (n.d.). *Crossborder Journalism Campus (Project No. 2021-1-SE01-KA220-HED-000030315).* Erasmus+. https://erasmus-plus.ec.europa.eu/projects/search/details/2021-1-SE01-KA220-HED-000030315

Gans, Herbert J. (2004 [1979]). *Deciding What's News: A Study of CBS Evening News, NBC Nightly News, Newsweek, and Time.* 25th anniversary ed. Evanston, Ill.: Medill School of Journalism, in association with Northwestern University Press.

Giddens, A. (1972). Elites in the British class structure. *The Sociological Review,* 20(3), 345–372.

Graves, L. and Konieczna, M. (2015) 'Sharing the news: Journalistic collaboration as field repair', *International Journal of Communication*, 9, pp. 1966–1984.

Grzeszyk, T. (2019) 'Diversity matters! How cross-border journalism calls out media bias', *Journal of Applied Journalism and Media Studies*, 8(2), pp. 169–189. https://doi.org/info:doi/10.1386/ajms.8.2.169_1

Hanitzsch, T., Hanusch, F., Ramaprasad, J. and Beer, A.S. (2019) *Worlds of journalism: Journalistic cultures around the globe.* Columbia University Press.

Heft, A. (2019). The Panama Papers investigation and the scope and boundaries of its networked publics: Cross-border journalistic collaboration driving transnationally networked public spheres. *Journal of Applied Journalism & Media Studies*, 8(2), pp. 191–209.

Heft, A. (2021) 'Transnational journalism networks "from below": Cross-border journalistic collaboration in individualized newswork', *Journalism Studies*, 22(4), pp. 454–474. https://doi.org/10.1080/1461670X.2021.1882876

Hostwriter. (2019). *Cross-border journalism booklets for downloading—hostwriterblog.* https://blog.hostwriter.org/cross-border-journalism-booklets-for-downloading/

Hulme, M. (2010) 'Problems with making and governing global kinds of knowledge', *Global Environmental Change*, 20(4), pp. 558–564. https://doi.org/10.1016/j.gloenvcha.2010.07.005

Kim, Y.Y. (2012) 'Comparing intercultural communication', in Esser, F.; & Hanitzsch, T. (eds.) *The handbook of comparative communication research.* Routledge, pp. 19–133.

Konow-Lund, M., Park, M. and Bebawi, S. (2024) *Hybrid investigative journalism.* Cham, Switzerland: Palgrave MacMillan.

Lewis, C. (2018) 'Tear down these walls: Innovations in collaborative accountability research and reporting', in Sambrook, R. (ed.) *Global teamwork: The rise of collaboration in investigative journalism.* Reuters, pp. 5–25.

Lunga, C. (2022). *Collaborative investigative journalism in Southern Africa.* Doctoral thesis, City University of London. https://openaccess.city.ac.uk/id/eprint/30062/

McDowell, L. (1998). Elites in the city of London: Some methodological considerations. *Environment and planning A*, 30(12), 2133–2146.

Mesquita, L. (2022). *Collaborative journalism and normative journalism: Intersections and implications of normative roles in the collaborative action of journalists, media practitioners and news organisations in Latin America.* Doctoral thesis, Dublin City University. https://doras.dcu.ie/27604/

Obermayer, B. and Obermaier, F. (2017). *The Panama papers. Breaking the story of how the rich and powerful hide their money.* Oneworld. (Original work published 2016.)

Örnebring, H. (2010). Technology- and journalism-as-labour: Historical perspectives. *Journalism*, 11(1),.pp. 54–74

Richards, D. (1996). Elite interviewing: Approaches and pitfalls. *Politics*, 16(3), 199–204.

Sambrook, R. (2018) *Global teamwork: The rise of collaboration in investigative journalism.* Reuters.

Schlesinger, P. (1978). *Putting'reality'together: BBC news.* Constable.

Singer, J.B. (2005) 'The political j-blogger: 'Normalizing' a new media form to fit old norms and practices', *Journalism*, 6(2), pp. 173–98. doi:10.1177/1464884905051009.

Smyrnaios, N., Marty, E. and Chauvet, S. 2019, "Journalistic collaboration as a response to disinformation online: The case of the CrossCheck project during the presidential election in France", *Sur Le Journalisme*, vol. 8, no. 1.

Solkin, L. (2022) 'Journalism education in the 21st century: A thematic analysis of the research literature', *Journalism*, 23(2), pp. 444–460. https://doi.org/10.1177/1464884920977299

Tuchman, G. (1978). Making news: A study in the construction of reality. *Free Pres*, 59(4), 1341–1342.

University of Gothenburg. (2021, June 17). *Pioneering journalism education to be developed with support from Erasmus+*. https://www.gu.se/en/news/pioneering-journalism-education-to-be-developed-with-support-from-erasmus

University of Pécs. (2018). *Research report of phase 1*. NEWSREEL Project. https://newsreel.pte.hu/news/research_report_phase_1

Ustad Figenschou, T. (2010). Young, female, Western researcher vs. senior, male, Al Jazeera officials: Critical reflections on accessing and interviewing media elites in authoritarian societies. *Media, Culture & Society*, 32(6), 961–978. https://doi.org/10.1177/0163443710379667

Vaughan, S. (2013). Elite and elite-lite interviewing: Managing our industrial legacy. In *Researching Sustainability* (pp. 105–119). Routledge.

Wahl-Jorgensen, K. (2014). WikiLeaks| Is WikiLeaks challenging the paradigm of journalism? Boundary work and beyond. *International Journal of Communication*, *8*, 12.

11

EXPLORING THE IMPACT OF NON-JOURNALISTS ON THE VALUES AND NORMS OF JOURNALISM IN AN AWARD-WINNING COLLABORATIVE INVESTIGATION

Carolyne M. Lunga

Introduction

Collaborative investigative journalism (CIJ) refers to the practice of two or more journalists and news organisations coming together to do investigative journalism. As the profession continues to face some challenges due to the onslaught of technology, declining revenues and unsustainable business models, CIJ is helping news organisations produce in-depth and impactful journalism (Jenkins and Graves, 2022). Some of the prominent and more recent investigations of a collaborative nature include those done by ICIJ, such as Swazi Secrets (2024), Cyprus Confidential (2023), and Pandora Papers (2021). A closer look at the practice demonstrates that journalistic and non-journalistic actors are collaborating due to a variety of political, social and economic factors. These non-journalistic actors or "those who were once strangers to the profession", as they are referred to by Holton and Belair-Gagnon (2018, p. 70), are extending the journalistic boundaries. Examples of new actors include legal experts, mobile application designers, data specialists, programmers, statisticians and money laundering experts, who are involved in various stages of the news production process (Holton and Belair-Gagnon, 2018, p. 70). The entrance of these new actors may have an impact on traditional journalistic norms and values, particularly objectivity and its associated values of impartiality and fairness, and may also blur the lines between journalists and non-journalists (Chua and Duffy, 2019; Holton and Belair-Gagnon, 2018). de Burgh and Lashmar (2021) note that journalism has become renewed with the entrance of new people and platforms while being characterised by new complexities. This chapter considers the impact of new actors on traditional journalistic norms in CIJ in an award-winning South African project known

DOI: 10.4324/9781003478157-17

as the #GuptaLeaks. As collaborations conducted in places outside the Global North are growing, the more important it is to conduct research that considers how they are being done, who is involved and how they are changing the profession. The chapter is part of a larger research project on collaborative journalism in Southern Africa and discusses new actors in CIJ, provides more information about the #GuptaLeaks and the actor-network theory, which is the theoretical approach informing this paper.

An Innovative Approach to Holding Power to Account

From a technological and professional point of view, CIJ can be said to be an innovative approach to doing investigations to uncover malpractices in the public interest, as those collaborating use advanced technologies and negotiate professional tensions to promote accountability journalism (Lunga, 2022). The concept of collaboration in journalism is not a new phenomenon (Sambrook, 2018). Collaboration in journalism is understood to have begun with American newspapers pooling resources together to cover the Mexican border conflict, resulting in The Associated Press News Agency, born in 1846 (Stonbely, 2017). In the 170 years since, journalists have continued to collaborate. Alfter and Cândea (2019) argue that cross-border journalism developed in the post-Cold War years, with many examples in the Anglo-Saxon investigative journalism tradition, which have coincided with the rise of computer-assisted reporting (CAR) and data journalism.

Previous research suggests that journalistic collaboration is motivated by political, economic, professional, and technological reasons, with academics noting that collaboration can have exponential benefits (Baack, 2016; Berglez and Gearing, 2018). Instead of journalists scooping one another, the need to collaborate has been considered a more viable option, even for legacy media outlets, particularly when investigating issues of common interest with huge consequences for those involved (Berglez and Gearing, 2018; Carson and Farhall, 2018; Stonbely, 2017). Benefits include promoting freedom of expression and information, creating access to shared resources, and promoting reach (Jenkins and Graves, 2019).

Collaborative journalism is also seen as "field repair" (Graves and Konieczna, 2015, p. 1969) where journalists deliberately engage in practices that are "expressly reformist" and seek to "protect journalism by changing it, legitimising new approaches to or definitions of professional, objective reporting". Meanwhile, some scholars see it as exemplifying journalism's transformation (Deuze and Witschge, 2018). Some collaborative teams are formed by taking advantage of existing networks of journalists, or can be formed after a story's facts have been established, and can have at least two journalists working together in "micro-collaboration" (Gearing, 2021). These develop organically, and journalists are invited to collaborate if they are known to be trustworthy, which makes trust a key factor in collaborations (Sambrook, 2018). Most collaborating journalists recognise that teamwork produces high-impact results for tackling global problems such as corruption, money laundering, wars, and organised crime, among other matters, which have become transnational (2018). To understand the new actors in collaborative investigative journalism, we need to understand the various CIJ investigations that are out there.

Models of Collaborative Investigative Journalism

A review of the literature shows that there are distinct models of collaborations. These models are continually evolving as journalists and media organisations collaborate with various actors and perform various tasks. Reviewing these models is useful for this chapter to uncover who some of the new actors involved are. These models are derived mostly from studying case studies in the Global North. In their research on case studies in three European countries, Jenkins and Graves (2019, p. 8) identify three distinct models:

> a permanent network of journalists and non-journalists (the Bureau Local). Legacy and start up news organisations working together on a single extended investigation ('L'Italia Delle Slot'). Regional news organisations sharing content through a collaborative newsroom (Lännen Media).

They argue that "these initiatives involve similar and divergent approaches to network building, project development and content distribution" (Jenkins and Graves, 2019, p. 5). Resource sharing (human and technical) and minimising competition are said to be at the centre of the three models (Jenkins and Graves, 2019, p. 5). In addition, all three models "feature diverse and dispersed networks, are dedicated to creating connections at the virtual and physical levels" (Jenkins and Graves, 2019). Journalists in these organisations see the benefit of collaborations in enabling them to report on issues they would not have been able to do themselves (Jenkins and Graves, 2019). The role of innovative technologies in these networks is important to consider as they offer networks of reporters an opportunity to overcome geospatial boundaries, time zone differences and the cost of international travel (Gearing, 2016). It can be argued that the Panama Papers, with its global outlook, transnational nature and multi-country, media, and journalists' involvement (Heft, Alfter and Pfetsch, 2019; Sambrook, 2018) aligns more with example (i) made up of a permanent and non-permanent network of journalists.

Another different model was studied in the United States and shows various collaborative models based on duration of time and degree of integration. In their analysis of 44 collaborations, mostly in the US, involving more than 500 newsrooms and other news and information providers, Stonbely

(2017, p. 21) came up with six different models of collaborative journalism, classified as:

> "Temporary and Separate," One-time/finite projects in which partners create content separately and share it. "Temporary and Co-creating," One-time/finite project in which partners work together to create content. "Temporary and Integrated," One-time/finite projects in which partners share content/data/resources at the organisational level. "Ongoing and Separate," Ongoing/open-ended collaborations in which partners create content separately and share it. "Ongoing and Co-creating," Ongoing/open-ended collaborations in which partners work together to create content. "Ongoing and Integrated." Ongoing/open-ended collaborations in which partners share content/data/resources at the organisational level.

Stonbely (2017) argues that several projects can fall into more than one category or have evolved into another model, which shows the dynamic nature of collaborations. Another model is one in which academics and students collaborate to investigate common issues of interest, and this is done across borders (Bacon, 2011). The increasing interconnectedness of people and issues around the world has also given rise to consortia of academics and student reporters, such as Europe and Australia's Global Environmental Journalism Initiative (GEJI) Gearing (2014, p. 63) and Canada's *Project Censored*, Australia-New Zealand-Pacific network's *UniMuckraker*, among others.

Sometimes, collaborative journalism is called transnational journalism, emphasising how the practice surpasses national states. For instance, Hellmueller and Konow-Lund (2019) argue that it "signifies journalism's concern with journalistic issues, practices, ideals that surpass national contexts". Meanwhile, in their study on transnational journalism in Europe, Heft, Alfter and Pfetsch (2019) note how cross-border collaborations reduce the imprint of nation-states. In another study, Heft (2021) argues that in another type of transnational journalism, journalists from different nations collaborate in sharing resources and creating content together, but publish stories to their audiences at a national level.

New Actors in Collaborative Journalism

As discussed above, different models of CIJ bring together diverse actors concerned with holding power to account. Jenkins and Graves (2019) argue that "collaborations are bringing together journalists from different news organisations and other actors – such as technologists, data scientists, academics, and community members – to report, produce, and distribute news". CIJ has seen the involvement of hackers (Lewis and Usher, 2014), app designers (Ananny and Crawford, 2015), and suppliers of web analytics (Holton and Belair-Gagnon, 2018) in journalism. For Sambrook (2018), CIJ entails the working together of professional news organisations, NGOs of various kinds, academia, and other public bodies, resulting in the opening of stories and issues which might otherwise go unreported. He notes that "editorial collaboration is different from public collaboration or citizen journalism and crowdsourcing which is a means of funding investigative journalism" (Sambrook, 2018, p. 26). In research on 155 cross-field collaborations across 125 countries, Stonbely and Siemaszko (2022, p. 3) argue that cross-field collaboration is a "partnership involving at least one journalism organisation and one civil society organisation (usually an advocacy organisation but not always) in which they work together to produce content in the service of an explicit ideal or outcome". The involvement of civil society in collaborations highlights potential ethical tensions that can arise in the process. Differences in collaborative models compel us to interrogate the variety of collaborations in diverse contexts to acquire a full understanding of who is involved and how they are working together (Lunga, 2022).

Collaborative Investigative Journalism in South Africa

This chapter is about a South African CIJ project. South Africa is the southernmost country on the African continent, bordered by Namibia, Botswana, Zimbabwe, Mozambique, and Eswatini. It is one of the largest economies in Africa and is well-known for its diverse landscapes, rich cultural heritage, and apartheid history, whose legacy still extends to the present day.

The #GuptaLeaks Investigation

One particularly well-known investigation in South Africa was a collaboration which brought together journalists from the country's three prominent news organisations – *Daily Maverick*, *AmaBhungane*, and *News24*. The #*GuptaLeaks* GuptaLeaks Stories (2017) was based on a huge data set leaked to journalists to uncover corruption. This is the case which is analysed in this chapter, to understand who was involved and the impact that their involvement had on journalistic norms and values. The investigation is lauded by industry for promoting public trust in journalism in a context where disinformation undermines media credibility (Allsop, 2018). The #*GuptaLeaks* involved over 300,000 emails, including images, attachments, bank statements and passports and has been dubbed the "African WikiLeaks" (AmaBhungane website). The investigation implicated the Gupta brothers, Rajesh, Ajay, and Atul, said to be working closely with one of the former president of South Africa's sons, Duduzane Zuma, in corruption involving the awarding of government tenders and contracts (Harber, 2020). The #*GuptaLeaks* investigation demonstrated how "state capture" came about. It included journalists from *AmaBhungane*, the *Daily Maverick*, and *News24* who collaborated to expose control of the state for personal gain (Harber, 2018b). Just like the Panama Papers, the whistle-blowers responsible for leaking the emails that exposed the *#GuptaLeaks* scandal have never been revealed. Despite the positive example of the *#GuptaLeaks* investigation and other examples in which media have exposed corruption within various government departments and the private sector, Daniels (2020) argues that exposing truth in the social media world has become tougher and more dangerous due to the prevalence of misinformation, disinformation, and propaganda and retrenchments. In 2024, one of the largest media organisations in South Africa, Media 24, announced that it will close five of its print editions and transition three of them into digital (Media 24). This move further impacts the role of media in holding power to account.

There are other challenges facing the South African media. Editorial lapses in *The Sunday Times* newsroom between 2007 and 2008 and brown envelope journalism also impact journalism standards (Daniels, 2020; Harber, 2020). Concerns about increasing state and private sector surveillance dominate the discussions on the safety of journalists and their freedom, particularly when they are known to be investigating those in power. Scholars argue that more than two decades post-apartheid, concerns about surveillance still exist in South Africa (Hunter, 2018). The 2021 revelations about the proliferation of Pegasus spyware in more than 30 countries worldwide have created more fears for journalists (Di Salvo, 2022). Surveillance is a great concern noted in Western contexts, which threatens the fourth estate (Lashmar, 2017). Technology gives governments new tools to track down confidential sources (Lashmar, 2017). Hunter (2018) further argues that the non-profit Right to Know (R2K) has shown considerable evidence of spying and that it affects all members of society. According to Hunter (2018), surveillance has been targeted at journalists who have uncovered corruption, state capture, and abuse of power and those who are known to be investigating the National Prosecuting Authority (NPA), the State Security Agency, and the Hawks. Despite these challenges, the South African media is seen in a better position when it comes to freedom of the press and being able to carry out investigative journalism in Southern Africa, albeit in a difficult environment (Daniels, 2020; Lunga, 2022).

Journalistic Values and Norms and Collaborative Investigative Journalism

By discussing norms and values of journalism, this chapter studies the basis through which journalists distinguish themselves from other professionals. This is useful to understand how they evaluate, criticise, and judge other journalists and ways of doing journalism. Principles such as truth, transparency, and accountability foreground what it means to be an investigative journalist. Investigative journalists play an adversarial role when they point out failures of systems or administrations of justice and serve the public interest by telling stories of victims and villains and bringing political and economic power to account (de Burgh, 2008; Ettema and Glasser, 1998; Schudson, 2008). Investigative journalism stories are framed on moral grounds, depicting the evil or wrong deeds that are done by people in power (Ettema and Glasser, 1988). Thus, investigative journalists do not claim to be objective as their reporting is subjective. As collaboration in journalism is bringing in new actors, the professional authority of journalists is eroded through the new actors' involvement in journalistic processes (Konow-Lund and Olsson, 2017). In terms of how stories are produced, investigative journalists thoroughly check documents for evidence and carry out lots of interviews over an extended period (Protess *et al*, 1991; Waisbord, 2000). In investigative journalism, journalists produce "enough evidence" to qualify a story as credible, and thereby significantly impacting audiences' lives (Aucoin, 2006, p. 2). The rise in huge data leaks require complex technologies and specialist knowledge and skills which has catalysed the collaboration of media organisations, professional journalists, freelancers, and actors from various geographical, media contexts and professions. To understand who these new actors are in collaborative journalism and the impact on journalistic norms, this research is informed by Actor-Network Theory (ANT).

Actor-Network Theory

The study is informed by the ANT, pioneered by Bruno Latour (2005), Michel Callon (1986and John Law from Science and Technology Studies (STS) in the early 1980s (Müller, 2015). ANT's intellectual roots are diverse, including sociology, philosophy, and semiotics (Müller, 2015). According to Couldry (2008), ANT seeks to explain social order through the networks of connections among human agents, technologies, and objects. In terms of the #GuptaLeaks, this is about understanding the connections between the journalists, non-journalists, the leak and various other tools employed in the investigation to uncover who/which had more power and the impact on journalistic values and norms. Latour (2005, p. 5) argues that the social is "a trail of associations between heterogeneous elements" and that sociology should be redefined as "*the tracing of associations*" (Emphasis in the original). According to the theory, components in the network shape and define each other and are always in a state of redefinition (Latour, 2005); hence, this chapter's focus is on understanding how those involved in the #GuptaLeaks interacted, shaped, and defined each other and more specifically, how they impacted journalistic norms and values. A central concept of the theory is translation, which refers to "the collaborative process in which diverse entities assemble, form new associations and disconnect..." (Mutzel, 2009, p. 879). Black boxing is another important concept of ANT (Stalph, 2019) wherein Latour (2005) argues that science, technology, and society are inseparable. This chapter sought to understand how the actors transformed each other in the #GuptaLeaks collaboration and the impact on journalistic values and norms. In terms of the limitations, Plesner (2009, p. 624) argues that the theory cannot offer "explanation and generalisation" and fails to adequately address issues of time, power, and interpretation. Müller (2015, p. 30) notes that ANT fails to "distinguish a priori between humans and materials, ignoring that humans are capable of intentions and pursue interests whereas things are not". Failing to consider power has potential limits on this study's ability to understand which actors wielded more power in the investigation and how it impacted the overall output. Focusing too much on associations is criticised for resulting in endless chains of associations and failure to appreciate reasons and differences in network formation processes (Müller, 2015). Informed by the ANT theory, the research seeks to answer the following questions:

RQ1: Who are the new actors in the #GuptaLeaks investigation?
RQ2: How do these new actors impact journalistic norms?

Method

The chapter employed a qualitative approach and used interviews with those involved in the #GuptaLeaks investigation. A non-probability sampling technique known as purposive sampling (Patton, 1990) was used to select the case study to help illuminate the research questions (Patton, 1990). I chose an award-winning collaborative project by industry as the best example of an investigative project which has had a major influence in the country and the media. I identified journalists and editors involved in the investigative collaboration project. They then directed me to the other actors involved, such as the technologist, while the other non-journalistic actor was not available for interview. Informed consent was given in written format, and where it was granted verbally, it was documented. The qualitative approach enabled me to acquire "rich descriptions" (Sofaer, 1999, p. 1102) on the way CIJ is undertaken in a different context and "enhanced my understanding of the context" of the investigation as well as the investigation itself. I interviewed 14 out of 19 participants who were part of the #*GuptaLeaks*, 1 CEO, 3 editors, 1 technological expert, and 9 journalists from Daily Maverick, AmaBhungane, and News24. I sought understanding and insights on who participated in the collaboration, how the relationships were negotiated, and the impact on journalistic values and norms.

Analysis

The #*GuptaLeaks* investigation model can be defined as a one-off collaboration which brought together a non-permanent network of journalists and non-journalists, thereby aligning with Stonbely (2017)'s temporary and co-creating model described as a one-time project which involves partners working together in story creation. In the words of ANT, the *#GuptaLeaks* investigation can be described as a translation process of a non-profit (*AmaBhungane*), privately owned online publications (*Daily Maverick* and *News24*), and non-journalistic actors namely an information technology and a money laundering expert who worked anonymously, the whistle-blowers responsible for the leak and the news sources used by the journalists to verify information. This was against the usual practice of individual journalists and media organisations doing investigative journalism separately as competitors.

> The #GuptaLeaks was different. We hadn't before done such a big collaboration except that we had participated in the ICIJ efforts
>
> *(Editor 1 interview: 9 April 2021)*

The quote above shows that the *#GuptaLeaks* investigation was the first collaborative project that brought the three media organisations together to work on a single project and share ideas, knowledge, and author stories with a common objective of promoting the public interest. It was different from cooperative agreements that media organisations and journalists enter with "shared access to material used for individual ends" (Heft, 2021, p. 457). Before the investigation, the three media organisations had publishing deals in which they co-published their stories for wider reach.

One editor said:

> There was a pre-existing, non-exclusive publication deal between amaBhungane and the Daily Maverick to start with – a partnership if you like. When the #GuptaLeaks came along, that partnership was taken to a different level. It was no longer just amaBhungane supplying stories which Daily Maverick would publish, but working together to obtain the leaks, analyse them and publish stories about them. The team was very quickly widened to include other journalists, experts, and media organisations, which turned it into what may be termed a full-scale collaboration.
>
> *(Journalist 1 Interview: 9 April 2021)*

The quote reveals that the partnership between *AmaBhungane* and *Daily Maverick* existed before the *#GuptaLeaks*. As the ANT calls for the identification of all actors, it is important to acknowledge other human actors involved in journalism production and distribution processes. However, these are often silenced or not recognised: "A news story is not solely the result of social forces. Multiple actors are associated in a complex network, from the truck to the cable man, from the easy-access notepad to a correctly held camera" (Primo and Zago, 2015, p. 42). The other human actors who indirectly participated in the *#GuptaLeaks* investigation such as telephone operators, personal assistants of the editors, the editors' drivers, the postal services that were used in transporting the leak between Johannesburg and Cape Town among others are "invisible" (Primo and Zago, 2015, p. 41). Their invisibility arises from the "limitation of what is considered an actor" in journalism (Primo and Zago, 2015, p. 41). In the interviews with the editors and journalists, they saw themselves as doing journalism and did not mention the existence and value of the "invisible actors". The "invisible actors" did not have a direct impact on the journalistic norms and values, as they did not directly participate in the news production processes.

With the rise in leaks in the present context, news organisations are forced to bring new actors into the investigations and employ technologies that will enable them to make sense of it. After receiving the leak, *Daily Maverick* and *AmaBhungane* had to decide how to work on the leak and brought into the collaboration a South African millionaire businessperson to fund the investigation. Due to fear of surveillance, hacking, and attacks from the Guptas, the investigative journalists decided that they will move to Ireland to analyse the leaks and publish stories from there. Specifically, the businessperson was invited into the project by the *Daily Maverick* editor to cover the expenses of relocating the whistle-blowers and funding the purchase of air tickets and accommodation costs for the team that was to go to Ireland. They later abandoned the idea of going to Ireland after being scooped by *The Sunday Times* and *City Press*, after the businesswoman had leaked the emails. The editors or *#GuptaLeaks* project leaders considered the businessperson part of the "*circle*" (Editor 1 interview: 9 April 2021). However, the businesswoman later pulled out after disagreements on how to go about the investigation.

The disagreement between the editors and the businesswoman on how to manage the leaks and conduct the journalism, as shown by the above quote, demonstrates two factors. First, there were power dynamics and misunderstandings in their association, which occurred due to different understandings of what journalism is and how it should be done. Second, the editors showed autonomy and the ability to exercise agency and power on how the investigation should be conducted, thus preventing external influence on editorial decisions. By refusing to i) work with politicians and ii) publish the leak on public platforms, in the "*Assange way*" as was being suggested by the businessperson, the editors asserted their power and reinforced the narrow understanding of journalism as an exclusive role done by those who research and author stories. In the editors' understanding, she was an outsider to the profession, and they were the insiders. This is a form of boundary work which journalists commonly do to protect the field from outsiders (Carlson and Lewis, 2015). In this case, it can be argued that they were protecting themselves from direct influence from politicians who may have wanted to use the leak for political reasons. The businessperson was not interviewed in the research.

Clashes over control and authority are common when new actors come into journalism (Carlson and Lewis, 2020). The editors perceived her actions as *non-journalistic* (my emphasis), therefore posing a threat to professional journalism. The editors also showed a commitment to wanting to fulfil their journalistic obligations and being ethical. Carlson and Lewis (2020, p. 127) argue that "claims to journalistic professionalism rely on the assertion that news judgments should be free from outside influences…". In defining what journalists do, Journalist 2 had this to say:

> We are journalists, and we know how investigations are done. We disagreed because she wanted us to work with the ANC (the South African ruling political party), but we said no so that we could do the stories the right way, talk to sources and verify information.
>
> *(Journalist 2 interview: 26 April 2021)*

The quote above reinforces the notion that the editors and journalists saw themselves as the ones doing journalism, and they were able to continue carrying out their fundamental role of holding power to account. It can be argued that disagreements in the way an investigation should be conducted can have unforeseen consequences and may require a change of strategy, particularly when an important actor like a funder pulls out. Additionally, tensions can occur when a network of journalistic and non-journalistic actors come together due to different understandings of how an investigation should be done, leading to them being perceived as threats and therefore expelled (Carlson and Lewis, 2020).

The technical complexity of leaks or huge data (more than 300,000 emails with attachments) in the #*GuptaLeaks* investigation necessitated the involvement of actors with backgrounds outside a newsroom, for example, the IT specialist, a computer science graduate, and the money laundering specialist. Their roles were important in the success of the investigation by helping to identify money laundering in the documentation, making documents readable, and identifying wrongdoing in the leak, showing a shared commitment to hold power to account. The investigation demonstrated that diverse actors and actants are contributing to journalistic processes (Primo and Zago, 2015; Ryfe, 2022). Actants such as the leak, computers, the internet, mobile phones, WhatsApp, email clients, the Optical Recognition App (OCR) app, Signal, and websites were part of the investigation showing how journalism is embedded within technology as they could not have been able to do the tasks they did without technology (Primo and Zago, 2015).

Verification of the emails was important, though the editors and journalists indicated that they did not doubt their authenticity because they had trust in the source. The money laundering expert influenced the agenda of the stories as he was the one who could assess the documents and tell journalists where money laundering was involved, thus enabling the journalists to uncover wrongdoing. There was no identified clash among the actors as they undertook the processes of verifying the information from the leak by contacting official sources and going through records. Another partner indicated that objectivity was not possible with investigative storytelling as there was a tension between adversarialism and objectivity since journalists are engaged in doing moral work when they use narratives that emphasise the pain and humiliation of a victim by a villain (de Burgh, 2008; Ettema and Glasser, 1988, 1998). Journalistic conversations in this research showed that objectivity is not an important pillar guiding their work, as they argued that it was impossible to be objective since their work involves making value judgements and siding with the oppressed. In the #GuptaLeaks investigation, journalists dominated the decision-making processes and saw themselves as the primary actors *doing journalism*. Other actors are seen as *"supporters"* who enable them to undertake journalism. Despite the key roles that the IT and money laundering experts played in identifying where the Guptas were involved in money laundering, they were considered supporters.

Conclusion

To fill the gap on how CIJ is being practised in the southern African region, this chapter has engaged with journalists, editors and other actors involved in #GuptaLeaks to identify the new actors involved in the collaboration and impact on journalistic norms and values. Both the actors and actants had agency, and technology is present in most of the activities done by the investigative journalists, which they would not have been able to do alone. Through ANT, the research considered the technologist, the money laundering expert, the funder, the public, sources, and whistle-blowers as key in the collaboration, and it allowed for the research to explore their interactions. In the collaboration, journalists managed to hold on to their professional values and principles such as truth, accountability and public interest. In terms of principles, such as objectivity and impartiality, journalists demonstrated that these were not possible, as investigative stories are told from a subjective point of view. Research limitations included the researcher not being able to see actors and actants in practice due to reliance on interviews and actors' accounts. Future research can use ethnography to acquire a holistic picture of how technology has become intertwined with collaborations and how its adoption influences investigative journalism.

CLASSROOM EXERCISE

- Find an example of a collaborative investigative project that brought together various players and state what roles they played in the success of the investigation.
- What are the potential benefits and challenges of these partnerships?

References

Alfter, B. and Cândea, S. (2019) 'Cross-border collaborative journalism: New practice, new questions', *Journal of Applied Journalism & Media Studies*, 8(2), pp. 141–149.

Allsop, J. (2018) *Were the Gupta Leaks South Africa's Watergate?* https://gijn.org/2018/09/24/were-the-gupta-leaks-south-africas-watergate/ (Last accessed 30 June 2022).

Ananny, M. and Crawford, K. (2015) 'A liminal press: Situating news app designers within a field of networked news production', *Digital Journalism*, 3(2), pp. 192–208. AmaBhungane https://amabhungane.org/stories/special-report-the-guptaleaks-and-more-all-our-stories-on-state-capture-2/ (Last accessed 1 September 2022).

Aucoin, J.L. (2006) *Beyond technological determinism: A model for understanding the new participatory networked news environment.* Kansas: University of Missouri Press.

Baack, S. (2016) *What big data leaks tell us about the future journalism and its past.* https://policyreview.info/articles/news/what-big-data-leaks-tell-us-about-future-journalism-and-its-past/413 (Last accessed 1 September 2022).

Bacon, W. (2011) 'Investigative journalism in the academy- possibilities for story telling across time and space', *Pacific Journalism Review*, 17(1), pp. 45–66.

Berglez, P. and Gearing, A. (2018) 'The Panama and Paradise papers: The rise of a global fourth estate', *International Journal of Communication*, 12, pp. 4573–4592.

Callon, M. (1986) Elements for a sociology translation: The domestication of coquilles Saint-Jacques and the fishermen of the bay of Saint-Brieuc. *Annee Sociologique*, 36, pp. 169–208.

Carson, A. and Farhall, K. (2018) 'Understanding collaborative investigative journalism in a "post-truth" age', *Journalism Studies*, 19(13), pp. 1899–1911.

Carlson, M. and Lewis, S.C. (eds.) (2015) *Boundaries of journalism: Professionalism, practices and participation.* New York: Routledge.

Carlson, M. and Lewis, S.C. (2020) Boundary work. In Wahl-Jorgensen, K. and Hanitzsch, T. (eds.) *The handbook of journalism studies.* 2nd edn. New York: Routledge, pp. 123–135.

Chacón, L.M. and Saldaña, M. (2021) 'Stronger and safer together: Motivations for and challenges of (trans)national collaboration in investigative reporting in Latin America', *Digital Journalism*, 9(2), pp. 196–214.

Chua, S. and Duffy, A.M. (2019) 'Friend, foe or frenemy? Traditional journalism actors changing attitudes towards peripheral players and their innovations', *Media Communication*, 7(4), pp. 112–122.

Couldry, N. (2008) Actor network theory and media: Do they connect and on what terms? In Hepp, A., Krotz, F. Moores, S., Winter, C. (ed) *Connectivity, networks and flows: Conceptualising Contemporary communications.* Cresskill, NJ: Hampton Press, pp 69–92.

Daniels, G. (2020) 'Disrupted for life: An analysis of journalists job losses in South Africa-at odds with journalisms function in a democracy disrupted for life', *Ecquid Novi African Journalism Studies*, 41(3), pp. 2–14.

Di Salvo, P. (2022) Information security and journalism: Mapping a nascent research field," *Sociology Compass*, 16(3).

de Burgh, H. (2008) *Investigative journalism.* New York. Routledge.

de Burgh, H. and Lashmar, P.(eds.) (2021) *Investigative journalism.* 3rd edn. London: Routledge.

Deuze, M. and Witschge, T. (2018) 'Beyond journalism: Theorizing the transformation of journalism', *Journalism*, 19(2), pp. 165–181.

Ettema, J. and Glasser, T.(eds.) (1998) *Custodians of conscience.* New York: Columbia University Press.

Ettema, J.S. and Glasser, T.L. (1988) 'Narrative form and moral force: The realization of innocence and guilt through investigative journalism', *Journal of Communication*, 38, pp. 8–26.

Gearing, A. (2014) 'Investigative journalism in a socially networked world', *Pacific Journalism Review*, 20(1), pp. 61–75.

Gearing, A. (2016) *Global Investigative Journalism in The Network Society*. Published thesis Queensland University of Technology, Brisbane. https://eprints.qut.edu.au/101275/4/Amanda%20Gearing%20Thesis.pdf (Last accessed 11 March 2020).

Gearing, A. (2021) *Disrupting investigative journalism: Moment of death or dramatic rebirth?* London: Routledge, Taylor & Francis Group.

Graves, L. and Konieczna, M. (2015) 'Sharing the news: Journalistic collaboration as field repair.' *International Journal of Communication.* **Vol. 9**, pp. 1966–1984.

#GuptaLeaks (2017) KPMG missed more money laundering red flags https://www.news24.com/fin24/companies/financial-services/guptaleaks-kpmg-missed-more-money-laundering-red-flags-20171124 (Last accessed: 12 June 2020).

#GuptaLeaks Stories (2017) https://amabhungane.org/stories/special-report-the-guptaleaks-and-more-all-our-stories-on-state-capture-2/ (Last accessed 25 September 2022).

Harber, A. (2018) *South Africa's Extraordinary Year: Journalists Turn the Tide Against Corruption.* https://gijn.org/2018/03/21/south-africas-extraordinary-year-journalists-turn-tide-corruption/ (Last accessed 10 May 2020).

Harber, A. (2020) *So, for the record: Behind the headlines in an era of state capture.* Cape Town: Jonathan Ball.

Heft, A. (2021) 'Transnational journalism networks "From below". Cross-border journalistic collaboration in individualized newswork', *Journalism Studies*, 22(4), pp. 454–474.

Heft, A., Alfter, B. and Pfetsch, B. (2019) 'Transnational journalism networks as drivers of Europeanisation', *Journalism*, 20(9), pp. 1183–1202.

Hellmueller, L. and Konow-Lund, M. (2019) 'Transnational journalism', in Vos, T.P., Hanusch, F., Sehl, A., Dimitrakopoulou, D. and Geertsema-Sligh, M. (eds.) *The International Encyclopedia of Journalism Studies*. Hoboken, NJ: Wiley-Blackwell, pp. 1–7. https://doi.org/10.1002/9781118841570.iejs0179

Holton, A.E. and Belair-Gagnon, V. (2018) 'Strangers to the game? Interlopers, intralopers, and shifting news production', *Media and Communication*, 6(4), pp. 70–78.

Hunter, M. L (2012) (ed.) *The investigative journalism casebook*. Paris: UNESCO.

Jenkins, J. and Graves, L. (2019) *Case studies in collaborative local journalism*. Reuters Institute for the study of journalism. https://reutersinstitute.politics.ox.ac.uk/our-research/case-studies-collaborative-local-journalism (Last accessed 7 March 2024).

Jenkins, J. and Graves, L. (2022) 'Do more with less: Minimizing competitive tensions in collaborative local journalism', *Digital Journalism*, 12(2), pp. 1–20.

Konow-Lund, M. and Olsson, E. (2017) 'Social media's challenge to journalistic norms and values during a terror attack', *Digital Journalism*, 5(9), pp. 1192–1204.

Lashmar, P. (2017) 'No more sources?' *Journalism Practice*, 11(6), pp. 665–688.

Lashmar, P. (2019) *Sources and source relations*. New Jersey: John Wiley & Sons.

Lashmar, P. (2021) 'National security', in de Burgh, H. and Lashmar, P. (eds.) *Investigative journalism*, 3rd edn. London: Routledge, pp. 30–43.

Latour, B. (2005) *Reassembling the social: An introduction to actor-network-theory.* Oxford: Oxford University Press.

Lewis, S.C., and Usher, N. (2014) 'Code, collaboration and the future of journalism: A case study of the Hacks/Hackers global network.' *Digital Journalism*, 2(3), pp. 383–393.

Lunga, C.M. (2022) Overcoming the Challenges to Investigative Journalism in Southern Africa https://gijn.org/tag/ijhub/ (Last accessed 26 August 2022).

Mesquita, L. (2022) *Collaborative Journalism and Normative Journalism: Intersections and implications of normative roles in the collaborative action of journalists, media practitioners and news organisations in Latin America*. Dublin City University (Unpublished thesis).

Müller, M. (2015) 'Assemblages and actor-networks. Rethinking socio-material power, politics and space.' *Geography Compass*, 9(1), 27–41.

Mützel, S. (2009) 'Networks as culturally constituted processes: A comparison of relational sociology and actor-network theory', *Current Sociology*, 57(6), pp. 871–887. https://doi.org/10.1177/0011392109342223.

News24. https://www.news24.com/ (Last accessed 23 August 2022).

Patton, M.Q. (1990) *Qualitative evaluation and research methods.* London: Sage.

Plesner, U. (2009) "An actor-network perspective on changing work practices: Communication technologies as actants in newswork", *Journalism Studies*, 10(5), pp. 617–633.

Primo, A. and Zago, G. (2015) 'Who and what do journalism?', *Digital Journalism*, 3(1), pp. 38–52.

Protess, D.L., Cook, L.F., Doppelt, J.C., Ettema, J.S., Gordon, M.T., Leff, D.R. and Miller, P. (1991) *The journalism of outrage: Investigative reporting and agenda building in America.* London: The Guilford Press.

Ryfe, D. (2022) 'Actor-network theory and digital journalism', *Digital Journalism*, 10(2), pp. 267–283.

Sambrook, R. (ed.) (2018) *Global teamwork: The rise of collaboration in investigative journalism.* Oxford: University of Oxford.

Schudson, M. (2008) *Why democracies need an unlovable press.* Cambridge: Polity Press.

Sofaer, S. (1999) 'Qualitative methods: What are they and why use them?', *Health Services Research*, 34(5 Pt 2), pp. 1101–1118.

Stalph, F. (2019) 'Hybrids, materiality, and black boxes: Concepts of actor-network theory in data journalism research', *Sociology Compass*, 13(11), e12738. https://doi.org/10.1111/soc4.12738

Stonbely, S. (2017) Report: Comparing models of collaborative journalism | Collaborative Journalism. Available at: https://collaborativejournalism.org/models/ (Accessed: 26 July 2021)

Stonbely, S. and Siemazkso, H. (2022) Cross-field collaboration. How and why journalists and civil society organisations around the world are working together. Cross-field-collaboration-How-and-why-journalists-and-civil-society-organizations-around-the-world-are-working-together-MAR2022.pdf

Waisbord, S. (2000) *Watchdog journalism in South America: News, accountability and democracy.* Columbia University Press. New York.

12

TEACHING INVESTIGATIVE JOURNALISM

The Centre for Investigative Journalism

Tom Sanderson

Introduction

This chapter aims to provide an understanding of the work of the educational charity, the Centre for Investigative Journalism (CIJ). It discusses some of the pressing issues facing investigative journalism and describes how the organisation is addressing these through its **Projects**.

It goes on to give an overview of the subject areas that form the foundation of an investigative journalist's skillset in the contemporary industry – the primary focus of the CIJ's **Training** provision. This encompasses a broad range of techniques and knowledge, and while it can be difficult to find space for all of these in already extensive curricula, all are essential to preparing students for such a career.

For each subject, the chapter provides some guidance on best practices for introducing the practical skills involved to students and outlines specific exercises that can help students to refine their own proficiencies.

The Centre for Investigative Journalism

The CIJ was established in 2003 by the late investigative journalist and film-maker Gavin MacFadyen and others as a response to a worrying decline in investigative reporting.

As MacFadyen (2012) himself later put it in evidence to the Select Committee on Communications: 'It should be said that, for the last 20 years, investigative reporting, as I am sure everybody here knows, has been on major decline in Britain from what it was—major television programmes like World in Action, This Week and Panorama—to where we are now; we have nothing,

DOI: 10.4324/9781003478157-18

really, that is comparable, or at least comparable with the depth and frequency that those programmes were'.

One core reason behind this decline was the economic problems within the wider industry, which stemmed in large part from the disruption to traditional business models brought by the digital age (Houston, 2010). These have been much discussed (Franklin, 2014) but were most keenly felt in investigative journalism (Lashmar, 2009), since the practice often requires greater resources in both time and expenditure, and carries greater risk than day-to-day reporting or features.

But there were other factors which MacFadyen and his colleagues were aware of. For instance, they saw a lack of innovation in the industry, especially when compared to the enthusiastic incorporation of new technologies in the United States, where Computer-Assisted Reporting (soon to become better known as Data Journalism) was already well established and the innovation in philanthropic funding models, pioneered by US organisations such as the Center for Public Integrity.[1]

In addition, there was a long-established tendency for investigative journalists to work as 'lone wolves'; much more comfortable competing with each other for stories than cooperating toward the same ends (Houston, 2010). It was becoming clear by the turn of the century, though, that there were many benefits to collaborations between investigative journalists, even those based at nominally competing outlets and especially where such collaborations reached across national borders. When the subjects of investigation, such as international financial flows, organised crime networks and multination corporations, work increasingly seamlessly across such divides, it becomes more and more important for journalists to build the networks that can sustain cross-border projects themselves.

Addressing these negative factors then became the central mission of the CIJ and is what still drives the organisation today. We fulfil it in several ways. First and foremost, we provide hands-on, skills-based training in a wide range of investigative methodologies and practices. The training is designed for journalists, but open to all, and we take care to ensure it is as affordable, accessible and inclusive as possible. Our provision differs from higher education in that all courses are short and participatory; we do not have assessments or formal accreditation, but this allows us to keep a sharp focus on the practical application of skills and tools. It works best to augment academic study or continuing professional development.

Our most frequent method of delivery is through **Scheduled training**, where we will work with an expert or team of experts to develop and schedule a course and then open it for bookings. We keep it accessible by charging for places on a sliding scale, where organisations sending staff members pay a higher rate based on their size and purpose, in order to subsidise cheaper places for freelancers and students. The CIJ is run on a non-profit basis, so any surplus to the costs of running the course is reinvested in further development and subsidies. In addition, we deliver **Bespoke training** where we work closely with an organisation to tailor our provision to the needs of their staff. We also provide guest lectures or supplementary training for journalism students at higher education institutions.

Much of this training is delivered online, since the advantages in terms of accessibility and affordability for people based outside of London and even across the world often outweigh the benefits of an in-person classroom setting.

However, our **Events** have an emphasis on networking and collaboration, and so work far better in person. These include our annual Summer Conference, Regional Conferences across the United Kingdom and our biennial Logan Symposia. Our events blend training workshops in all the investigative skills we specialise in with talks, panels and lectures from leading practitioners and authors of high-profile investigations.

Finally, we also deliver training through our **Projects**, which are externally funded via grants. This allows us to target specific groups or areas where we feel the application of more advanced investigative methods can help to alleviate a problem or redress an imbalance or injustice. Often, these projects allow us to deliver training free at the point of use, ensuring we get practical research skills to people who can apply them for the greatest impact.

Projects

Open Climate Reporting Initiative

As Hopke (2022) noted, 'everyone is a climate reporter now'. At the end of another year of broken temperature records and seemingly relentless climatic disasters across the globe, her words ring with ever clearer prescience.

The point is not just that journalists from every geographic patch, whether local, national, or international, cannot ignore the impact of anthropogenic climate change in their reporting, but that every thematic beat, from politics and business to sport and fashion, must also understand and address climate change causes and impacts if they are to inform their audiences with contextual honesty.

This reality became the driving force behind the CIJ's largest project to date, in terms of both scale and ambition, the Open Climate Reporting Initiative (OCRI).[2] We began by identifying the major gaps in the current landscape of climate reporting.

The first two gaps were areas the CIJ was well-equipped to address; limited access to the skills, tools and understanding required to critically analyse and explain climate change; and an investigative focus to ensure that while journalists report on what is happening as the climate crisis unfolds, they are also able to tell stories that show why each event occurs, covering not just the scientific drivers behind heatwaves, wildfires, droughts and floods, but also the neglect, corruption and vested interests that have led to such events, despite decades of warnings and research (for example, Shukla et al, 2022) into available mitigation and solutions.

To deal with the third element identified as lacking in mainstream climate reporting, though, we needed to engage with partner organisations throughout the globe. Despite widespread recognition that populations of the Global South face the greatest threats from a changing climate, though their contributions to the crisis have been far smaller than those in the global north, the voices of Global South journalists and communities are still marginalised in international reporting (Donovan, 2023). Far too often, large news organisations send white Europeans and Americans to report on disasters in Africa, Asia and Latin America and treat professional journalists working in such regions as fixers and sources, despite their greater experience and far-reaching knowledge of local contexts.

To help address this, it was crucial to work collaboratively with journalist associations and media development organisations within the regions, to ensure that the training and support we could provide reached journalists who came from and understood the communities they were reporting on. The project is now entering its third year, but across 2022 and 2023, we partnered with 20 organisations to deliver training, networking, mentoring and project support across 53 countries from Mexico to Bangladesh.

We were clear from the outset that our aim was to build skill-sharing networks, rather than send Western experts to teach journalists what we thought they needed. If the project was to have meaningful impacts, it needed to be responsive to different regional and national contexts. We fostered constructive dialogue with our partner organisations, worked with them to implement preparatory research to identify the areas that mattered most to journalists working in each region and collaborated on developing tailored curricula based on the findings the groundwork unearthed.

Data journalism techniques featured heavily, as did open-source intelligence, satellite imagery and mapping. An important innovation was the development of a handbook designed to support journalists in reporting the annual Conference of the Parties (COP) process, which has now been made available for free download.[3] Many of the training programmes maximised their impact by providing expertise to new cohorts of trainers who were then equipped to disseminate the necessary knowledge and skills to others in their own networks.

Alongside the practical training, we supported live projects, across several forms including mentoring, development workshops and story grants; work which helped many projects reach publication. So far, the project has supported 143 published investigations. There is insufficient space to discuss all of them here, but highlights include Sechaba Mokhethi's investigation into the missing $15Bn that had been earmarked to build windfarms in Lesotho

(Mokhethi, 2022); an analysis of the delays and insufficiencies of multilateral funds intended to mitigate climate impacts in Costa Rica (Soto and Fallas, 2023); and a series of projects examining the decline of mangrove forests across Cameroon (Mbonge and Mounde Ngamo, 2022).

One element that has become clear through OCRI is the impact of involving editors at established newsrooms in the push to improve climate reporting. We partnered with the United Nations Educational, Scientific and Cultural Organization (UNESCO) to deliver a pilot project which built on our work: Climate Change in News Media targeted editors and teams of their staff in newsrooms across Nigeria, Ghana, Cameroon and Gabon. Enlisting the help of previous partners in both regions, we were able to build dedicated training curricula to help embed climate reporting into their ongoing editorial schedules.

An important next step for the CIJ will be to take the insights gleaned from our work on OCRI and build it into an ongoing course that is flexible, practical and above all investigative. The aim is to deliver Climate Investigations training across the journalism industry. Hopke (2022) was right when she wrote, 'a fundamental shift is needed in how news organizations cover climate issues, and that starts with training'.

Lyra McKee Bursary Scheme

Another problem we address is closer to home. Diversity and representation in the UK journalism sector have historically been poor. Those from ethnic minorities, the working class and LGBTQ+ backgrounds face barriers in attaining secure employment within the industry (Spilsbury, 2023).

This means that the mirror of society that journalism presents is skewed in damaging ways. Issues that matter are too often reflected upon through a distorted prism that foregrounds the concerns of a wealthy, well-connected few who have little experience in common with wider society. Not only does this result in important stories being overlooked and underreported, but it also feeds into the growing mistrust of the media as a profession, at a time when access to accurate information and nuanced opinion is more important than ever (Ross Arguedas et al, 2023).

In early 2019, one CIJ alumna was spectacularly bucking this trend. Lyra McKee was a young and courageous Irish investigative journalist. Despite personal disability, the need to care for her disabled mother, as well as fighting the in-built bias against working class entrants to journalism, Lyra was in the early years of what promised to be an illustrious career when she was shot dead by dissident republicans in Derry in April 2019.

Having known Lyra through our training and conferences, we were immensely saddened by the news, but we remain inspired by her determination, and so in May 2019, we launched a bursary scheme as our way of honouring her memory.

Jointly funded by our long-standing supporter, the Lorana Sullivan Foundation and members of Lyra's family, the aim of this six-month bursary scheme is to support people from underprivileged backgrounds who aspire to become journalists or who are at the very early stages of their journalism career.

The scheme provides investigative journalism training on investigative methodology, data journalism, using the Freedom of Information Act and open-source intelligence tools, as well as access to the CIJ Summer Conference.

Alongside this training, the scheme offers additional assistance designed to help participants make the most of the opportunity and ensure they feel prepared to take the next steps once they graduate. Each participant is assigned a mentor with whom they have a series of one-to-one meetings throughout the scheme, giving them a chance to ask questions about applying the skills they've learnt, discuss their story ideas and get tips for navigating the wider industry.

This has proven to be a crucial component – participants frequently stress how important mentoring is. We are very lucky to have dedicated and generous mentors in Jenna Corderoy of Open Democracy and Emma Youle, the former special correspondent at HuffPost UK, both award-winning journalists and editors.

Towards the conclusion of the programme, all participants prepare a pitch which they get the chance to put to a panel of working editors across the UK media and several of the stories pitched have been commissioned and gone on to be published (See for example, Hughes, 2022, and Gouveia, 2024).

Since the mentoring aspect was introduced in 2021, 31 people have been trained and mentored under this scheme. Each year, about 40–50% of the trainees get jobs in the industry and have their stories commissioned and published and win further scholarships to do more journalism training.

Destinations for alumni of the scheme and their stories include BBC, Open Democracy, the Belfast Telegraph, Tortoise Media and the Northern Echo. One has even established their own community journalism outlet, The Leicester Gazette, following the model of the Bristol Cable.

Community Journalism Projects

A long-standing concern at the CIJ has been the increasing death spiral of local journalism, particularly the capacity for investigations at this level. The problem is well-documented and not unique to the UK. A combination of concentration in local media ownership, declining advertising revenue and subsequent job losses and paper closures have meant large areas of the country lack a dedicated news provider and left journalists working local patches with minimal time and resources to pursue much more than regurgitating press releases from the local authority (Barclay *et al*, 2022).

There are, however, people working to address the issue, running independent, hyperlocal and community-focused outlets. These organisations are frequently pioneering innovative structures, whether that's through coopera-tive models, membership schemes or what are known as Community Interest Companies. These new approaches hold the potential to build a more partici-patory, two-way relationship between journalists and their readers, alongside the prospect of finding new ways to fund public interest reporting that avoids the editorial influence of either advertisers or state funding.

It is undoubtedly very hard work. We spoke to many of the people engaged in these efforts back in 2016 to identify the primary barriers they felt pre-vented them from doing more investigative research. Unsurprisingly, the main answer was a lack of time and money.

We didn't feel well-placed to address either of these issues directly. We rec-ognised that there were already organisations doing excellent work supporting the new outlets in these ways, such as the Centre for Community Journalism,[4] the Bureau Local project at the Bureau of Investigative Journalism[5] and the Independent Media Association.[6] But we reasoned that we could provide ac-cess to skills and training to help them make the best use of what time and money they do have.

With this in mind, we organised a series of workshops during 2016 and 2017 that we took to 11 different cities, reaching all four nations of the UK as well as the Republic of Ireland. These workshops covered a range of different skills, including Data Journalism, Media Law, Company Accounts and FOI (Freedom of Information) Requests.

The next year, we built on the project's success, working directly with some of the most established outlets we had supported. In partnership with the Bris-tol Cable,[7] the Manchester Meteor,[8] Portsmouth's Star and Crescent[9] and The Ferret[10] in Scotland, we ran six-week-long programmes of training, expanding the subjects covered and going into greater depth, allowing them to build new cohorts of skilled contributors from their existing supporter networks.

In addition, we ran our own story lab focusing on more advanced data jour-nalism techniques, which we delivered to a hand-picked group of community journalists who already had some investigative projects under their belts.

We had planned to follow this up with a new project focused on local inde-pendent media in some of the most deprived boroughs of London, where the problems of news deserts and local accountability gaps are just as acute. This two-year in-person programme was planned to launch at the start of 2020, but the global pandemic meant we had to adapt.

We ran an online pilot of the programme on a reduced scale, support-ing an in-depth investigation into a controversial development in the London borough of Haringey. The project then ran in full online as the Collabora-tive Community Journalism programme, which brought together small teams comprised of an independent news outlet from one of the identified boroughs, a community campaign group and an early-career journalist with a connection to the local area.

The programme ran for two years and covered a range of important issues. From Greenwich (Lowe, 2021) council's misuse of funds supposedly ring-fenced to help those living with disabilities, to the offshore links and under-hand tactics of the property developers behind the gentrification of the famous Brick Lane (Kehoe, 2023) in Tower Hamlets, the stories that came out of the project showed the power of building genuine links across a community in a way that most local journalists in the UK rarely get the time or opportunity to do these days (Barclay *et al*, 2022).

Alongside supporting community journalists with investigative skills, we've also put time and effort into helping journalists establish new community-focused outlets, disseminating the best practices and the lessons learnt from those pioneers of the emerging sector. Alongside Rachel Hamada, one of the founders of the Ferret, we developed a participatory workshop on 'New Business Models for Journalism', helping those considering taking the leap into community journalism to think through the different options for organising, funding and building their own community outlets.

Some excellent organisations have subsequently been set up by participants in these workshops, including the award-winning Greater Govanhill,[11] which covers the south side of Glasgow, featuring community campaigns and an inclusive style, frequently translating articles into Polish, Czech and Româna. While it takes huge amounts of hard work to successfully establish new outlets like this, we hope the space and advice provided by our workshop played a small part in that success.

Training

Data Journalism

One of the core areas the CIJ has always focused on is Data Journalism. We began training on the subject before the term was widespread in the UK. Even in the US, it was more commonly referred to then as Computer-Assisted Reporting or CAR. Helped by the foresight of our Founding Director, Gavin Mac-Fadyen and the generosity of pioneers of data journalism, such as David Donald, we played a major role in disseminating the practice and establishing it firmly into the workflow of newsrooms in the UK and Europe (Hewett, 2015).

It can, of course, be argued that good journalism has always been data journalism, since datasets are fundamentally collations of information. Any journalist who has been producing work without reference to collated information is unlikely to be doing a decent job. Broadly, though, when we talk about data journalism, we mean leveraging computational processing power to collect, analyse and present information.

Though this has been producing excellent investigative research for decades – see Philip Meyer's coverage of the 1967 Detroit riots (Meyer, 1968),

Bill Dedman's 1989 Colour of Money project (Dedman, 1989), or Stephen Doig's reporting on Hurricane Andrew in 1993,[12] all of which won Pulitzer Prizes – the more recent exponential increases in the power and accessibility of software for data analysis have revolutionised the practice of investigative journalism, both through drastically reducing the research time required and by opening up areas for investigation that would simply be impossible without these new tools.

It should be noted at the outset that most good examples of data journalism have few, if any, numbers or statistics contained within the final published pieces. The data here is driving the journalism, but the focus is still on storytelling and during our analysis, we must always remember the human stories that lie behind each data point (Hudoon, 2021).

Because of the ongoing innovation around the subject, 'Data Journalism' is a term that encompasses a wide range of separate, though interrelated, techniques and the tools and practices for these are constantly evolving. While they're all useful for investigative research, it's perfectly possible to produce solid data journalism with just a decent grasp of standard spreadsheet functions and some knowledge of data cleaning tools like OpenRefine. Even those who don't self-identify as 'data journalists' should understand that knowing their way around a spreadsheet is an essential competency these days. Otherwise, they risk closing off many avenues of investigation for themselves.

We generally teach data journalism at a range of different levels. Our introductory course, 'Finding Stories with Data', assumes no knowledge of spreadsheet functions and aims to get participants comfortable with cleaning, sorting and filtering datasets, as well as performing calculations and analysis through Pivot Tables.

Of course, these are the kind of data analysis skills that are taught across a huge range of disciplines. One element that makes data journalism training different is the need to recognise that trainees will have quite specific objectives in their use of data.

These will range from finding story leads by identifying extremes and outliers through comparison, building evidence cases to support an existing investigative hypothesis or examining the wider context around a subject, issue or finding that is already a focus of a developing story.

The underlying framework for this training is the concept of 'interviewing' data. The idea that any given dataset should be treated as a source like any other tends to make the prospect of data analysis more conceptually accessible, even to those journalists who have an ingrained dislike of statistics or numbers. To see data analysis as no different from asking questions of an interviewee allows us to relate to the journalistic objectives of data research somewhat more readily than conceiving of it as dry quantitative analysis.

In many ways, a dataset is an ideal interviewee – it may be terrible at small talk, but it does not have off days, and we don't need to work to win its trust.

It also has an incredible memory for numbers, dates and facts, and it cannot lie to its interviewer, though we must bear in mind that it might have been lied to by others.

Alongside the conceptual framework of a data 'interview', and at least as important in communicating the necessary skills, is the provision of examples and exercises with which participants can put their learning into practice. There is a huge range of datasets which can serve as good sandboxes on which to practise data journalism skills, but several factors make some datasets more effective than others in this role.

An ideal dataset holds information with clear relevance to the public interest, allowing us to show the potential stories that can be gleaned from it, although it must also have enough data which is too granular or irrelevant to be of interest, providing a demonstration of how analysis quickly brings information of interest to the surface.

A dataset should also not be too clean. Instances of duplicate or incorrectly entered information provide a means by which we can show the importance of cleaning a dataset prior to drawing conclusions from our analysis, as well as allowing us to demonstrate the cleaning process. However, it must of course not be so messy that it requires a long process of cleaning before coherent questions can be asked of it.

Once the fundamental tools have been demonstrated, students should be given some sample questions to ask of an example dataset. We have found that, at least in the UK context, the data on political donations published by the Electoral Commission[13] works well, but it is worth bearing the above criteria in mind when looking for other datasets to use as examples. Try to find similar datasets with local or thematic elements that carry relevance to a particular group of participants. Look out for excellent newsletters published by data journalists, such as Sophie Warnes' *Fair Warning*,[14] or *Data is Plural*[15] from Jeremy Singer-Vine. Both regularly highlight potentially interesting datasets, which can make good training exercise material.

Once familiar with the fundamental functions with which journalists can 'interview' a dataset, we encourage participants to take our more advanced course, 'Data-Driven Investigations'. This course reinforces the learning from the introductory course and embeds a focused investigative mindset within the techniques. Practical work on participants' live projects is threaded throughout the course.

Though building familiarity with the primary functions of spreadsheet software will go quite far in terms of incorporating data analysis into journalistic research, students of data journalism should be encouraged to explore coding. Some of the best data-driven investigations would have been impossible to conduct using spreadsheets alone, due to the size or complexity of the datasets involved, but coding can save time and increase efficiency in data projects of any scale.

The flexibility and automation possibilities that applying programming languages such as R or Python can bring to data analysis can be transformative in terms of the time and effort required to draw meaningful conclusions from large datasets. Accordingly, the CIJ now runs dedicated courses using both these languages for data journalism projects.

Coding also allows journalists to build their own datasets for analysis through web scraping. This term refers to automating the collection of information that is available on a website or websites but is not provided in an analysable form. Far too often, public authorities providing data in the interests of transparency manage to find incredibly inaccessible and inconvenient ways to publish it. In these and other circumstances, web scraping can be a huge help.

Wherever information could be collated into an analysable dataset through copying and pasting, a web scraper will be able to do the job with a minimum of time and effort. As Jonathan Stoneman, one of our core data training team, often says, 'if a data journalism task is boring and repetitive, you're probably doing it wrong'. In such cases, coding and web scraping are often the best solution.

One further element in data journalism that can be facilitated through the application of coding is the presentation of data to an audience to ensure clarity and accessibility. This is often termed data visualisation, but it also encompasses personalisation or interactivity, in cases where it makes sense to allow a reader to change the way data is presented to them to enhance its relevance. The classic case is explanatory reporting around budget announcements,[16] where readers can enter details about their own financial situation and view the ways in which changes might affect them, but there are many other examples where this can be applied.

Platforms for building visualisations of data without code are available, such as Flourish or Datawrapper, but learning Python or R will allow journalists to build visualisations themselves both easily and quickly. Besides the technical skills to create them, though, it is key for journalism trainees to learn the principles behind visualising data: which form will work for which story or dataset and the design choices that can maximise clarity and minimise superfluous or misleading elements, what is often termed 'chart junk'. If this understanding is properly covered, then the process of building visualisations will be far more effective regardless of the platform or programming language used.

So, what of the future of data journalism? In such a rapidly evolving practice, it is very difficult to make solid predictions, but many claim that the integration of AI will radically change the discipline (Simon, 2024). Similar claims have been made about nearly all aspects of human endeavour, of course, but it does seem likely that there will be significant impacts for data journalism. Almost certainly, there will be opportunities to eliminate even further the 'boring and repetitive' aspects, and we must hope that this allows greater scope for future data journalists to tell more impactful data-driven stories in new and innovative ways.

Open-Source Intelligence

A more recent development in the CIJ's training provision is the incorporation of open-source intelligence, or OSINT. The term originates from security services jargon and refers to information that is freely available, primarily from digital sources. OSINT is a category that sits alongside HUMINT (human intelligence, or informants) and SIGINT (signals intelligence, or the kind of large-scale, dragnet surveillance that was revealed by Edward Snowden in 2013[17]).

Since the rise of the practice among state security circles, OSINT has been adopted and adapted by those working toward more public interest objectives. Among the first to do this were loose-knit teams of amateur internet sleuths, from which emerged the organisation Bellingcat, though more formal organisations were also pioneering elements of the discipline around the same time. Forensic Architecture has been developing the techniques of OSINT and applying them to investigations into war crimes, state violence and environmental harms for many years now.[18]

Over the last decade, the benefits of OSINT have been recognised and incorporated into investigative research by a huge range of other actors, including international NGOs, such as Amnesty International[19] and Global Witness[20] and a wide range of newsrooms from the BBC[21] to the New York Times.[22]

Like data journalism, OSINT covers a broad spectrum of different practices and techniques, from the fundamentals of refining online searches to be as specific as possible, through targeted social media analysis to find details and connections of people, organisations or political movements, to verification, geolocation and satellite imagery. Even within these practices, there is a range of different use cases and objectives from everyday newsgathering to complex in-depth investigations such as the 2020 BuzzFeed News investigation into internment camps in Xinjiang, China.[23] This is one factor that means the teaching of OSINT skills to journalism students is best served by focusing less on the exact skills and tools involved and more on the mindset required to conduct this type of research, alongside the problem-solving and know-how which will facilitate students' ongoing self-directed learning on the subject.

A further – and arguably more important – factor that leads to the above conclusion is the fast-changing nature of the discipline. The practice of data journalism has evolved significantly since its emergence as a field, and other skills still require regular updating, but OSINT practices change on a far more rapid timescale.

Social media platforms amend their infrastructure and render formerly essential tools defunct as happened with Facebook Graph Searching; online projects providing information and search capabilities useful for OSINT lose funding or support and go offline; information law changes remove access to actionable data as the General Data Protection Regulation (GDPR) did with the 'WhoIs' registration records for web domains; the best tools and platforms frequently go behind prohibitively expensive (even for a national newsroom budget) paywalls, restricting previously core OSINT techniques to corporate intelligence and law enforcement.

The unstable nature of the field means that solely providing students with in-depth training on the current tools and techniques is almost guaranteed to become obsolete, sometimes even before their graduation. Far more effective is to use OSINT examples and use cases to instil in students an understanding of the types of problems that OSINT can solve and then provide them with the resources and resourcefulness which will allow them to seek out the tools and techniques that are currently effective as and when they face one of these problems.

That said, it is still worth students getting to grips with the kind of problems that current OSINT tools can solve. Useful exercises for these might include finding the location of a building from a photo[24] or profiling a local politician or business figure using Google operators and people finding tools.[25]

The saving grace for OSINT as a practice for journalism is the active and generally welcoming online communities that have built up around it. Incorporating access and involvement in these communities into OSINT provision for journalism students is an important further step in ensuring that graduates are both informed and capable of keeping themselves up to date when it comes time for them to use the techniques in live research projects. Inclusion in reading lists of the many newsletters, resource platforms and online community discussions about journalistic OSINT,[26] as well as encouraging active participation in OSINT Capture-The-Flag (CTF) events[27] and engagement with online courses, are all important ways to ensure OSINT teaching is and will remain practical and relevant.

Safety and Source Protection

While you can make a lot of progress in an investigation from published data and open-source information online, most projects – especially those that lead to wide-ranging and lasting impacts – will at some point require journalists to speak to human sources, whether that's to provide additional context, corroborate a hypothesis formed during initial research or provide crucial evidence to stand up a story.

In the most extreme cases, journalists need a whistle-blower from inside a company or organisation to explain what's really going on and provide the proof required to publish. Whistle-blowing is a difficult act which takes courage and conviction and comes with inevitable stress and often great risk. A journalist can never fully alleviate these factors, but they can be mitigated by practising good source protection processes.

This starts with keeping a source's identity confidential and, in the digital age, this requires a good working knowledge of information security and secure communication tools. In light of Snowden's revelations about the global digital surveillance capabilities of security services, and the many examples where these have targeted journalists and those who pass them information, it is clear that the task of maintaining confidentiality for sources and communication with them is becoming harder and harder.

Reports in 2021 (Kirchgaessner *et al*, 2021) showing Pegasus spyware was bought by governments and law enforcement from 50 different countries and used to spy on nearly 200 journalists underline how careful we need to be when communicating digitally. This software was implicated in the especially gruesome case of Jamal Khashoggi, the Saudi journalist brutally murdered in 2018 after his family and close associates were surveilled using Pegasus by security agents linked to the United Arab Emirates (Priest, 2021).

Even in the face of greater spyware sophistication, there are ways to minimise risk. For students, it is important to instil a solid grounding in good digital hygiene, the kind of processes and practices that everyone should be mindful of such as using strong unique passwords (and preferably a password management software such as 1Password, KeePass or Bitwarden), setting up 2-Factor Authentication on your accounts and encrypting your hard drives. Alongside teaching journalism students how to set these up and become comfortable with using them, it is important to ensure they understand why they are particularly important for their chosen career.

Quite apart from the ethical imperative to protect the confidentiality of your sources, it is particularly important for career progress. A journalist who has failed to protect a source is unlikely to win the trust of others, or indeed maintain the trust of any people they have previously spoken to. Conversely, those journalists who have treated their sources' confidentiality with care and have been seen to respect that duty will be far more likely to be approached by new sources who wish to reveal information in the public interest. Many high-profile scoops have come to journalists at least in part because they have worked hard to build a reputation for being able to protect the identity of those who pass information to them.

However, while digital security is imperative for any good investigative journalist, it is not the only aspect of good source protection and general safety processes. Anti-harassment strategies are becoming more and more important. While many people who target online abuse at journalists are acting alone, or are part of decentralised internet subcultures, the rise in organised and sometimes state-sanctioned and funded 'trolling' (Reporters Without Borders, 2018) has made this an essential skill for journalists, and especially those who are likely to anger powerful actors as should be expected in the course of conducting good journalistic investigations.

Strategies to mitigate and counter online harassment have much in common with source protection strategies, but are focused more on the protection of a journalist's own personal data and often require some coordination with their friends and families. One excellent practical exercise that can help students understand the online vulnerability of their personal data is 'self-doxing'. Guiding students through the act of searching for their own personal data online will show them the weak spots in their online privacy and allow them to identify measures to protect themselves in future.[28]

A further, interlinked consideration is mental health, which the profession of investigative journalism can often put at great risk. It is important to make students aware of the ways in which the profession impacts mental health and provide access to resources to instil resilience and preparedness before they encounter situations where this impact will become clear. The Dart Center for Journalism and Trauma should be the first port of call for such resources,[29] and at the very least, students should be signposted to the support and guidance that the Center offers.

In partnership with the US-based Freedom of the Press Foundation, we have developed our Source Protection Programme, a flexible course of training and resources which aims to help journalists at all career levels to protect their sources, themselves and their stories (in that order).

Financial Investigation

While investigative journalism can be categorised as a 'beat' in and of itself, akin to sports, travel or indeed financial journalism, there are still specialisms within investigative journalism. Whether regional or thematic, investigative journalists tend to gravitate towards an expertise. However, regardless of the areas in which they specialise, if a journalist's work is in any way investigative, then they will inevitably need to access and understand information about companies and corporations.

There are many investigations where this is key, whether looking into corruption, organised crime, money laundering, sanctions evasion or misuse of public funds (Davies, 2022). But, in truth, almost any project will benefit from a grounding in financial investigation.

So much of our world is managed through the framework of these entities, especially in our age of ever-increasing outsourcing of public services to the private sector, that there are vanishingly few avenues of investigation in which the actions and decisions of companies and their directors do not play important roles. Therefore, a decent grasp of where such information can be found and how it should be meaningfully understood and explained is now essential for investigative journalists of all stripes.

Journalists in the UK (and, given the popularity of UK-registered businesses with their largely unfounded veneer of respectability, journalists everywhere) are lucky in that information on UK companies is free and easily accessible on-line through the Companies House website. Becoming familiar with searching the system and understanding what the different categories of stored information and documents can tell you about a company should be taught to all journalism students.

It has many flaws – from the lack of connections shown between registrations made by the same person but with different accounts, to the fact that directors can be found in the system named Adolf Tooth Fairy Hitler,[30] Santa Claus (with an occupation listed as philanthropist)[31] and Jesus Christ (country of residence: Heaven)[32] – but there is still a wealth of useful and largely reliable information available there without cost.

Indeed, to give credit where due, the recent requirement for records on Companies House to declare 'Persons with Significant Control' (PSC) has been fairly well enforced and often makes it a simple task to identify the beneficial owner of a company at a glance. Of course, with many of the companies that warrant investigation, this task is complicated by the use of complex structures of ownership through other companies, meaning that the PSC record often leads only to the next company up the ownership chain.

Following the chain of ownership may lead outside the jurisdiction of the UK, frequently to jurisdictions in which financial secrecy is a selling point for potential company owners, such as the Channel Islands, the British Virgin Islands or Delaware. In such cases, it is necessary to use other tools to continue the research, at least as far as transparency allows.

Open Corporates[33] is a transparency organisation which brings together company registration information from a wide range of jurisdictions, making it the natural next step for following the money offshore. The information they are able to provide is naturally limited by the disclosure requirements, or lack thereof, in each jurisdiction, but it is nevertheless an essential resource in financial investigations.

It is also worth noting that where a line of inquiry leads to a secrecy jurisdiction, it is not necessarily a dead end. Even in notoriously secretive locations, it is possible to get further information on a particular company, though often this will require a fee, so judgement (or a budget) is required to decide when it is worth paying for documents.

In the worst cases, very little information will be available regardless of what you can afford, but even here, there are still further avenues to try. The barriers around financial information have become increasingly leaky in recent years, with several large caches of documents being passed to journalists. Probably the most high-profile have been the Panama Papers,[34] but there have been many others, both before and since.

The International Consortium of Investigative Journalists (ICIJ), the team that coordinated the collaborative Panama Papers project, have published data contained in that and other leaks. Though partially redacted, it is available to search for free in their **Offshore Leaks Database**.[35] It is always worth checking if a person or company of interest is included, as it can reveal hidden links or details, and the ICIJ have been known to share additional documents with journalists where there is a clear public interest in doing so.

Another source of access to leaked company information is the vast **Aleph**[36] database, maintained by the Organised Crime and Corruption Reporting Project (OCCRP). This contains documents from a range of leaks alongside other useful information and is free to access, once registered for an account. All students of investigative journalism should be encouraged to make such an account and familiarise themselves with the system.

To help students get used to finding specific information through these systems, it helps if you can provide a focus for their practice. This can be any company or person, but it generally works best if you can find a target that will have some relevance. For instance, one of the companies that came up during your data journalism exercises analysing political donations can make a good example target to ask students to find information (perhaps the ultimate beneficial owner, or a map of subsidiaries and parent companies in the same corporate structure) about. Similarly, a local or national business figure can be a good dummy target for an exercise that asks students to navigate these systems to identify information (directorships, links to other people) from the starting point of a person rather than a company.

Accessing such information is an important step, but understanding it in enough depth to draw meaningful conclusions can be even more difficult. Guidance for this takes far more than the space available here, but in this regard, Raj Bairoliya's handbook **The Investigative Journalists' Guide to Company Accounts** (Bairoliya, 2018) should be required reading.

Events

CIJ Summer Conference

The final pillar of the CIJ's activities is our events, centred around practical investigative training, but also fulfilling important purposes that are difficult to replicate in any other way. Everyone in attendance, from student delegates to keynote speakers, is treated as an equal, and we strive for a collegiate and welcoming atmosphere throughout. This means that networking opportunities are wide and varied, and advice on pitching a story or coding a web scraper is freely given.

Alongside peer-learning and collaboration, the Summer Conference gives us a chance to champion both new practices and courageous work. It's especially important to us that we bring different perspectives, and we work hard to ensure diversity in terms of nationality, ethnicity and background.

One central way in which we do this is through the Gavin MacFadyen Memorial Lecture. Since our founding director passed away in 2016, we have, every year, sought out a speaker who has produced exemplary investigative work under some of the most difficult circumstances.

Previous speakers have included Maria Ressa, the fearless founding editor of Rappler, the investigative outlet in the Philippines, who was targeted for both online abuse and lawsuits by the regime[37]; Wa Lone, the Reuters journalist jailed by the Myanmar government for his investigation into military abuses of the Rohingya people in Rakhine state[38]; and Meera Jatav, who co-founded Khabar Lahariya, a grassroots newsroom in rural Uttar Pradesh, India, staffed exclusively by Dalit caste women.[39]

In recent years, we have also started to host Regional Conferences, bringing the same opportunities for learning and networking to other cities in the UK, including Newcastle, Belfast and Glasgow.

Logan Symposia

Supported by the Reva and David Logan Foundation, the Logan Symposia are held biennially and focus less on training and more on the wider environment in which investigative journalism is conducted. It allows us to interrogate more radical subjects, such as surveillance and censorship, propaganda and conspiracy theories, or whistle-blowing and leaks, in more experimental ways.

The programmes have welcomed a range of speakers and a variety of different forms. Alongside panels including a direct conversation between Edward Snowden and Ai Weiwei,[40] the Logan Symposia have also hosted documentary films, plays, live music and art exhibitions, all with themes relevant to surveillance, technology and investigation.

All this makes the Logan Symposia a more eclectic, artistic forum than our Summer Conferences, though no less focused on important issues and debates. It does still cover practical skills, though. In 2018, the Symposium played host to **Investigative Practice**, a series of high-level participatory seminars that each evaluated an important question or challenge, from winning the trust of sources within secretive online groups such as Anonymous, to building machine learning into open-source intelligence. The report (Sanderson, 2018) summarising all the discussions from these seminars is available to download and remains relevant today.

Each iteration has allowed the CIJ to establish and cement partnerships with a range of other organisations in the space, including Der Spiegel, Tactical Tech, The Intercept, Disruption Network Lab and Reporters United. The ways in which the event brings together organisations to collaborate and share insights speak to one of the most important functions we perform in the wider sector.

Conclusion

Over the past 20 years, the CIJ has been working to address the factors behind the decline that prompted its formation. Unsurprisingly, our success has not been comprehensive, but we feel we've made some significant impacts on bringing greater innovation to investigative practice, both in the UK and further afield, as well as playing our part in building more collaborative models of working, both between those within journalism and between the industry more broadly and with other disciplines and sectors.

There is, admittedly, much more to be done. The improvements seen are far from total or perfect, new challenges are constantly arising and attempted solutions often prove not to be as effective as first hoped. For instance, the difficult economic circumstances for the industry remain and continue to claim victims, as seen by the recent collapses of BuzzFeed's investigations units (Warren, 2023) and Vice News (Kale, 2024).

Nevertheless, investigative journalism has not died the death that many feared was looming two decades ago. In significant ways, the practice is vibrant and thriving. Unarguably, it has been forced to adapt, but from within that adaptation have come the foundations of myriad revelations of wrongdoing and corruption, some with global import. As many mistakes as successes have been made during the process, but if investigative journalism ever stops adapting, then surely that will be cause for more serious concern than ever before.

We continue to work towards helping that adaptation be as smooth and effective as possible, and hope that this chapter has provided some insights from our experience of teaching investigative skills to a wide range of learners, from students to veteran reporters and editors.

CLASSROOM EXERCISE

All local councils in the UK are required by law to provide data on any spending over £500.

- Find your local council's most recent spending data.
- Use a pivot table to identify the top five recipients of council spending.
- Look up at least one of the companies listed there through Companies House and find the relevant Person with Significant Control.

Notes

1 See https://publicintegrity.org/
2 See https://tcij.org/ocri/
3 https://thecjid.org/document/cop-reporting-handbook-for-journalists/

4 See https://www.communityjournalism.co.uk/
5 See https://www.thebureauinvestigates.com/local/
6 See https://www.ima.press/
7 https://thebristolcable.org/
8 https://themeteor.org/
9 https://www.starandcrescent.org.uk/
10 https://theferret.scot/
11 https://www.greatergovanhill.com/
12 For a summary of Doig's work, see Johnson, JT. (2000), The Guardian, https://www.theguardian.com/media/2000/jul/03/newmedia.mondaymediasection2. Published 3 July 2000.
13 The portal for searching through political donations data is available here: https://search.electoralcommission.org.uk/. You might start students off with some sample questions to ask of this data (e.g. What was the largest single donation?; Which party or MP received the most overall?; Which company donated the most?), before asking them to come up with their own interesting questions the data might be able to answer.
14 https://fairwarning.substack.com/
15 https://www.data-is-plural.com/
16 See for example, https://www.theguardian.com/uk-news/2024/mar/06/budget-calculator-2024-better-worse-off-interactive-tool-chancellor-tax-spending
17 See Greenwald, *et al* (2013) The Guardian, https://www.theguardian.com/world/2013/jun/09/edward-snowden-nsa-whistleblower-surveillance. (Accessed 10 September 2024).
18 See https://forensic-architecture.org/
19 See https://citizenevidence.org/
20 See https://www.globalwitness.org/tagged/investigation/
21 See https://www.bbc.co.uk/news/uk-65650822
22 See https://www.nytimes.com/spotlight/visual-investigations
23 For a description of Killing's work on the project, see https://exposingtheinvisible.org/en/podcasts/alison-killing/
24 To find and develop your own exercises for this it is best to run through a few OSINT exercises yourself and find ways to replicate them using images or information that will be relevant to your students from a local or thematic perspective. A good starting point for geolocation challenges are the online exercises (and walkthrough solutions) hosted by Sofia Santos at https://gralhix.com/.
25 The objective of such an exercise would be to familiarise students with some of the techniques for finding information about specific people online. Once you've identified a suitable public figure, you might ask students to use google operators (a good starting point with examples can be found here – https://researchclinic.net/googlesyntax.html or here – https://expertisefinder.com/google-search-tips-journalists/) and some people finding tools such as pipl.com or 192.com and ask them to find some simple pieces of information, such as addresses, emails or social media accounts for the example target.
26 For instance, the newsletter Week in OSINT (https://sector035.nl/articles/category:week-in-osint) or the resource page OSINT Dojo (https://www.osintdojo.com/resources/)
27 These are online competitions structured around OSINT and online investigation, designed to teach and refine OSINT skills. OSINT Dojo's resource page maintains a list of CTF events.
28 You might, for instance, repurpose some of the people-finding tools highlighted in the OSINT section above and ask students to use these on themselves and see how much of their own personal data is available online to anyone with basic OSINT know-how. This is a good way to introduce the topic of leaving digital footprints

online and emphasise the importance of caution when using the internet for both self and source protection.

29 See https://dartcenter.org/resources.
30 See https://find-and-update.company-information.service.gov.uk/officers/TuA9z MlZy5LtlglBOTPtYoOXhYM/appointments
31 See https://find-and-update.company-information.service.gov.uk/officers/ffVJIV LdD9IopKmR3xT5nmv2blM/appointments
32 See https://find-and-update.company-information.service.gov.uk/officers/Ny3nt St6u9tDvF1X-PQtftuvfv8/appointments
33 See https://opencorporates.com/
34 See https://www.icij.org/investigations/panama-papers/
35 See https://offshoreleaks.icij.org/
36 See https://aleph.occrp.org/
37 See https://www.youtube.com/watch?v=5ii4v2Fl-lQ
38 See https://www.youtube.com/watch?v=XSXNlCj6_7s
39 See https://www.youtube.com/watch?v=q6pcsGomtkE
40 See https://www.youtube.com/watch?v=REv-6YSJrPc

References

Bairoliya, R. (2018) *The investigative journalist's guide to company accounts.* 2nd edn. *The Centre for Investigative Journalism.* Available at: https://tcij.org/handbooks/the-investigative-journalists-guide-to-company-accounts/

Barclay, S. et al. (2022) 'News deserts in the UK', *The Charitable Journalism Project.* Available at: https://camri.ac.uk/blog/articles/news-deserts-in-the-uk/ (Accessed 10 September 2024).

Davies, G. (2022) 'His companies made a deal for £138m of taxpayers' money. Where has it gone?', *The Bureau of Investigative Journalism.* Available at: https://www.thebureauinvestigates.com/stories/2022-07-15/his-companies-made-a-deal-for-138m-of-taxpayers-money.-where-has-it-gone (Accessed 10 September 2024).

Dedman, B. (1989) 'The color of money', *The Atlanta Journal.* Available at: https://powerreporting.com/color/. Published May 1988-Jan 1989 (Accessed 10 September 2024).

Donovan, R. (2023) 'Climate journalism needs voices from the Global South', *Eos, 104. Available at:* https://doi.org/10.1029/2023EO230085 (Accessed 10 September 2024).

Franklin, B. (2014) 'The future of journalism: In an age of digital media and economic uncertainty', *Journalism Studies,* 15(5), pp. 481–499. Available at: https://doi.org/10.1080/1461670X.2014.930254 (Accessed 12 September 2024).

Gouveia, F. (2024) 'Stormont pays out more than £6m on empty buildings and disused land', *The Belfast Telegraph.* Available at: https://www.belfasttelegraph.co.uk/news/politics/stormont-pays-out-more-than-6m-on-empty-buildings-and-disused-land/a1124210548.html (Accessed 10 September 2024).

Greenwald, G. et al. (2013) The Guardian, https://www.theguardian.com/world/2013/jun/09/edward-snowden-nsa-whistleblower-surveillance (Accessed 10 September 2024).

Hewett, J. (2015) 'Data journalism grows up', in Felle, T., Mair, J. and Radcliffe, D. (eds.) *Data journalism: Inside the global future.* UK: *Abramis,* pp. 27–38. Available at: https://openaccess.city.ac.uk/13924/1/Data%20Journalism%20chapter%20.pdf (Accessed 10 September 2024).

Hopke, J. (2022) Everyone is a climate reporter now', *Nieman Reports.* Available at: https://niemanreports.org/articles/climate-change-journalism-education/ (Accessed 10 September 2024).

Houston, B. (2010) 'The future of investigative journalism', *Daedalus*, 139(2), pp. 45–56. Available at: https://direct.mit.edu/daed/article-abstract/139/2/45/26836 (Accessed 12 September 2024).

Hudoon, F. (2021) 'Data at First Sight: Telling the human story through numbers', *Exposing the Invisible*. Available at: https://exposingtheinvisible.org/en/articles/data-stories/ (Accessed 11 September 2024).

Hughes, F. (2022) 'Universities 'illegally hitting disabled students with extra housing costs'', *OpenDemocracy*. Available at: https://www.opendemocracy.net/en/disabled-students-equality-act-adapations-accessible-rooms/ (Accessed 10 September 2024).

Kale, S. (2024) 'Vice's cunning, irreverent journalism is dead – and executives with bloated pay cheques helped kill it', *The Guardian*. Available at: https://www.theguardian.com/commentisfree/2024/feb/27/vice-clever-irreverent-executives-helped-kill-it (Accessed 10 September 2024).

Kehoe, C. (2023) 'The Truman Brewery development: The community reaches boiling point', *Whitechapel London*. Available at: https://whitechapellondon.co.uk/truman-brewery-development-community-reaches-boiling-point/ (Accessed 9 September 2024).

Kirchgaessner, S. et al. (2021) 'Revealed: leak uncovers global abuse of cyber-surveillance weapon', *The Guardian*. Available at: https://www.theguardian.com/world/2021/jul/18/revealed-leak-uncovers-global-abuse-of-cyber-surveillance-weapon-nso-group-pegasus (Accessed 11 September 2024).

Lashmar, P. (2009) University of Westminster, Journalism in Crisis Conference, London, May 2009. Available at: http://bura.brunel.ac.uk/handle/2438/4337 (Accessed 10 September 2024).

Lowe, Y. (2021) ''Smoke and mirrors' hide cuts hitting Greenwich's most vulnerable people', *Greenwich Wire*. Available at: https://greenwichwire.co.uk/2021/11/05/smoke-and-mirrors-hide-cuts-hitting-greenwichs-most-vulnerable-people/ (Accessed 10 September 2024).

Macfadyen, G. (2012) House of Lords Select Committee on Communications 'Oral Evidence: Third Report, The Future of Investigative Journalism'. Available at: https://publications.parliament.uk/pa/ld201012/ldselect/ldcomuni/256/25602.htm (Accessed 12 September 2024).

Mbonge, M, & Mounde Ngamo, M. (2022) 'Environ 31 de mangrove perdue en 5 ans a bonaberi', *Data Cameroun*. Available at: https://datacameroon.com/environnement-environ-31-de-mangrove-perdue-en-5-ans-a-bonaberi/ (Accessed 10 September 2024).

Meyer, P. (1968) '1968: A Newspaper's Role Between the Riots', *Nieman Reports*. Available at: https://niemanreports.org/articles/1968-a-newspapers-role-between-the-riots/ (Accessed 9 September 2024).

Mokhethi, S. (2022) 'Gone with the wind: Lesotho's $15-billion energy pipe-dream', *Mail & Guardian*. Available at: https://mg.co.za/business/2022-09-22-gone-with-the-wind-lesothos-15-billion-energy-pipedream/ (Accessed 11 September 2024).

Priest, D. (2021) 'A UAE agency put Pegasus spyware on phone of Jamal Khashoggi's wife months before his murder, new forensics show', *Washington Post*. Available at: https://www.washingtonpost.com/nation/interactive/2021/hanan-elatr-phone-pegasus/ (Accessed 10 September 2024).

Reporters Without Borders. (2018) 'Online harassment of journalists: Attack of the trolls', *RSF*. Available at: https://rsf.org/sites/default/files/rsf_report_on_online_harassment.pdf (Accessed 8 September 2024). This report's appendices also include a short but useful guide for journalists who find themselves the subject of online harassment.

Ross Arguedas, A., et al. (2023), 'News for the powerful and privileged: how misrepresentation and underrepresentation of disadvantaged communities undermine their trust in news', *Reuters Institute*. https://doi.org/10.60625/risj-jqny-t942. Available at: https://reutersinstitute.politics.ox.ac.uk/news-powerful-and-privileged-how-misrepresentation-and-underrepresentation-disadvantaged (Accessed 11 September 2024).

Sanderson, T. (ed.) (2018) 'Issues in Investigative Practice', *The Centre for Investigative Journalism*. Available at: https://tcij.org/handbooks/investigative-practice/ (Accessed 8 September 2024).

Shukla, P.R., et al. (2022) Intergovernmental panel on climate change: *climate change 2022: Mitigation of climate change. Contribution of working group III to the sixth assessment report of the intergovernmental panel on climate change*. Cambridge University Press, Cambridge, UK and New York, NY, USA. https://doi.org/10.1017/9781009157926 (Accessed 9 September 2024).

Simon, F.M. (2024) 'Artificial intelligence in the news: How AI retools, rationalizes, and reshapes journalism and the public arena', *Columbia Journalism Review*. Available at: https://www.cjr.org/tow_center_reports/artificial-intelligence-in-the-news.php (Accessed 10 September 2024).

Soto, M. and Fallas, H. (2023) 'Millonario fondo climatico es insuficiente para frenar calentamiento global en 1,5°C', *La Data Cuenta*. Available at: https://ladatacuenta.com/2023/01/31/millonario-fondo-climatico-es-insuficiente-para-frenar-calentamiento-global/ (Accessed 10 September 2024).

Spilsbury, M. (2023) 'Diversity in journalism', *National Council for the Training of Journalists*. Available at: https://www.nctj.com/wp-content/uploads/2023/05/Diversity-in-journalism-2023-4WEB.pdf (Accessed 10 September 2024).

Warren, T. (2023) 'The 'Moonshot' Newsroom: An Insider's Account of the Meteoric Rise and Fall of BuzzFeed News Investigations', *Global Investigative Journalism Network*. Available at: https://gijn.org/stories/the-moonshot-newsroom-an-insiders-account-of-the-meteoric-rise-and-fall-of-buzzfeed-news-investigations/ (Accessed 10 September 2024).

INDEX

Note: – *Italicized* page references refer to figures and page references with "n" refer to endnotes.

For Product Safety Concerns and Information please contact our EU
representative GPSR@taylorandfrancis.com
Taylor & Francis Verlag GmbH, Kaufingerstraße 24, 80331 München, Germany

www.ingramcontent.com/pod-product-compliance
Ingram Content Group UK Ltd.
Pitfield, Milton Keynes, MK11 3LW, UK
UKHW021848150925
462929UK00011B/312